UNDERDOGS

How a man and a street dog
form an unbreakable bond and
a life-changing friendship

Gray Freeman
with Brendan Freedog

CONTENTS

INTRODUCTION.

This is a book about a friendship between two people – except one of them is a dog. It is the story of how I took on a rescue dog, Brendan – he came with his name. The term "rescue dog" is ambiguous, because in so many ways he rescued me. Not in a brave and selfless way, you understand, as some dogs might. No, unless the rescue involved having a nap or watching Watercolour Challenge, then it's not for him. He saved me by being himself.

ABOUT THE AUTHORS

Gray Freeman is a dog lover, traveller and writer... in no particular order. He is the author of several walking and cycling books. More recently, he has penned a short play about Alzheimer's, which was performed twice in Manchester. People cried, shook his hand and told him how much they could relate to it. It is currently being recorded as a radio play. He is anxiously waiting for a call from Hollywood. (He is starting to get concerned that Hollywood might have misplaced his number.)

Brendan Freedog was a street dog in Bulgaria. He was saved by a charity and brought to Britain in a Transit van. He's had a hard life and is afraid of almost everything. He hates uniforms and anyone carrying anything, such as a stick, a bag or a grudge. He isn't a people person. Or indeed a person. Hobbies include: sniffing, weeing, sitting down and sleeping. He likes to think of himself as an international ambassador for rescue dogs. Just not a very good one. Favourite colour: the colour of Bonio. Relationship status: available!

The Odd Couple

Our website: https://grayfreeman.wixsite.com/mysite

Facebook: https://www.facebook.com/BrendanFreedog

Email: the2underdogs@outlook.com

CHAPTER 1: THE BRENDAN WHO CAME IN FROM THE COLD

Brendan was a street dog. He ran all day through the narrow, cobbled alleyways of Bulgaria, scavenging, possibly busking, probably scamming tourists. I'm guessing, because I don't know very much about his secretive past.

While he was making a nuisance of himself on the shores of the Black Sea, I was spending an unhealthy amount of time standing at my window, in England, looking out over the waterlogged lawn. It was cold and wet; it *always* seemed to be cold and wet, but that didn't matter, because I didn't have to go out; I had nowhere to go.

In the past year, my life had been turned upside down. Through no fault of my own, I'd lost a job which I loved and I had reluctantly started a legal battle with my former employers. I don't know how I got through that time, but I did and I won. It should have made me feel good, but by then the damage had been done and it didn't feel at all like winning. I was paid off and cast adrift. I had no job and no idea where I was going in life, apart from nowhere. I avoided going out if at all possible. It was getting very difficult to speak to people – even people I knew – and it felt safer to stay inside. My immediate goals were to try and regain some confidence and attempt to leave the flat without having a panic attack or throwing up on a stranger's shoes.

I was in a very dark place – a place so dark that even putting the big light on couldn't illuminate it. I couldn't sleep at night and I couldn't stay awake during the day. I had nightmares, palpitations, tremors, saw flashing lights and heard voices, felt dizzy, disorientated, confused and paranoid, in fact, probably all the effects of a hallucinogenic drug, but the nearest I've ever come to one is when I once ate an over-ripe kiwi fruit and it tasted slightly fizzy. My life was falling apart; I felt like someone was pulling the rug from beneath me, but it wasn't a rug, it was my last shred of dignity, so I stood fast.

Throughout all this turmoil, which lasted for well over a year, standing by my side – metaphorically if not always physically – was my long-term partner, Nicky. Although we had been together for a long time, ours was an unconventional relationship. For a start, we didn't live together at this point, though we had in the past. We both had our own lives; in many ways we led separate lives, but we led them together. But separately... and not always all that together. But we were inextricably linked, whilst also being individual. We were soul mates and we were poles apart. It's complicated. Our set up was one that a lot of people were quite envious of, especially couples with children. (We didn't have children and had never wanted any.) Ours was a brilliant arrangement in some respects and very imperfect in others.

Whilst Nicky had her cats, Hector and Pixie, I lived alone. My last dog, Jake, died a decade ago. I only had him for two years when he died in my arms, of something like a stroke. He wasn't old, but he was highly strung and constantly anxious. He departed this world far too young and he left a huge gap, but I vowed I would never get another dog, because they become such a large part of your life and then they die. But being alone isn't really healthy; it's not generally good for your mental state and it's not good for your confidence.

I hadn't realised yet, but there was a very obvious dog-shaped hole in my life.

* * * * * * * * * *

Somehow, Brendan's life of liberty, rough sleeping and food stealing in Bulgaria was brought to an abrupt end when he was captured. (I'm assuming he didn't turn himself in voluntarily – though it wouldn't surprise me.) He was taken, along with all the other waifs, strays and trouble-causers, to the local kill shelter. He was given a number, and had that number pinned to him through his ear. The dogs get a short amount of time to be bought and rehomed, and if they aren't – as the name suggests – they are killed. He was literally on Death Row.

I *wasn't* a prisoner, but I felt like one. I rarely left my flat; my big trip out was the weekly pilgrimage to see my therapist at the local hospital. I'm a very private person; my innermost feelings are rarely on display, so being assigned a therapist was bizarre and pointless. If someone asks how I am, I'm very British and I say I'm fine. If they probe further I either deflect with humour or run away. The fact that the person might be a qualified therapist, counsellor or psychiatrist doesn't change this.

My current therapist – I'd had a few – looked like Barbara Windsor in a *Carry On* film and I'm just not convinced this is an appropriate look for a member of the psychiatry department of a busy hospital. She came clopping down the corridor in her dangerously high stilettoes and barged into the room without smiling. She was wearing a black mini skirt and a tiny black bolero jacket. She had a mass of peroxide hair piled up on her head, balanced there precariously. She looked like a Barbie Doll, probably *Office Barbie 1980*. She sat down and began the session. It became apparent that after several weeks, she had now run out of all the textbook clichés, so she had basically run out of things to say.

In desperation – presumably – she told me I should get a dog and take it for long walks. It seemed such an irresponsible and inappropriate thing to say. Does she say this to everyone? Because some people really *shouldn't* have a dog. I didn't *want* a dog and, besides, I wouldn't be allowed a dog in my rented flat, so I dismissed this ridiculous suggestion immediately. This was the moment I completely lost faith in this rather brusque healthcare professional. I headed home feeling very depressed and hopeless. I decided to take a break from counselling, because it just wasn't working for me and I was continually coming home feeling worse.

****

Brendan was saved from the kill shelter. He was bought by a charity called *Street Hearts*, along with numerous other inmates. He was shipped over to the UK in a specially converted transit van. The journey took days. Consequently, Brendan has travelled across most of Europe. I suspect he is a wanted felon in many of the countries he passed through. He wound up at a sanctuary on the outskirts of Manchester. He was rehomed, at least once, but because of his behavioural issues he kept bouncing back to the sanctuary. That was where our paths crossed on a breezy day in March.

Nicky loves animals. She used to be a dog person, but she's morphed over the years and is now more of a cat person. She also loves rabbits and rats – and any animal really. I haven't asked how far down this list I appear, because I probably wouldn't like the answer. I wouldn't describe myself as an animal lover, though I actually do love animals, but I don't want to be surrounded by them or constantly watch clips of adorable kittens on YouTube doing hilarious or cute things.

Nicky had learned of a new sanctuary in the area and had offered our services as dog walkers, as they were desperate for people to take the dogs out and give them some decent exercise. It was about half an hour away. We came off the motorway and drove along a narrow, rutted, single track lane, then an even further drive along a meandering, potholed driveway. It was actually the countryside, but not very nice countryside; it was a scrubby wilderness, open but barren, with dry reeds and acres of dead bracken stalks blowing in the cold wind. It looked very much like a grassed-over landfill site. There were very few houses in this vast area of nothingness and it had an "end-of-the-world" feel to it.

We went wrong several times, but eventually found a collection of old farm buildings, isolated and slightly dilapidated. It all looked foreboding and unwelcoming. We could hear a lot of dogs barking, so we knew it was the right place. Ten minutes later, we were sitting on a settee in the extended kitchen talking to the two female live-in staff. One was seemingly very friendly; the other wasn't.

A tiny lamb wearing a nappy walked past, paused to look at us, bleated, then continued on his way. The kitchen door opened and several dogs slinked in. The first one came directly towards us, climbed onto my lap and curled up, with his head on my chest. He closed his eyes and within a minute he was breathing steadily, fast asleep. The two staff members stared open mouthed.

"Oh... my... god..."

"I can't believe that!"

This was Brendan, apparently, and he didn't like people and he especially didn't like men-people or strangers – and I fit into at least some of those categories.

"Be careful..."

"He changes suddenly without warning..."

"He snaps at people..."

"He can be quite aggressive..."

"Don't make any sudden movements..."

Brendan was still sound asleep. His head was inches from my face, but I had no fear whatsoever. And neither did he. We were both calm and relaxed. It was like we'd always known each other and this was meant to be.

We stayed like this for some time, until Nicky decided we really ought to take some dogs out, which was the purpose of our visit. I took Brendan, on a filth-encrusted fabric lead; Nicky took another dog. We headed off along the trackway, through the harsh scrubland, with the sound of the motorway ever-present and the reeds and bare hawthorn branches crackling. It wasn't actually raining, but it was a grey day. There was a cold breeze and no colour anywhere.

The hostile landscape didn't matter at all, because I couldn't take my eyes off Brendan. The first thing that struck me was that he looked exactly how a dog should look. If you were showing an alien what a dog looked like, you'd probably choose Brendan as your model. Or if you were designing the ideal dog, I'm sure it would come out something like him. He looked so "doggish". He had an athletic body, a slim waist, like a greyhound and was slightly too thin, almost ribby. In contrast to his regal frame, he had a terrier-like face, with a scruffy, straggly beard and sideburns. If he was a person, he might well be a market trader in the Nineteen-seventies.

His colouring was amazing, he was predominantly black on his back, but sandy underneath. His head, face and legs had touches of russet, chestnut and copper, such rich and deep colours; he was quite stunning. He had long legs; he looked a bit like he had dressed in a hurry and put the wrong legs on. They're *very* long legs.

(In the future – which we're not up to yet – people will constantly stop me and ask what type of dog he is, then tell me "He's definitely got some Airedale, Terrier, Labrador, Alsatian, whippet, beagle (and so on) in him". The list is actually endless, but I'm cutting it short there. And I have never agreed with any of them. He is what he is.)

There was something about this dog; he'd really got his claws into me. He was exactly the kind of dog I liked... the kind of dog that I'd choose... If I was looking for a dog, that is... which I wasn't. So that was that.

We walked a long way through the eerie wilderness. None of the dogs were allowed off their leads, as many were former street dogs and reverted to type when let loose: they just ran off and probably started busking in shopping centres. Brendan pulled enthusiastically and seemed interested in his surroundings, happy to be out in the open air.

We stopped for a break and sat on a log. We took a few photographs of ourselves with the dogs, as a memento. (It amazes me, but we have photographs of us each cuddling Brendan. Knowing him as I do now, I can't believe he let us do that when we had only just met him. It makes my blood run cold. But it also speaks volumes.)

When we drove home in the Saturday evening traffic, we talked about all the dogs we'd met that day, but I only really wanted to talk about Brendan.

"You should try fostering him." Nicky said.

"I don't think so."

"You're a dog person. You should have a dog."

"I can't have a dog at my flat, can I?"

"It wouldn't matter if you were just fostering."

I shook my head. "No…"

"Anyway, your landlord wouldn't mind."

"No… I can't." I said dismissively.

"You *need* a dog."

"I don't *want* a dog."

But she was completely right. About everything. It was already a *fait accompli*. I'm not saying Nicky was orchestrating events or that I was being manipulated by a divine power, but I almost feel things had already been decided and I suspect Brendan was sitting patiently at the sanctuary with his case already packed.

****

Apparently, Brendan had previously been adopted by a lesbian couple, but once at his new home he had become possessive and over-protective; he wouldn't let anyone in their house. They tried their best, but he became more aggressive and was unpredictable and they were frightened of him. In the end they returned him to the sanctuary, where he remained.

We also returned to the sanctuary – to walk the dogs. We took out a variety of different animals; we never saw the same faces twice, apart from Brendan. The ones we'd met previously had always been re-homed. Nicky had persisted in saying I should try fostering Brendan, that it would be good for me, that I'm a dog person and needed a dog. I had continually resisted, but I was getting increasingly concerned that one day we'd come here and he'd have gone, having been re-homed. I felt a connection to him, something inexplicable. I felt he was a dog who needed special attention.

We tried to speak to the staff about Brendan's troubled past, which they'd vaguely and enigmatically mentioned, because so far we'd seen no evidence of the issues that they'd alluded to. However, they were very reticent and quite dismissive. Eventually, as a favour, I agreed to foster Brendan for a single night while they were having work done at the sanctuary. He was brought to my flat by a volunteer called Debbie. She would do the required home check at the same time and if all seemed suitable she would leave Brendan with me.

I answered the door to them and let them in. Brendan stood there looking very sorry for himself. He'd been really sick in the car and looked terrible. He let me greet him and give him a cuddle. (Again, with hindsight this is quite amazing. And this was the first time I'd met him outside of the sanctuary.) They came up to the flat. It's a studio flat, so the bedroom and the living room are one. Brendan leapt onto the bed and settled himself down. Debbie laughed. "I don't think we need to worry about him. He's made himself right at home." And he had.

"He'll probably just sleep. They get no peace and quiet at the sanctuary, so when they get fostered or adopted they usually sleep for a week."

Brendan, feeling a little bit worse for wear after his car journey to my flat.

He lay there on my bed (henceforth "our bed") and never left.

****

Brendan is five. Apart from the vaguest details, his past remains a complete mystery to me. It's upsetting to think about how he lived or how he was treated and I can't begin to imagine the traumas he's suffered. Sometimes he has a faraway, haunted look, but sometimes he looks like an inquisitive puppy. Occasionally, he looks like a sad old man. He's got whiskers and a beard, which can make him look like he's performing Dickens at the Opera House. As far as I know, he isn't, but then there is so little about him that I *do* know.

Debbie left Brendan with me and headed home. Suddenly I was alone with my boy. He just lay on the bed with a certain look. I'm sure he felt like a piece of luggage, shipped from pillar to post, and I'm certain he thought "Here we go again... and when I'm bad (which is inevitable) I'll be returned to the sanctuary." Although I was only fostering him – and it was supposedly for one night – I knew he was never going back again.

I took him for his inaugural walk and introduced him to the local field. It's a small area of green surrounded by houses, with a few trees around the perimeter. It isn't great, but it's the nearest open space in our suburban area. He had a good sniff, smelling all the smells for the first time, the smells that he would come to know, come to expect, come to enjoy and come to wee on.

Brendan insisted on sitting down in the middle of the field for a very long time. At first I wondered if there was something wrong, perhaps his legs were hurting or he had some other ailment, but he seemed quite contented, sniffing at the air, casually looking around and admiring the view. I would come to learn that this is his favoured style of exercising. The sitting down bit, I mean, much more so than the actual walking.

A woman with a retriever came up to us and the dogs had a sniff and a bit of a playful dance.

"He's gorgeous. What's he called?"

I wavered. "Erm... Brendan." I said reluctantly. "He came with his name. I'm just fostering him."

She laughed. "Brendan! Oh, it suits him."

"Right... OK."

I don't think it suits him at all! I don't think it suits *anyone*, least of all a dog. I'll let you into a secret: I can't stand the name! "Brendan" is Gaelic for "prince". He's not Gaelic, nor a member of the aristocracy, so it's ludicrous. I don't mind human names, per se. Some are quite funny. There's a Trevor who goes to the field, and a Tony, Dexter, Ed, Dougie, Charlie and Bruno. Those names all work, for a variety of reasons, but "Brendan"... It just doesn't do it for me. (At the field I tend to shout "Boy" or just "B". "Brendan" is saved for a last resort... and I always shout it as quietly as possible, which defeats the point of shouting.)

In my experience, sanctuaries generally aren't good at naming; they have so many animals coming through their doors that they must run out of good names and are scraping the barrel. I think names should come to you naturally when you meet an animal, rather than be forced. For Brendan, the first name that sprang to mind was Skippy, because when he lay on his back, his paws and his face looked like the eponymous kangaroo. He could also look like Wile E Coyote on occasion. And Bill Sykes as portrayed by Oliver Reed. But I couldn't see myself at the field shouting either "Wile E Coyote!" or "Bill-Sykes-as-portrayed-by-Oliver-Reed!", but I *could* see myself shouting "Skippy! Skip!

Here boy!" Unfortunately, because I was just fostering him, I didn't think it was my place to rename him, though annoyingly, he didn't seem to know his name at that point. Or perhaps he just chose to ignore it out of embarrassment.

As he was Bulgarian, I looked up the most popular Bulgarian names. Georgi, Alexander, Ivan and Dimitar all cropped up near the top of the list. I thought he could carry any of those off really, they all sort of suited him, especially Ivan, which is terrible, but I think it also has a certain cuteness to it. I could really see myself shouting "Come on, Ivan!".

Ivan/Brendan ate a lot of grass, to combat his travel sickness; he seemed a lot perkier afterwards. He was very interested when other dogs arrived at the field and was friendly at first, but once he'd sniffed them thoroughly he cut them dead and didn't seem to want to play. Sniffing was his thing; I'd never known a dog so smell-orientated. Dogs learn so much from a quick olfactory inspection. Obviously they have a far superior sense of smell to humans, otherwise we'd be sniffing out drugs at the airport instead of them. They say, for a dog, having a sniff is like reading a newspaper. The headlines might be: LATVIAN CHARLIE WEES ON NETTLES; BRUNO'S HAD ANOTHER BATH; DAISY'S CHANGED HER FOOD; SOMEONE ROUND HERE IS UN-NEUTERED. These might not sound like riveting stories to us, but to a dog they're click bait.

They also say a ten minute leisurely sniff-stroll is the same as a one hour energetic walk and tires the dog out, because when they get home they go to sleep and assimilate all the information. ("They" are presumably the dog professors, by which I mean *human* professors who are experts on dogs, not professors who *are* dogs. Although something like a weary bloodhound in a white lab coat would look very plausible as a scientist.)

Dogs love smells, which is ironic, because Brendan really smelled. I mean he actually *smelt*. He *stank*. He absolutely *hummed*. His fur was greasy and lank. Usually you'd probably give a new rescue dog a bath, but I didn't have a bath, only a shower and I couldn't see that working too well. Also, considering his history and his alleged nervousness, I didn't want to upset him in any way, so I sponged him down with some spray-on "dry" animal shampoo foam and rubbed it off with a cloth. The cloth went completely black. He was filthy. He stood there very obligingly and wasn't at all bothered. I'd got a lot of dirt off him and already I could see that there was even more colour to him than I'd previously thought. He still smelled, but less so. It would take a while for that cloying biscuity dirty dog smell to completely wear off.

When he was fully dry, I gave him a good grooming. His skin was covered with crusts of scurf. A lot of dry flakes and scabs came out with the brushing, but he seemed to really enjoy it. Already he looked much better.

Our first day had been successful, uneventful really, but nice. Brendan so far seemed no trouble, he came across as quite relaxed and at ease. He responded passively, but not affectionately, when I made a fuss of him. He didn't make an effort to sit close to me or anything: he lay on the bed in the evening and didn't sit on the sofa with me, but he seemed contented, if self-contained.

That night he slept on the bed. He seemed a little quiet, but not depressed, perhaps a bit wary, because it was all very different. He took over most of the bed and I was squashed on one side, trying to give him as much room as I possibly could and not disturb him. I looked at him sleeping beside me. He made me very sad. I couldn't imagine what sort of life he'd had and what terrible things had happened to him and what he could remember. He started to jerk and whine and chatter; he was having a dream. I've had several dogs, they've all dreamed and sometimes those dreams didn't seem like golden holiday memories, but Brendan's dreams were obviously terrifying nightmares. I gently stroked him and he became still.

Whilst stroking his head, I became aware of a lump on his ear. It felt like it might be a scab on the underside. When I examined it closer, I found there were two of them and I realised they were permanent scars from the ID ear tag he'd been given in the kill shelter. I held him and started to cry. He sighed loudly in embarrassment.

****

Having spent the night in his new home, Brendan seemed to accept that this was where he lived now. In the morning he trotted happily towards the field, but he was a different dog now. It was as though during the night he had gone on line and purchased the field and the adjacent streets, because he walked along as though he owned them. Anyone approaching us was treated to a growling, snapping frenzy. He wouldn't tolerate intruders on his patch. This was obviously the start of the behaviour they had mentioned at the sanctuary.

Brendan barked at men in general. He hated most men. He hated tall or big men. But he also hated short, fat or thin men. He hated old men with grey or white hair, but he also disliked men with brown, black, or ginger hair. Or fair hair. Or no hair. Most of all he despised men in any type of uniform, not just militarised uniforms like the police, but postmen, council workers in hi-viz jackets, painters in all-white overalls, anything at all that resembles a uniform in the loosest sense of the word.

Women were less of a problem, but not always totally exempt. Often he ignored them without incident, as long as they kept their distance. Regardless of gender, Brendan also didn't like joggers. Not one bit. Jogging, running, call it what you will, even someone speed-walking, it was a big no-no for him. He didn't like people running *at all*, but the very worst thing you could do was run *towards* him. If you absolutely *had to* run, run *away* from him. Fast.

So, we walked to the field, crossing the road repeatedly to avoid people, edging round parked cars to create a barrier and either hanging back to let people get a safe distance away or running ahead and trying to lose them. Once at the field he was a lot calmer, because nearly all the people there were accompanied by dogs, which made them just about acceptable.

Brendan sat down in the middle of the field, idly looking around him. I picked up a stick and tried to entice him. "Look what I've got!" He looked at me impassively. "Go and get it, boy! Fetch!" He watched motionless as I threw the stick. When he didn't react I ran after it, picked it up, all the time showing exaggerated excitement about the lovely stick. He just sat and watched with a blank expression. Today I learned that if I throw the stick, I must go and pick up the stick.

****

I wanted Brendan to feel happy and secure in his new home. I wanted to spoil him, so I spent a small fortune – which was actually a *large* fortune – buying the most luxurious, sumptuous basket I could find, with a cosy fleecy lining, plenty big enough but not too big, in a nice manly grey and black colour scheme. If it had come with ample parking I would happily have moved in myself. This beautiful, well-appointed basket would suit a medium dog, young child or very small newlyweds. It seemed very reasonably priced for its size and quality, so I whipped it to the till ASAP, before some over-zealous shelf-stacker realised the mistake and re-priced it accordingly.

The over-smiling assistant asked excitedly how my day was going and then bibbed the barcode; it came up as *twice* what I was expecting. I nearly choked, but being British I just smiled uneasily and said nothing. I'm not afraid to speak out when something's wrong, but I felt the mistake was probably mine, because I should have known this deluxe basket had obviously been placed or dumped on the wrong shelf beneath the wrong price, so I swallowed hard and paid for it. I couldn't refuse it anyway, because it would make me feel like I was trying to scrimp on my boy and I'd never do that.

I installed the luxurious and expensive new basket in the flat and then tried to lure Brendan into it. He came sauntering over to investigate, yawned, stretched and then finally sniffed at it curiously. He looked at it lingeringly, with mild disinterest. I'd rather he'd shown contempt or something with more fire – a basket this expensive deserved to elicit extreme emotions – but this half-hearted apathy was insulting. I put some treats in the basket to coax him into it. He's no fool though and he very gingerly lifted the treats from the basket, with the precision and care of a bomb squad expert. He carried them to a safe distance, defused them and ate them. (It took a while for him to accept the basket, possibly until it started to lose its alien smell of the world outside and began to take on the smell of us and home. Eventually, by which I mean several days later, he slinked into it, curled up and went to sleep.)

Brendan has become really patriotic towards his adopted nation. His Union Jack pillow means he can be patriotic without making any effort.

Although he often sat on the sofa and lay on the bed, once he'd accepted the basket as his own, he retreated there each night for Big Sleeps. When I was in bed, I could clearly see him in his basket: it was a studio flat, so I could see almost everything from the bed. I often used to sit there in the lamplight just looking at him, curled into a tight ball, a ball so much smaller than could scientifically be possible for a dog his size. Occasionally, he would raise his head to check where I was and would catch me watching him. He would sigh and drop his head heavily down again and I know he was wishing it was a two bedroom flat, so he could have his own room.

****

We walked to the field. I took Brendan's macho blue dumbbell squeaky toy with us. I squeaked it and he reacted, standing alert. I threw it and he bounded after it and picked it up. It worked! Sort of. He dropped it again and sat down. I picked up the dumbbell, squeaked it and threw it again. This time he didn't move, he didn't react, he didn't flinch. He looked at me, a certain look... not contempt, not scorn, but *disappointment*; he thought less of me, because this was basically the stick game, but I'd foolishly tried to pimp it up with a squeaky novelty toy. He turned away. We walked home in an awkward silence, with me carrying the dumbbell.

****

Brendan meeting the neighbours was never going to be a good experience for anyone. As the weeks went by he began to get increasingly protective towards his home, which was something of a problem. There are six flats in this Edwardian house, so there are five sets of neighbours coming in through the communal front door, into what Brendan seems to think is his personal property. He barked every time he heard a door, or footsteps, or conversation. Sometimes he barked if he heard none of these things, just to keep me on my toes. There was never a dull moment. There was certainly never a quiet one.

Whenever we left the flat, I did my best to check that the coast was clear, to minimise the risk of encountering anyone. It became second nature to listen at the door, then open it a crack, peer out cautiously, then hurry down the stairs as quickly as possible, dragging a languorous Brendan after me. But this approach was never going to work every time.

The first person we encountered was Mike, who lived directly above us. Most of the time it sounded like we were in the same flat as him, rather than there being a floor and ceiling between us. I could hear every word he said. Every row he had with his girlfriend felt like I was in the same room, standing between them. They slammed doors, they screamed and shouted, they ran up and down the stairs at all hours, they had friends round all night and jumped up and down in the kitchen on the laminate floor at 4am for no apparent reason. I also had a front row seat on their sex life, and I had certainly never willingly bought a ticket. Their bed was immediately above mine and was clearly an ancient and clapped out affair; it was very noisy and groaned and creaked constantly. Fortunately, the sex only occurred about once a month and it never lasted very long. It sounded like someone very slowly and half-heartedly sawing a small piece of wood.

Mike was an odd fish. At first glance, he came across as quite youthful, but he was in his forties. He had shoulder length hair; I think he was going for a Madchester look, but from a distance he looked like Take That's Mark Owen; from close up he looked like a scrotum.

We came back from shopping one day (*I'd* been shopping, Brendan had waited in the car). We entered the flat, I was struggling with several heavy bags, as well as Brendan's lead, so we barged through to the kitchen, momentarily leaving the flat door open. I put the bags down, then returned to the living room and leapt backwards as I saw Mike *attempting* to creep stealthily into the room, though he was actually staggering clumsily, but he was clearly *trying* to be quiet. Fortunately, I hadn't had time to unclip Brendan's lead. We all froze. For a moment I stared at Mike. For a moment Brendan stared at Mike. For a moment we both stared at Mike. And he stared back with his mouth open. Then Brendan flew at him, snarling and snapping ferociously, until he reached the extent of the lead and he stood on two legs clawing and snapping at the air.

Mike retreated towards the hall. "I saw the door was open..." he blurted out. "...and I just wanted to make sure you were OK."

If that was genuinely the case, he shouldn't have been so shocked when he suddenly came face to face with us *in our own flat*. It doesn't really help that he was always complaining about having no money and about the price of alcohol and cigarettes. I decided to keep him at arms-length... or further. (It was some months later that I found out he'd also done it to the new couple downstairs.)

If dogs *do* communicate via their urine, as scientists believe, that evening at the field Brendan would be doing his best to wee the headline: LOCAL HERO BRENDAN CATCHES PISSED UP BURGLAR.

The next time we encountered Mike was on the driveway, thankfully not as he was clearing out our wall safe of priceless diamonds. The thing about Mike was, he was constantly drunk, so he was always staggering, reeling and falling over, which made him quite a threat and a liability to Brendan. (One night, Mike had come out of his flat and toppled over the banister, falling down two storeys and landing crumpled in the stairwell. As he was blind drunk, he had fallen well and only broke his collar bone. Having no body fat to cushion him didn't help, but then he also had no weight to increase his velocity or impact; it would have been like dropping a toothpick).

On this occasion, coming face to face with Brendan outside, Mike loomed right up to him. He could barely stand upright, so he kept pitching forward and Brendan was clearly afraid. Dogs often display fear through aggression, so Brendan displayed all the aggression he could muster. And it was quite a lot. His teeth were bared and his whole face contorted. He looked demonic and a completely different dog to the lazy boy that sprawled across my bed and looked like Skippy.

Mike said he loved dogs and to be fair to him, over the weeks he tried all sorts of tricks to win Brendan over, but Brendan wasn't for being won over. Lastly, Mike decided that if Brendan saw him shaking hands with me, it would show him that we were friends and he was no threat. So we duly shook hands, but Mike forgot to let go and we ended up standing there – in the street – shaking hands for about five minutes. The actual "shaking" part of the handshake was getting slower and slower, so that in the end we were basically just standing there holding hands. All the time, Mike was pitching very gradually forwards, it was like he was falling in very, very slow-motion, until it was only our handshake that was effectively propping him up. When I finally managed to disengage from him, the ploy clearly hadn't worked, and I had to drag Brendan away in a brutal snapping frenzy.

Mike gave up after that and just steered clear of him. He had tried his best to get on Brendan's good side, but sometimes it seems Brendan doesn't actually have a good side. Then again, Mike had established himself as the pie-eyed burglar who had broken into our flat and it seemed Brendan was never going to forget that.

We had similar experiences with the other tenants; most chose to run away when they heard us approaching. Unfortunately, it didn't end with the neighbours. A few weeks after Brendan's arrival, Tim, the landlord's handyman, had to come in and check something. He knocked on the door and Brendan immediately barked and howled like a really vexed banshee. Tim is one of the nicest people you could hope to have poking around your fuse box. He is apparently very highly educated, but has turned his back on academia in favour of a simple life working with his hands and fixing things. I really admire that and can identify with him, although I'm not an academic and I don't much like working with my hands, but I'm with him in theory. Sort of. He's presumably a free spirit, as implied by his huge beard.

Brendan doesn't care about any of these things and as I opened the door, he was making it quite clear that he didn't want people to come into his flat. Brendan and Tim were of one mind, because Tim clearly didn't want to come in either, but he needed to. I think at this point he was regretting not taking the career path as an academic. I held Brendan's collar, while Tim ran into the kitchen. All the time Brendan was straining furiously to get at him. Tim looked quite ashen. He quickly did his checks and made a rapid exit.

I remembered what they'd said at the sanctuary, that when he'd been rehomed previously, Brendan had become possessive and wouldn't admit people into the house. It was now obviously starting here. The upshot was that we no longer had visitors. At all. Ever. This wasn't such a problem for me, as I didn't really welcome people coming into my home. On the plus side, having Brendan meant I no longer had to bark myself to ward people off.

Looking at him sprawled out on the bed, completely relaxed and at ease, he'd made his home here and I vowed that no matter what it took, we'd find a way through this and he would never have to go back.

****

We walked to the local field. I found a tatty old football. It had a slow puncture. Well, isn't that just the perfect metaphor for life? I kicked the abandoned ball towards Brendan. He flinched and cowered. He thought I was attacking him. I gave him a reassuring cuddle and we tried again, with me kicking the ball *away* from him this time. He still reacted to the delayed, dull thud of my foot against the slightly sagging sphere. I gave him another cuddle, ruffled the fur on his head and told him not to be such a softie. I tried rolling the football for him, tenpin bowling-style. He sidestepped it and then eyed it suspiciously, as though it might explode. He didn't bother with it again.

We walked home from the field without the football.

Unlike Brendan, I have always liked walking. I have always gone for walks. Preferably in the countryside, but if not, around the neighbourhood, along secret footpaths, across golf courses, around playing fields, down to the Mersey valley, along abandoned railways. The only problem is that as a solitary man, you're very often viewed with suspicion: seen as a threat, a mugger, a rapist, a paedophile or at least a wandering random nutter. All too often people have crossed the road to avoid me, or seen me in the distance, looked at me, looked again and then disappeared rapidly down a side road. I may look like a killer, but I've hardly ever killed anyone.

Being out with Brendan gives a legitimacy to walking;

people no longer suspect me of being a criminal (simply of harbouring one). The downside though of being out with Brendan is... *Brendan*. Nothing is ever simple with him. The walk to the local field takes five minutes if you dawdle, sniff and wee on a few gateposts, but even that can be a stressful ordeal because of the people and obstacles we might encounter en route. I might look like a serial killer, but I'm not. Conversely, my dog might look like a gorgeous, smiling, huggable puppy – at a distance – but underneath he's got the attitude of a psychopath. And not a very nice one at that. He's definitely less Teddy Bear and more Ted Bundy.

****

They say people are like their dogs, or vice versa. I'm not saying we look alike physically, we absolutely don't... except we both have long legs... and a beard... and we both look miserable most of the time. We certainly share some characteristics. I actually wonder if we were drawn to each other *because* we're similar. Probably not, but I find it intriguing all the same. We are undoubtedly kindred spirits. For a start, we both like dogs and dislike the majority of people. I'm polite on the surface and keep my rage under wraps, so people always think I'm nice. I suppose that could also apply to Brendan. He looks relaxed at the field, sitting calmly and occasionally sniffing the air, with the rage under the surface, hence the countless comments about what a chilled, relaxed and happy dog he appears to be.

But there are also marked differences between us. Brendan enjoys a walk; so do I, but he enjoys walking to the field and then sitting down for an hour. I'm less keen on this. While I'm very guarded with my emotions, Brendan very much wears his heart of the sleeves that he hasn't got. He enjoys sitting in public and looking mournful and miserable. In an alternate reality somewhere, where canines are the dominant species, Brendan is the lead singer of the Smiths.

I admire the way *most* dogs live in the moment and enjoy life; that's the canine aspect I'd most like to take on board. Meanwhile, Brendan wants to be more like a human. He likes the way humans can wear hats; his just fall off.

Brendan is quite flighty in relationships; one sniff and he's off. I hardly ever do that.

He sleeps an awful lot. I don't, instead I spend most of my days feeling tired. He is very much a thinker. I like to believe I also have a philosophical leaning, but while I'm pondering the meaning of life, Brendan's deciding what he's going to wee on next.

We have learned a lot from each other. He has learned how to manipulate me. I have learned that if I throw the ball, I must go and retrieve the ball.

Brendan is Bulgarian. I am British. His first language is Bulgarian. Mine isn't. We communicate primarily via a mixture of mime, body language, telepathy and pidgin English. As long as I understand everything he's trying to tell me and act swiftly to fulfil his needs, we usually get on fine.

Brendan enjoys napping, sniffing, big sleeps, sitting down, going-to-the-field-and-sitting-down and sunbathing. He dislikes travelling. He likes staying at home. I have a partner; Brendan doesn't, he's single. He recently took part in an "anything goes" bisexual orgy at the field, which was designed by the dogs solely to embarrass their attendant humans. It succeeded.

****

We walked to the local field. I took along a tennis ball. I threw the ball and Brendan chased it and picked it up. He carried it for a matter of seconds and then dropped it. Forever. (Can you see a theme here?) We walked home with me carrying the ball.

****

Almost from Day One, I started leaving Brendan in the flat for short periods of time while I took the rubbish or recycling down. This was to get him accustomed to being home alone. He was always glad to see me when I got back. I left him with music playing and also various treats. He never touched the treats while I was out; he ate them ravenously when I came back in.

The plan was to steadily increase the time, because we had imminent theatre tickets and – because of his unpredictable behaviour – we didn't dare ask anyone else to look after him.

We went to the theatre. I was worried about him the whole time and it was no fun at all. When I got home I found the internal door into the living room wouldn't open and I had to force it. Blocking the door were piles and piles of wool-like fibre from the carpet that he'd clawed and chewed into oblivion. He was ecstatic to see me, in an uncontrollable frenzy of excitement, which was both touching and upsetting. I wasn't cross with him, despite all the damage. A three foot square section of carpet nearest the door had been completely destroyed. I felt so sorry for him, because he must have been frightened and I felt guilty having left him. I took him out immediately and we ran round the block without stopping; he was absolutely wired.

Once back inside, he wolfed down all the various treats that were scattered around, ate two bowls of food and then fell into a deep, exhausted sleep. I had obviously left him too long, too soon, but it couldn't really be avoided and I was keen to establish that we each had our own lives and couldn't be together all day every day. He had decimated the carpet and I would need to replace it. (I still haven't.) I will have to pay for the damage and it will cost a fortune. But more worryingly, I felt I couldn't leave him alone again.

The first time the carpet was chewed up.

I felt trapped. It made me feel resentful towards the people who said I should get a dog and to all the people

I met at the field who constantly told me how chilled Brendan was. I had felt like a prisoner before I got him, trapped in my flat, unable to go out. Now I still felt like a prisoner, trapped in my flat, unable to go out. But with a dog.

****

We walked to the local field. We walked there a hundred times. At various points I took a squeaky dumbbell, a tennis ball, a partially deflated football, a rope toy, a squeaky Christmas cracker, a rugby ball, a rubber pull toy. I threw them, I threw each of them, I threw them all. I threw them repeatedly. Brendan ran after each of them precisely once. And once only.

I stopped taking toys. We walked to the field; Brendan had a sit down; we walked back.

****

No one could accuse Brendan of being the happiest dog on the block, but then he probably says that about me. It very quickly became obvious that there was a lot in life that Brendan didn't like. He had baggage. He'd had a troubled past. He was aggressive to people because he didn't trust them and he had good reason not to. There's a certain safety in keeping people at bay. (I realise I've just described my own philosophy.)

Nicky started calling us the Odd Couple. We went everywhere together; if I went, my dog went. You invited me, you got my dog. If you didn't want my dog, you didn't get me; that's what I told people and I'm sure Brendan told his friends the same too. That could explain why we rarely ever got invites.

It wasn't really by choice, because it would have been healthier if we'd had time apart and had our own friends, our own hobbies, but Brendan had torn up the flat; it happened several times and the area of floor covered by carpet was getting less and less. It was clear I couldn't leave him in alone or he'd destroy everything. Also, several of the neighbours worked irregular shifts, so I was very conscious about leaving him in and him barking when they were trying to sleep. This was compounded by Mike and his girlfriend upstairs setting him off barking with their arguments, doors slamming and monotonous sex. It was mainly due to these complications – or so I tell myself – that Brendan became my constant, night and day, all-weather, come rain, come shine, all-growling, all-snarling 24/7 companion. So: the Odd Couple.

We quickly established a routine at home, one that suited us both. Correction: Brendan quickly established a routine at home, one that suited him, with complete disregard for anyone else. He liked to sleep in late; he definitely wasn't a morning person. I got up at seven and gave him a cuddle in his sumptuous basket. He sighed and grumbled, then curled up tighter in the hope that I'd go away. He was never ready to go out before ten, often much later. I don't know how his bladder coped, but he steadfastly refused to go out early without me dragging him all the way. Eventually we slipped into a pattern: unless we had an appointment, we worked to his timetable.

Brendan barked a lot in the flat, at the neighbours,

at birds in the trees... and at the trees themselves, at any noises at all. But that was nothing compared to the commotion he created when we ventured out into the world; a world full of all the things that Brendan hated, loathed, despised and barked at. He barked a lot. Apart from neighbours and strangers, he also barked at my dad and Nicky's mum, which is very unfortunate, because they tried so hard and they just wanted to love him.

Brendan didn't only bark at people. Oh no. He didn't restrict himself. Whilst we were out walking, I lived in constant fear of a plane flying overhead. Brendan absolutely hated planes: they were loud and frightening; they tore open the sky, they hovered overhead and were quite unnatural, powered by witchcraft probably. He seemed to think planes were an invading force and he would bark furiously at them to ward them off. Once or twice he chased a plane right across the field and frightened it away. By his reckoning, he had saved his beloved adopted country from invasion by aircraft on countless occasions.

Brendan hated lights at night. This was especially unfortunate, because night was generally the time when you got an increase in lighting. He went into a frenzy when he saw the moon, especially a full moon. Even the regular street lamps presented a problem and we had many a nocturnal stand-off with them. Then there were flashing burglar alarms, movement-triggered security lights, approaching car headlights and UFOs. Brendan would categorically *not* like to have been abducted by a UFO. And the aliens probably wouldn't have enjoyed it much either.

Brendan hated wheelie bins, so I dreaded Bin Day. You possibly call it Tuesday, but to us it was always Bin Day. It was a nightmare. Wheelie bins lined the streets like colour co-ordinated daleks. Brendan would rather leap into traffic than walk near a bin... and he tried, on many occasions, to do just that. The first problem was that he was fastidious and didn't like things being out of place; the bins didn't *normally* line the streets, then suddenly there they all were, blocking every pavement. It was as though they had received an unheard command from their mother ship and swarmed out of hiding and amassed on our carriageways. They were everywhere and you couldn't avoid them. Worse still, after they'd been emptied, on very windy days, they had been known to skitter across the pavement and chase us. Finally, the bin lorry was huge and noisy; it smelled rank and left a cloying fug – reminiscent of mouldering soup tins – in its wake. It came with an army of human slaves, all men* and all wearing hi-viz clothing. It was like most of Brendan's "hate list" rolled into one. He unequivocally did not like Bin Day. It was rubbish.

* Bin Women are also available. Probably.

Actually, there was an awful lot that Brendan didn't like. I'm picking the highlights, because the full list was very long. I'm not too sure what he actually *did* like. Probably nothing.

All this negativity and barking – apart from being highly stressful – made me wonder if Brendan was really happy here or whether I had actually done him a disservice by wrenching him from the sanctuary. I was concerned that he was essentially a pack animal and I had taken him away from his pack. He clearly liked dogs and very clearly didn't like people. He had obviously been badly mistreated during his secretive past life that we never spoke about. At best he viewed humans with suspicion; at worst he viewed them as items on the menu.

Living in close proximity to other people – the neighbours, I mean – wasn't really suiting Brendan. He wasn't getting used to the noises of their comings and goings and he barked at everything... at all hours of the day and night. His behaviour wasn't really getting any better; he was aggressive with most people, most of the time. He seemed constantly edgy and on high alert, never able to fully relax.

When we left the field he pulled frantically to get home. I took this as a good sign, that he felt safe there and he liked it. Once inside he would leap onto the bed with excitement, but a few minutes later he looked depressed and miserable. Of course, you can't project human traits onto animals. Dogs are different to humans – humans hardly ever run around the field wearing nothing but a collar and dogs seldom wear flip-flops – but we still tend to bestow them with human characteristics, we just can't help it. So, even if it's anthropomorphically invalid, I've never known a dog look so miserable.

It seemed the evidence was mounting that he needed to be back at the sanctuary, because living in a one human/one dog relationship wasn't going to work for him. I hated the thought that in trying to help him I was forcing an alien lifestyle on him that was making him feel unhappy.

Technically, I was only fostering him on a semi-permanent basis, so in theory he "belonged" to the sanctuary still. I had regularly toyed with the notion of taking him back there for a visit, to see how he reacted, as a way of reassuring myself about what *he* wanted and needed. If he clung close to my legs, I'd assume he wanted to stay with me, but if he ran off and didn't want to come with me at home time, then that would be a clear indication that he wanted to remain there. Don't get me wrong, if he chose to stay I would be very upset, but I was genuinely thinking of him. I know I'd be devastated without him, but I was prepared to go through that if it was the best thing for him.

In one of their more pro-active moments, the sanctuary suggested that before doing that, I should contact a dog behaviouralist, who had worked successfully with them on a number of occasions. It seemed a reasonable idea, so I gave him a call. His name was James. He said he would prefer to come to us, so he could see us in our natural environment and gauge where we were going wrong.

On the day, he phoned to say he was outside; I put Brendan on his lead and we went down to meet him. I had expressed my concerns about Brendan being aggressive towards him, especially with it being a man who was going to invade our home. James had said, "It's OK. Keep him on his lead, but allow him to come towards me." I opened the front door tentatively as James was coming up the drive. He was in his thirties; he apparently had three dogs of his own and a new baby

– and he looked understandably tired.

Brendan flew at him snarling, halted mid-flight, of course, by his lead. James stopped, but showed no fear. He was wearing a pouch on his belt, from which he scooped a handful of cheese and ham cubes, which he flung towards Brendan; they hit the uneven crazy paving, bounced and scattered in an arc. The Boy immediately started snuffling around for them and eating them in a frenzy. Once he'd found every morsel, the growling resumed, so James threw some more. This went on for some time.

I was disappointed that Brendan was being so easily manipulated, I would have thought he'd have seen through this very obvious ploy to win him over, as I would have done. Perhaps we weren't so similar after all. I wouldn't do whatever James said just because he threw bits of food for me. Unless it was cake, then I probably would.

Within a few minutes of feeding Brendan treat food, he was able to kneel down and stroke him. Brendan wasn't a complete push over though, and every time the treats stopped he would revert to snarling, so he was showered with another handful of cheese and ham.

"I guess we're OK to go inside now." James said. I think; he had an almost impenetrable Irish accent.

I led the way upstairs; James followed, but when he tried to enter the flat, Brendan lunged at him aggressively. The cheese and ham raining down immediately derailed him.

"This is the secret. Get yourself a treat pouch. Cut up tins of luncheon meat and cheese. Give them to him at all stress times, so if someone approaches or something startles him, distract him with some treats. De-escalate his moods before they set in."

I asked a lot of questions about this, because to me it seemed like rewarding him for aggressive behaviour, but James assured me it would work. We talked for a long time, James asking questions about Brendan and our routine. Brendan calmed down completely and he and James seemed like old friends.

I asked about Brendan's seeming low mood. Poor James must get sick of confronting the same questions every day of his working life, but then again, it's his job. Lying on a bed didn't mean a dog was depressed, he said. Dogs sleep for around twenty hours a day. I think Brendan would argue that wasn't nearly enough. James asked how far we walked. I was going to Dad's twice a day at this point, which was at least forty minutes each way. He said that was too much and I should be aiming for two hours exercise a day and that slow sniff walks were as good or better than long, energetic walks.

At James's request, we took him to our local field. He lent us a ten metre training lead, which trailed after Brendan, so he could have a run about. The idea was, you could stand on the end of the lead if he started to run off, but because of the treat pouch, Brendan didn't stray far. James miraculously got him chasing squeaky toys and running around like a puppy, which was lovely to see.

38

I think the most revealing thing James said, which I had never heard before and never read about in any of my online researches, was how stressed dogs can get, how they carry stress with them and how the stress would build up in them, weakening their heart and reducing their lifespan. I think it's easy to see dogs as simple creatures who enjoy the good things in life, like a run and food and being with people. It was quite an eye opener to hear that the truth is almost the opposite.

I asked about Brendan barking all the time, at noises, at the neighbours, at people in the street. Apparently, he's alerting me to a possible threat to him and he wants to be sure I'm aware of that threat and will protect him. I've noticed that if he's lying on the bed and he hears a noise in the garden, he'll bark, but he doesn't leap up and go and investigate the threat, as I would have expected; he stares at me until I go to check. I'll go to the window and his eyes will follow me expectantly. I will look out and check there are no vagabonds scaling the walls or no badgers snuffling under the apple tree. I'll say: "It's OK, boy, relax." He will then settle down again. It's touching really, this trust he places in me... But also not at all touching, because he's essentially using me as cannon fodder.

Each time I suspect stress is clearly building up in him, such as after an incident or after a firework has gone off, or he's felt threatened by someone in jogging bottoms, I have to de-escalate with a treat, which will hopefully distract him, so he'll forget why he was anxious in the first place. The bottom line is: throw food at the problem. Literally.

Finally, I voiced my fears about the suitability of Brendan living here, because I felt I had taken him away from his ideal lifestyle, running wild at the sanctuary as part of a pack. James' response was quite reassuring; he said that at the sanctuary, Brendan – and all the dogs – would be on high alert all day, every day, as they needed to constantly assert their place within the pack. This was very stressful for a dog and they could never fully switch off. He was certain that if Brendan went back to the sanctuary, it would have a detrimental effect and he would probably only get to half his life expectancy. He insisted that living here with me was a better life for him and he felt confident that in time Brendan would bond fully; he would realise this was his home and he would feel safe and secure here. He was quite adamant that no matter how it seemed on the surface, if I took Brendan back to the sanctuary, I would effectively be cutting his life short.

That was all I needed to hear to reassure me. He was definitely here for keeps.

****

My life had changed completely and unimaginably – *twice* – in a relatively short time. Firstly, I had gone from a challenging job of fifty-plus hours a week, many of them unsociable hours: evenings, weekends, including trips away and being on call… to nothing. I had lived and breathed work, I got calls at all hours of the day and night and I never switched off. I wasn't a high powered executive juggling stocks and shares, I wasn't a CEO, I wasn't Bill Gates, I was simply a support worker for people with learning disabilities, and latterly – and very grudgingly – I was steered into managing the team I had been a part of. That all finished overnight.

Despite having been paid off – so I had money in the bank – and finally having time on my hands, I found I was struggling to leave the house and finding it increasingly difficult to interact with people. Then Brendan came along and moved in with his tatty, foul-smelling carrier bag of possessions. Immediately, my whole life revolved around him. I was never alone; we were together twenty-four hours a day. We were a unit, a team. We belonged together. We were like two pieces from a weird jigsaw that had been left behind in a charity shop that no one wanted to buy, even though it was a really, really special jigsaw.

Being part of a really special jigsaw was fine, but life was still very difficult and stressful and challenging. I was constantly trying to avoid people so Brendan wouldn't fly at them. We had to avoid moving vehicles, the moon, wheelie bins, visitors, relatives, neighbours, rush-hour, people with walking sticks, people with shopping bags, people wearing headphones, planes, gardeners, runners and so on… Weeks turned into months and he didn't seem to be getting any better and I thought something had to give.

I had no job, so I had time on my hands. I'd had a pay-off from work, so I had money in the bank. I had a camper van. It had long since been a dream and a plan to travel around the coast of Britain. I had started last year, but then Dad had got ill and my van broke down – conveniently at the same time – so I came home. Dad was now much fitter and stronger and Social Services had arranged for carers to call in three times a day, so he no longer needed my constant attention. The sun was shining and there would never be a better time for taking a trip. I decided that Brendan and I should take this trip together; travelling is always a bonding experience. It's true that his ideal trip would be over to the field for a sit down, but I know he was also keen to become better acquainted with his newly-adopted homeland. I'm para-phrasing, but I think I know my dog well enough to feel sure it's exactly what he wanted.

****

Dog facts:
A dog's nose print is unique, like a human's fingerprint. In all likelihood, Brendan's nose print is on the criminal databases of most European countries.

Brendan, on one of his so-called "walks".

CHAPTER 2: GONE WEST: THE UNDERDOGS HAVE A BREAK DOWN

It's after midnight and I'm driving through the darkness, heading south, along the M6 – not very fast, due to roadworks. Eagle One is the only vehicle that isn't a huge lorry. She's my trusty Citroen Relay camper van, supposedly a four berth, but that's ridiculous; she's adequate for one person if you pack light and enjoy being cramped. The pull-out "double bed" is five foot square. I'm six foot four, so whichever way I lie, it's just too small. Add a dog into the equation and things become quite challenging.

Talking of which, my new and somewhat reluctant travelling companion is asleep in the back. Brendan: he came with his name… and his luxury basket, which takes up a considerable amount of the available space. He's had his travel sickness pills and is breathing easily. Driving is much better for him at night. As we crawl ever-southwards, Brendan is having a nightmare and is jerking his paws, whining, barking and growling. When I gently awaken him, he sees his nightmare is indeed a reality: he really *is* in a campervan, driving down a motorway.

Ahead, the corridor of white lights curves into the distance. I'm suddenly feeling a bit daunted by the trip, overwhelmed and panicky. I always miss Nicky the most on the first day of a voyage. I'm feeling alone and lonely, despite Brendan being only inches away. So I turn up the music and sing my way through the night.

I doze for an hour or so in various services, but it's cold, very noisy and not very relaxing. Eventually, the sun comes up and it turns into a fresh, crisp, early morning. I pull into Severn View services for another break. For me a trip or a holiday only really begins at the first brew stop. After what he considers to have been a tiring journey, Brendan decides he wants to stay in the van and have a nap.

I step out alone onto the dirty, stained tarmac, with the constant roar of traffic from all around. I buy a coffee, then go for a short walk – without my dog – to the viewpoint over a metallic sheet of water, the Bristol Channel. Striding across it is the stunning Severn Bridge, which is a feat of engineering, with its twin uprights and gracefully arched cables. It's an iconic landmark; Brendan will be sorry he's missed this. (He won't.) I've come away to share new experiences with my dog, but he's slept all the way and – unlike any normal dog – has passed up the chance for a walk in favour of a post-slumber nap.

Despite the fact that we've been driving for several hours, this bridge is the symbolic start of our journey. It has long been my ambition to travel and explore the coast of Britain. I began in the early autumn last year, at the start of England, the Solway Firth. I drove anti-clockwise, heading south, through the northwest and then through Wales. * By the time I got to the Welsh side of the Severn Bridge, my van, Eagle One, needed some serious attention and my dad had become ill, so I had to abort and return home. I didn't know whether I'd ever be able to continue, but my van and my dad have both been repaired. Eagle One has had medical attention and been in respite, and my dad has been welded back together. But now I'm back, carrying on from where I left off. I was alone before, but this time I have my dog with me, man's best friend… and yet I'm still standing here alone.

So far Brendan has made absolutely no difference to this trip whatsoever. But I miss him. And I'm really glad he's here.

* * * * * * * * * *

We set off into the heart of Somerset, famously a county big on producing cider, known locally – or if you're in a cheap comedy sketch – as "zyder". Specifically "Zomerzet zyder".

We stop in Portishead. I wake Brendan; he yawns and blinks slowly. Very reluctantly, he rises from his basket, and – with ongoing encouragement – we set off to explore this pleasantly suburban small town.

Locals sit on benches looking across a boating lake, enjoying the sunshine. I have to rein Brendan in every time we pass a man, especially an older man… or a young man, or any man. We only touched down a matter of minutes ago and already it's really stressful. The lakeside is too busy, so we continue to the beach, which is deserted. For a reason. The word "beach" is perhaps upgrading it somewhat; it's rocky and looks like a quarry. Brendan potters amongst the rocks and stones and has a sniff and a sit down. For all I know, this may well be his first experience of the sea, though technically it's just the wide Severn estuary at this point, with hazy views of Wales opposite.

Because it's our first day it seems fitting to have lunch out, so we find a nice pub. Only one other table is occupied, by a middle-aged grandma accompanied by her young granddaughter, Shirley Temple. The kid is complete with ringlets and a lisp. As we walk past their table, a secret dog underneath starts yapping furiously.

"Sorry." Grandma says to me, "He's just very noisy. Ignore him."

I do. Surprisingly, so does Brendan. He can tell from the high-pitched bleating that it's a small dog and not worth his while. (When Brendan barks, it's the bark of a huge dog, the bark of a dog that means business. If Brendan barks at you, you don't assume he's dishing out platitudes; you hand over your wallet and run.)

I hear Shirley Temple say precociously: "Grandma... why didn't you tell that man what type of dog Harvey is?"

Grandma continues with her food. "Because he didn't ask."

"Grandma, *why* didn't you *tell him*?"

"Because not everyone wants to know."

"Hello! Hello! *Hello!*" I realise Shirley Temple is shouting to me. I turn round. "He's a bichon frise!"

"Oh... right." It could well be a lie, because I never lay eyes on the dog.

Brendan is brilliantly behaved while I eat my rich vegetable curry, whereas Harvey is petulant, spoilt and irritating. He keeps yapping and howling: all unseen. Brendan is fine with all the staff who approach the table, until one poor young man comes to clear the plates and Brendan goes off on one. Harvey goes very quiet after this, probably realising that he very definitely *isn't* the top dog around here.

* * * * * * * * * *

My impression of Portishead is of a pleasantly genteel town and I could happily stay longer. (Be careful what you wish for!) But Brendan's pretty much exhausted the place. His favourite bits so far include sitting down near the lake and barking at pensioners, a sit down on the beach, a nap under the table in the pub – followed by barking at a waiter – and a leisurely sit down at the marina, so he's covered all the highlights.

We get back onboard Eagle One and set off. Straight away I can tell something is very wrong with the van, with the noisy bit at the front, that some call the "engine". As we pull out of the car park people turn and stare, which isn't generally a good sign. As we drive along the main road people stop on the pavement and gawp open-mouthed. There's a terrible screeching, which is both high-pitched and low at the same time: a grinding, a grating, a squealing with a deep undertone. I've never heard that sound before; I've never heard a noise quite like it. I'm no mechanic, so I do the only thing I know how to do, which is turn the stereo up. Brendan is curled up in his basket – after his strenuous morning of sitting down – seemingly relaxed and oblivious to the cacophony. I decide that if I drive on and ignore the noise it will most probably go away, so that's what I do.

The beautiful Eagle One: my van.

Our next port of call is neighbouring town, Clevedon. It looks promising, but as I approach the seafront there's a dull clunk and it sounds like the whole engine has dropped out. The gears are gone and we're losing motive power. I jab at the hazard lights and steer towards the side of the road. We cruise, ever-slower, into a bus stop and come to a halt. No gears, no forward motion. I grip the steering wheel and watch the hazard lights blinking on and off. I feel numb. It's our first day and I can't believe this is happening. As far as Brendan's aware, this might be how every day "on holiday" pans out. I can tell he's not a fan. He sits up, alert, looking around, realising something is awry.

I call the AA and as ever they are efficient and helpful, instantly deploying their nearest operative. This turns out to be Mike. Mike's big, friendly, bearded and local – not necessarily in that order. He hops in the driving seat and jiggles about for a while. I'm on pins because Brendan is only inches behind him, but he's strangely passive. It's almost as if he knows Mike is trying to help us. But Mike *can't* help us. It isn't the gearbox as I'd suspected, but the clutch. The clutch has gone. It's gone west.

Thankfully, Mike takes charge of things, because I can't focus on anything other than the words circling around in my head: "Don't bite Mike! Don't bite Mike!" Weirdly, Brendan is still being a model citizen. Mike makes a few calls and gets us booked in at a garage back at Portishead for the work to be done the next day. He arranges for us to stay on the industrial estate in the van overnight. He tows us back "on the bar", which means I stay at the wheel, steering and braking, which is quite an experience. We set off slowly, but once Mike's confident in my abilities, he turns onto a dual carriageway and puts his foot down. It's exhilarating in a way that only terror can be. It must be fairly smooth, because Brendan has curled up again in his basket.

We arrive unscathed on an industrial estate in Portishead, which is full of men: young men, middle-aged men, men holding spanners, men carrying wrenches, men in baseball caps and men in overalls, which in Brendan's eyes constitutes a uniform. He barks at all of them, all of the time. They're all very good and very patient with him. Several of the mechanics look under the bonnet and tut a lot. I stand on the street with Brendan pulled close to my leg, snarling continually.

Mike comes over. "Right, I'm off." He shakes my hand firmly. "Good luck."

He bends down to stroke Brendan. My heart is in my mouth. "Oh, no, Mike... He's..."

"It's OK. I'm great with dogs... He can smell my dog, can't you boy?"

Brendan seems quite relaxed and appears to be nuzzling him, but I've seen this before.

"Mike, it's just he's very unpredictable..."

"He's fine, he's fine, aren't you, boy?"

Brendan rubs his head against Mike's hand in a seemingly affectionate manner, then it's as though he detects that Mike has now served his purpose and is no longer any use to us. He suddenly flashes round and snaps at the mechanic's leg, unprovoked and without any flicker of a warning. Mike leaps backwards; he is clearly shocked and taken completely by surprise. His over-trousers are ripped towards the top, inner-thigh area, just below crotch level, but dangerously close.

"Oh god, I'm sorry, Mike! Are you OK?"

Mike's staring at his crotch in dismay. "Oh no... These were new on this morning! They're ruined!"

All things considered – if the only damage is to his AA-issue over-trousers, then we can chalk this up as a success, because it was very nearly a whole lot worse.

Mike had been so helpful, knowledgeable and friendly, but he doesn't hang around after this. He says a clipped goodbye and shuffles off with his tail between his legs – for which he should be grateful.

* * * * * * * * * *

It's late afternoon. We leave Eagle One on the industrial estate and retreat as far away as possible from all the milling mechanics. We end up at the new harbour development, known as Port Marine. Most towns with water have reclaimed their derelict docklands and quaysides; Portishead has done exactly that. It is an eclectic mix of French windows, Georgian doors, balconies; a mish-mash of architectural styles and shapes, all designed to make you think life is cosmopolitan and fun; that life is for *living*.

Brendan the Thinker in Portishead.

It's sunny and warm, people are cycling home or

strolling for drinks after work. Brendan has a sit down amongst the uprights of a modern sculpture and gazes out across the Bristol Channel to a dark smear of land where Wales ought to be.

A passing lady with a lapdog gazes at my boy in awe. "What a lovely looking dog! What's he called?"

"Brendan. He came with his name. I didn't choose it."

"Bernard? What a nice name. It suits him."

I laugh. I wish he *was* called Bernard, it really *does* suit him.

I set off with "Bernard" along the main waterway, overlooked by newbuild apartments, with a vaguely Scandinavian feel, painted in subtle pastel shades. A huge gang of Norwegian Hell's Angels roar quietly and sedately into town in single file, so maybe we *are* in Scandinavia after all. Brendan watches them with interest, his head cocked to one side, as they park neatly and sensibly, get off their bikes *en masse*, feed money into parking meters and then stand chatting in a hushed, civilised, almost business-like manner, which just seems so *Scandinavian.* They probably do a litter pick before they move on – they're just so *nice* and considerate.

I can tell Brendan is eager to get back to the van for a rest. We tramp along the footpath with weary paws. All the day workers have gone home from the industrial estate, but rather than being empty, the streets are now filled with a dozen articulated lorries, parked up for the night. The drivers are obviously still inside, some have curtains drawn, others are sitting up eating or staring into space. At least we won't be here alone in the small hours, though our van is conspicuously the only vehicle not a lorry.

It's eight o'clock in the evening. In Portishead, the church bells are ringing over the corrugated roofs of the rather drab industrial units. The sunlight begins to fade and Day One draws to an end. It's not been the first day I had planned, certainly not what I had hoped for – we're parked up overnight on an industrial estate – but we're not despondent. We're determined to put our best foot forward – Brendan's got more choice than I have – and make the most of everything. We're resolute.

We're both really tired after a long day, so I make up the bed, have a cup of tea and we snuggle down for a good night's sleep. At least that's the theory.

* * * * * * * * * *

At around midnight, the burglar alarm in the nearest industrial unit goes off. Brendan leaps off the bed and is jumping up and down barking. There are flashing lights and a shrill, ear-piercing electronic alarm. There's nothing I can do. I can't even drive off to avoid the sound. I try and pacify Brendan and eventually he calms down. I'm fully expecting the police to screech up, but they don't. No one comes.

The alarm goes on for over an hour. Just when I'm getting used to the undulating rhythm and am starting to filter it out, it stops. The sudden harsh silence is now just as disturbing. Brendan sits up abruptly, looks around, hesitates, then flops down again. I try and get comfortable and attempt to get used to the huge nocturnal void.

A few hours later, we're jolted awake again, when the horn of one of the huge lorries parked across the street starts blaring, repeatedly and frantically. It isn't like a car horn, it's a deep, dangerous, gut-punching baritone. It vibrates and throbs: it's three dimensional. Again, poor Brendan is on his feet, standing on the bed, his eyes wide, his tail tucked between his legs.

There's shouting. A man shouting, I can't hear the words, just a high-pitched and hysterical tirade. Brendan looks at me, then quickly lies down and curls up tightly. He's obviously decided not to challenge this one. The horn carries on sounding, it's rapid and repeated. I realise it's doing SOS. I'm up, sweating, peering out of the window. It's still dark, lit with orange street lamps. I can't see any movement or lights. In all the other dozen lorries the cabs are curtained and no one appears to be stirring, which seems odd, because I would have thought they'd go to the rescue of one of their own, a fellow lorry driver.

I pick up my phone and dial 999. Before the call connects, the horn has stopped and I can hear voices; no longer shouting, but talking. It all sounds calm and relaxed. I cancel the 999 call. I hear an engine start, a deep, low, rattling engine, then hear a lorry drive slowly away. My heart's racing and I'm wide awake, pumped full of adrenaline. Brendan is stretched out now and dozing peacefully. I know I won't be able to sleep again because I'm far too agitated, so I decide to brew up. I'm English; there is never a time when brewing up is a bad idea. I tip the remains of my final water bottle into the kettle. It's less than a thimbleful. I'm now completely out of water, apart from the inch in Brendan's bowl. I consider syphoning some of it off, but it's full of hairs. I get back into bed and lie awake for hours, while Brendan starts to snore.

* * * * * * * * * *

In a complete contrast to yesterday, I wake up to find today is bitterly cold and windy. It isn't raining yet, but it certainly looks like rain is imminent. I start to put the kettle on, but remember there's no water. Brendan is dozing peacefully, curled up tightly. As the workers start to arrive on the industrial estate, I have to rouse him and he isn't pleased about it. He is definitely *not* bright-eyed and he's far from bushy-tailed this morning. And I'm the same. We're both very tired and very cold.

We head to the site office to hand over Eagle One's keys. Mechanics and admin staff scatter like marbles as we approach. Brendan doesn't single anyone out; he barks at all of them. Continually. I'm told the van will be ready by five at the latest, so off we go, through the damp back streets of Portishead. We're a bit less resolute today. And we're tired. And we're hungry. And we're cold. We gravitate towards the marina, which is cold and grey. Everything is cold and grey. Rigging on the moored yachts chinks and rattles. The water is dark and choppy. All colour and life seem to have gone from the place. It's still early and very few people are about. None of the cafes seem to be open. It's like a ghost town; a cold, grey shadow of its former, vibrant self.

Brendan drags his paws beside me. This isn't his idea of how to start the day. He's mastered the hangdog expression perfectly. Every time we stop to cross a road he sits down and yawns.

We wander aimlessly with nowhere to go and nothing to do. I just want to find somewhere to get warm; Brendan just wants to go back to bed. It takes a very long time to get to nine o'clock, when a café bar on the quayside opens its doors. At first it looks like a hideous pre-fab factory, but it's actually made from twenty-eight old shipping containers. Inside is a comfortable lounge area with rugs and mismatched sofas and armchairs, all retro and vintage and other words meaning "old and bought from a house clearance sale". It's really welcoming and it's warm. We are the first and only patrons.

Brendan is contented, stretched out on a deep, red Persian rug. I drink my crisp leaf tea and order a breakfast. I try reading for a bit, *On the Road* by Jack Kerouac, because it's about travelling and we're travelling. Sort of. Supposed to be. I keep reading the same sentence over and over. My blinking is getting very laboured and I know I can't fight the lure of sleep much longer. And worst of all, if I do fall asleep, I will most probably awaken to find Brendan has eaten the staff and robbed the till.

After an hour and a half of slow blinking and my head lolling backwards, I can't delay the inevitable any longer. We set off outside. It's still freezing, which really wakes me up. We bump into an eccentric old lady, who is bizarrely strolling along through the fog carrying a flimsy multi-coloured parasol. "Oh, what a lovely dog... Is it a boy? What's he called?"

"Brendan. He came with his name."

"Ah, hello Brenda!"

To prove a point, Brendan – a male dog with a male name – proudly raises a hind leg and starts licking himself. I retreat hastily, dragging him after me.

Throughout the morning, I receive several texts from Nicky. She seems quite concerned about us. "Are you OK?" "Any news about van?" "How's B doing?" "Are you VERY stressed?" "Are you upset about van?" "Are you coping?" But I *am* coping. No one's more surprised than I am, but I'm taking everything in my stride. I actually feel very chilled. Well, freezing to be honest. I'm just getting along, filling my day and coping with this unexpected interruption. My main ordeal and limiting factor is Brendan, because it's so difficult to go anywhere with him.

The day eventually warms up, warm enough to sit outdoors, so we sit on benches, we sit on grass and we sit on rocks, logs and railings. We sit down *a lot*, which is fine, because it's Brendan's number one hobby.

Brendan is loving Portishead – well, we both are, which is just as well, because it doesn't feel like we'll ever be leaving. At five o'clock I receive a call – a call I don't want to receive – from the garage. They had fitted the new part, it was the wrong part and it had broken. The van wouldn't be finished today. But worse still, Eagle One is currently twelve feet up in the air on a ramp, with her engine loose, held in place by supports and jacks, so we can't sleep in her tonight.

They suggest we stay in a Travelodge. I almost say yes, but then I glance at Brendan who's having another sit down. It suddenly seems unfeasible to get a room in a hotel with him, with strange noises and people coming and going constantly. It just wouldn't work.

To their credit, having already experienced Brendan, they take this on board. Instead, they kindly arrange for us to stay in one of their offices. It turns out that most of the industrial estate is owned by one man, I'll call him Ryan to protect his identity. Further down the street, he has a self-storage business. We're installed in a dusty, disused office at the front on the ground floor. Ryan himself jets over in his open-topped sports car to show us around and, I think, to vet us and give the thumbs up for us staying on his premises. He's a sun-tanned businessman in a pink polo shirt, who – apart from his gold jewellery – seems very down to earth and approachable. He's very easy going and likeable... at first... until, Brendan takes an instant *dislike* to him and snarls and barks savagely. Like Mike the Mechanic, Ryan seems a little less friendly after this and is probably regretting his impetuous kindness.

"One of the lads in the office upstairs will leave you with a key. There's a camera in the room. We can't switch it off." Ryan indicates an old fashioned camera in a corner with its red light blinking away. "A security firm views the cameras and responds to any call outs... so don't do any naked dancing." He mimes a hands-in-the-air, hip-grinding dance, which must be how he dances when he's naked. I assure him naked dancing isn't on the cards. Not by me anyway and I think Brendan is too tired.

Locking The Boy in the office, I'm taken to the garage where Eagle One is suspended from the ceiling. I'm allowed to climb a ladder and go inside to get any essential overnight luggage, but it's one trip only, so I need to be selective and I need to be quick. The most important item is Brendan's basket. And Brendan's food. Brendan's water bowl. His brush. His chew toy, his treats and his Travel Scrabble. I forget virtually everything I might possibly need for myself, apart from my sleeping bag.

A friendly bloke from the office upstairs hands me a silver key. "That's for the front door. Have a good night. I'm the last one and I'm off now. I'll lock up when I leave."

A moment later I hear his footsteps bounding along the corridor. The front door opens and closes. I hear the scraping as the lock slides home. There is the screeching of tyres and the rapid accelerating of a small, but souped-up car and we're alone... Probably... Because then – and several times throughout the evening – we both hear what sounds like footsteps in the office above us.

Brendan eats all his tea and drinks a bowl full of water, then slinks into his basket and goes immediately into a deep sleep. He's had a long and strenuous day and a lot of stress with traffic and lots of men and now he's been thrust into a strange and alien place. He's flaked out.

I decide that he's so tired I can afford to nip out to Sainsbury's at the end of the road to get myself something nice, but cold, for my tea. I go to the front door, a typical modern, double-glazed, metal-framed, office door. I slip my key into the lock – and discover that not only are we alone, we're locked in. The key doesn't turn. It's the wrong key. I try several times. I try being gentle, I try being forceful, I try being aggressive, I try swearing at it, I try threatening it, but none of these things work. We're locked in.

What if there's a fire, flood, earthquake, famine or some other emergency? Being locked in is actually quite scary. There are two windows in the office, but they're specially adapted to only open a couple of inches. If there was a fire, I'd break the windows or the front door. They are all double glazed, so it would be difficult, but I'm confident it wouldn't present too much of a problem. I start to relax.

I decide I'd better not report this to Nicky or she'll panic. She's already worrying because my phone is running out of power and I've not brought my charger out of the van. I decide I can survive on the rations I've brought. Some chocolate, a small packet of nuts and a Tupperware box of cherry tomatoes, radishes and beetroot. I eat as much of the salad as I can stand, then find half of it has gone off, but unlike meat, this won't cause a lethal issue, it's just not very nice. I'm trying to save the chocolate, but I'm really hungry, so I eat it.

I'm still hungry and have a brainwave: hunger can sharpen the mind; it can also make you eat your companions, but that's generally reserved for being stranded in the Andes and is frowned upon in Somerset. I will look up a Chinese takeaway that delivers and get them to slide me the cartons of food through the letter box! It's a *brilliant* idea, but on closer inspection, the letter box is sealed up on the outside. I go back to the plan of making do. I still have my nuts. (Unlike Mike the mechanic.) I eat the nuts, but they do nothing; I'm still ravenous. Then I realise Brendan has drunk a *huge* bowl of water and he won't last all night, so we *have* to get out.

I find a number for the alarm people and speak to a suspicious, confused, impatient and disgruntled, elderly security guard. We embark on a surreal conversation, because he won't actually *listen* to what I'm saying.

"So... let me get this straight... You're telling me *you broke in*... and now you can't get out?"

"No! Where did you get that from? I was given a key..."

"So... you work there and you overslept..."

"*What?* No!"

"Are you saying one of your workmates locked you in on purpose? For a joke? Because that's very serious and it's not a joke and..."

"*No!* I've already said, I..."

"Well, I don't like this! I don't like this one bit! *And I don't trust you!*"

I explain it several times. And then several more times. Slower each time. He still doesn't understand and he doesn't believe me, but he knows I'm where I claim to be, because he can see me on the monitor.

Five minutes later, Ryan-the-boss himself phones up, having been alerted by the security guard. He's very apologetic and very friendly, due to the safety of being on the other end of a phone and not in the room with Brendan. He says he'll sort it. True to his word, he sorts it. Before long, the happy chappie from upstairs is back in his tiny souped-up car and we're free. Brendan is very ungrateful and howls the place down. I'm given the correct key and with another screech of tyres the happy chap is gone, home to his tea and we're left alone again.

I have to drag Brendan out for a short walk before bed. He isn't interested and is keen to get back to his basket. He curls up and goes straight back to sleep.

I buy some food and eat it. I try reading *On the Road* for a bit and then watch Brendan sleeping peacefully. Outside it goes dark. The orange-lit street is filled with the over-night lorries, curtains drawn around their cabs and flickering lights inside. I miss Eagle One.

The night in the office is eerie. I try not to look at the security camera and try not to think about it, but it's unsettling being observed at all times. Especially when getting undressed. There are occasional noises from upstairs, which sound like footsteps, moving from one side of the room to the other. It's not my imagination, because it wakes Brendan and he glances upwards, then looks at me. He sees I'm awake and can deal with any issues, so he immediately flops down and returns to sleep.

I venture out into the corridor and creep gingerly up the stairs in the dark to check the first floor office. The door is locked, but has a glass panel in it. It's a small room filled with desks and computers, only lit by the orange street lamps shining in. There is no one inside.

I creep back down the stairs again, passing a locked door on the ground floor. It had been open during office hours and I had seen inside. It leads into a huge warehouse filled with aisles and aisles of self-storage units: small lock-ups with roll-down doors. It's the perfect setting for a slasher flick. Who knows what's hidden within those lock-ups? Probably nothing of any significance, no severed heads or body parts, but still, it's mighty spooky.

Back in our office, Brendan checks I've returned to the room and then settles himself down again. I switch out the light, get into my sleeping bag and lie down on the hard floor. I lie awake for a long time. It's quite unsettling, but I feel comforted by Brendan's steady breathing. At least if we're murdered in the night there will be footage; I look up at the corner of the room, at the pinpoint red light blinking continually in the darkness.

* * * * * * * * * *

It's another cloudy and grey morning as we set off into

Portishead for the third day in a row, trying to vacate the industrial estate before the mechanics arrive. We're starting to feel like a permanent fixture. Brendan seems to regard this town as home and as far as he's aware we might never leave. I'm also thinking that might be the case.

I'm feeling like – and resembling – a rough sleeper, a homeless person, wandering aimlessly, dishevelled, unshaven, carrying a large rucksack and in the company of a scrawny street urchin dog. Café owners are starting to recognise us. Probably because of the smell. (I haven't had a shower for days; I've had to make do with a stand-up wash when and where appropriate.) They're wise to us already; we buy a coffee and sit in their warmth for two hours, falling asleep. Or stretched out on their Persian rugs.

It's absolutely freezing. We end up at the marina again, because we've been everywhere. Twice. At least. The sun comes out and it starts to look like summer, but it feels like winter. We sit on a bench overlooking the water, rippled by a cold breeze.

A man bends down to stroke Brendan. "Hello, fella."

"Oh, please don't... He's..."

"What a smashing face! What's his name?"

"Brendan. He came with his name. But please be careful... He's very..."

"Benji! What a lovely name! Suits him!"

I drag "Benji" away as he's about to lunge.

We walk to the sea, where Brendan has a sit down. I join him, looking out over the brown water, with white-crested cappuccino waves rolling in. Many people walk past and it strikes me that I'm sitting here, the hood of my hoodie up, cuddling my dog for warmth; Brendan's water bowl is in front of us, which could at a glance be mistaken for a begging bowl. Now we really must look like homeless man and dog – and d'you know what really annoys me? As pitiful, desperate yet handsome as we must look, not one person throws us any money!

I phone the garage for a progress report. There's no news, except the promise that it will definitely be completed before closing, but it's starting to sound like a line. They specify a time: 5pm, but not a day.

We carry on walking. We walk everywhere we have so far walked, because we've walked everywhere there is to walk in Portishead. At one point, Brendan starts limping, then he turns and holds his front paw up to me. When I examine it, there's a huge thorn sticking in his pad. I pluck the thorn out, then he licks my hand as though in thanks. It's probably just because my skin is salty with sweat, but it seems so lovingly symbolic. This is the highlight of the day – *of the trip* – so far.

* * * * * * * * * *

Eagle One is finally finished at the end of the working day. I'm way too tired to drive, almost delirious with lack of sleep, so we end up on the forecourt of the self-storage warehouse for the night, which all the overnight lorries seemingly use as a turning circle, so it's like Piccadilly Circus. (If you're not familiar with London, it's like somewhere very busy near you.) Of course, Brendan barks frantically each time it happens, so it's another bad night of fitful sleep and tension.

This is our first trip together, our joint adventure, discovering the secrets of Britain. It isn't going how I'd planned... but it's different, it's memorable, we're together, and what doesn't kill you makes you stronger. Probably. Tomorrow morning, first thing – touch wood, fingers crossed – we will leave Portishead.

* * * * * * * * * *

Dog facts:
Greyhounds are the fastest dogs on Earth. They can reach a top speed of 45 miles per hour. Brendan has a similar physique to a greyhound, athletic with a very slim waist. But his preferred speed is a steady 0 mph.

Brendan reclines on a Persian rug in a café. It was 9AM... an hour before his preferred getting up time. Notice his yellow bandana, bearing the words I NEED SPACE.

CHAPTER 3: WESTWARD! HO! (BRENDAN! IN THE WEST COUNTRY!)

The next morning we're finally leaving Portishead, having got to know it well... and better than expected. And better than necessary. As we drive along the M5 to Weston-Super-Mare, it feels like a new start after all the van trouble. Me and my boy are on the road! This feels like Day One and we're filled with excitement. Well, *I'm* filled with excitement.

We park on the prom. It's not yet 9am but there's a smell of chips in the air. Penny arcades seem to be the first things to open and Brendan pulls to go in every single one. I'll never know all the secrets of his past, but I'm guessing he has a gambling addiction.

It's hazy across the bay, but in that way that implies it's going to be scorching later. We walk along the beach, a proper beach, unlike Portishead, with the waves lapping at the golden sand. For all I know, this is Brendan's first time actually experiencing the real sea, being confronted by it. He scampers gleefully up to it; he's about to run into the foaming shallows... but then he backs away rapidly, because it moves. *It actually moves!* His head tilts to one side as he watches, processes the data and learns: it comes towards you, but if you bark it will retreat, so he chases it down the beach, barking and snapping, but then it builds up the courage to come back again, so you have to keep barking; it's really tiresome. As a spectator sport though, it's quite fun.

An elderly couple approach us, making a beeline for Brendan. "Hello boy." A hand is offered to him. Brendan sniffs tentatively. I tense. Brendan is uninterested, but doesn't growl or snap. "What's his name?"

"Brendan. He came with his name. I didn't choose it."

"Oh, hello David!" (David! This is the best yet!) "Isn't he lovely?"

I shrug. "Well... the jury's out at the moment."

We return to Eagle One and slip across the border into Devon, green and pastoral, home of clotted cream, cream teas and the Cornish pasty. Yes, Devon claims to have invented the Cornish pasty.

We pitch up at our pre-booked campsite. It has idyllic views in every direction for as far as the eye can see. It's sunny and very hot. Brendan has a sit down on the grass. I join him, drink a can of beer, eat a Pot Noodle and go to sleep. This is our first night on a site, rather than on an industrial estate or in an office. It's very exciting and I'm enjoying being here with my boy. He makes even the simple act of sitting on some grass seem special.

We go for a short walk before bed. The sky is covered with an array of pinpoint white specks; there's no light pollution at all. It's breath-taking. Brendan wees on a hawthorn hedge and shrugs; he's less than impressed. Then he turns and spots the piercing white light of the almost-full moon and starts howling hysterically.

This marks the end of our nocturnal stroll through the pleasantly balmy evening air. And the end of our amicable relationship with the other campers.

Once in the van, we get ready for the night. The bed pulls out in the back and occupies virtually all the floor space, so Brendan's basket is on the bed, beside me. I would like the curtains open, so I can gaze at the stars, but that isn't going to happen. Brendan hops into his basket and curls up. As long as the curtains are all tightly shut, I won't hear from him again until mid-morning. So we go to sleep in our tightly sealed steel tomb.

* * * * * * * * * *

Ilfracombe. I came here as a child, though I can barely remember it. Brendan has never been, as far as I know. The harbour area is very pretty, with nice pubs and cafes overlooking the quay and moored yachts bobbing on iridescent water. It's very busy, and it's a full time job weaving Brendan in and out of the meandering holidaymakers and avoiding incident.

The day is getting unbearably hot. After a chip and pea luncheon I'm feeling a bit lethargic, but there's no way I can let my equally lethargic dog leave the town without climbing Lantern Hill, a grassy crag overlooking the harbour and the sea. I sit on a bench close to the top. Within a minute I'm lying down on the bench, sunbathing, which is what lazy people call sleeping when the sun's shining. Brendan sensibly lies underneath the bench in the shade. From this vantage point, he can bark at everyone passing by and they can't see him, so he can startle them *and* perplex them. He's loving it. He has worked this strategy out for himself; he's so intelligent. And devious.

I would never usually sit on a bench in such a public place, because someone would inevitably sidle up, sit down and start telling you about their politics or their bunions, but with Brendan that's not a problem; no one comes near. I would certainly never usually *lie down* on a bench in a public place – as I am doing now. It would be unthinkable. But Brendan has increased my confidence hugely. With Brendan the unthinkable has become... *thinkable*.

I sleepily watch the sea through one half-open eye. The ocean stretches away, slate grey, to meet a cornflower blue sky. Tour boats chug out into the bay and do a circuit of the headlands: I keep getting exactly the same three minutes of dialogue from the various onboard tour guides as they turn out of the harbour until they've sailed out of earshot, punctuated by furious barking from below. It's all rather perfect, if repetitive and noisy.

As it hasn't rained for days, all the puddles have dried up. Brendan loves to drink from puddles, in fact he'll usually *only* drink from puddles. Perhaps this is a habit left over from his street days, when the only drink available was from a pothole in the road. Tap water, boiled water and even bottled water isn't good enough for him. It has to be a puddle. If it's brown, drink it down; the dirtier, the better. This is quite common, apparently. He's currently having water sneaked into his food to keep him a hydrated and happy boy. And he needs hydrating, because it's so hot!

This afternoon, back at the site, they're having a Champagne and Strawberry Garden Party. I mentioned it to Brendan, but he doesn't like champagne or strawberries or gardens or parties... or people... so he was less than enthusiastic. I already know we won't be returning to the site until long after everyone has staggered back to their own vans for a post-champagne siesta. We spend the rest of the day dodging the sun and languishing in the shadows. Because of this, Brendan is finally starting to warm to the idea of holidays.

* * * * * * * * * * *

A new morning, a bright Devon day. We arrive at Bideford, once a bustling port, now... not. Tourists amble along the waterside path or sit on benches in the morning sunshine. We walk along, happy that the sun is shining, happy that we're away from home and happy that we're together. Brendan wees on a lamppost then looks up at me; he must wonder why I never wee on lampposts. I think he'd feel much happier if I did. (But I don't.)

I hear a voice on the other side of a hedge; it's a middle-aged man saying: "Well, we've all got to die sometime!" He says it quite gleefully, as though it's high on his *to do* list and I wonder what prompted the statement.

It's a Sunday and it feels like a Sunday; like a Sunday decades ago: closed. It's not an unattractive little town by any means. There are some very narrow cobbled and flagged alleys with traditional workers' cottages on either side. It feels old and rooted in history.

We call in a café, the only place that seems to be open. I order a tea and a flapjack. A smiling, singing young waiter passes our table and bends down to stroke Brendan. My heart's in my mouth – as is the flapjack – and suddenly I'm spluttering and spraying chewed up oats, trying to warn him, but Brendan doesn't bark or bite; I think he's been caught off guard and doesn't have time to react, before the unsuspecting waiter has moved on and is clearing plates and singing at other people. The whole episode seems to exhaust Brendan and he flops down for an emergency nap. When we're leaving, I make sure the young waiter is busy elsewhere so we can sneak out without him coming to say goodbye, because Brendan won't be caught unawares a second time.

I walk back along the river, chatting to The Boy. I suddenly realise I talk to him *all the time*, usually small, inconsequential things, observations or thoughts, pointing out things he might be interested in. ("Look at that dog; he's cute. Not as cute as you, obviously. That's a nice old tree. Bet you'd like to wee on that!) The worrying thing is, I used to do this anyway, before I had him; he just makes the practise more socially acceptable.

We leave Bideford, still chatting, and drive through Westward Ho! It is famously the only town in the United Kingdom to officially contain an exclamation mark in its name! We don't stop! We continue southwards along the narrow winding lanes, which are banked and lined with hedges bursting with colourful wild flowers: buttercups, gorse, red and white campion and cow parsley. It's beautiful. Brendan is doing so well with all the travelling. He has his travel sickness tablets every day we're in transit and they seem to be doing the job. It also helps that he usually travels in his basket, which gives him some extra support and stability.

Quite suddenly, the scenery goes very moor-like, with large, open fields of rough grass. It looks more like Cornwall now than the soft, rolling landscape of Devon. That's probably because – I realise much later – it *is* Cornwall. We've crossed another border. We're really racking up the miles now and ticking off the counties.

As the early evening descends, we're on our campsite in Bude. We head out for an evening walk around the site and bump into one of the staff, a helpful and friendly man, Tom. His eyes light up when he sees Brendan and he bends down to stroke him. Time slows down. I tighten my grip on Brendan's lead. I start to issue a warning, but Tom cuts me off with the words I dread. The world goes into slow motion.

"It's... OK... I'm... a... dog... person..."

No, no, no! History is about to repeat itself.

"Look..." Tom says, "They can tell if you like dogs. See..."

He strokes Brendan; Brendan nuzzles him affectionately. Déjà vu.

"See... There we... *God!* Oh god!"

Tom leaps back as Brendan snarls and snaps fiercely, straining at his lead and clawing in vain at the air. That's the problem; he's so unpredictable.

"Oh my god!" With a hand to his chest, Tom recovers from the shock and takes a slow step backwards. Surprisingly – and thankfully – his friendly demeanour doesn't change and neither does his sage-like wisdom. "Well, I can see he's nervous... I should have left him alone. It's my fault. I'm sorry. Sorry, fella! There are no bad dogs, just bad people."

I wholeheartedly agree with this, though I do think Brendan can be just a little bit bad sometimes.

We return to the van and have a relaxed evening, apart from all the barking, the growling and stress. We love our evenings in Eagle One. We both love being out in the open in the day, but I think we also enjoy that time when we can close the curtains on the outside world and relax together. We sit side by side on the sofa; Brendan usually sleeps solidly. I have travel Monopoly, Cluedo and Scrabble, but he's not interested. So he sleeps and I usually read or watch a DVD, but we're together and I generally have an arm around him. Then we go to sleep, side by side. Apart from his nightmares, Brendan usually sleeps very deeply, probably dreaming of the day when he can affford a larger van. Or a hotel room. For one.

* * * * * * * * *

The next morning we're up early. Well, one of us is. Brendan consents to weeing on a thistle adjacent to our pitch, but that's all. I don't know what it is about prickly plants, but he loves weeing on them, which always surprises me, because one slight miscalculation and he's going to know about it. He retracts his cocked leg and leaps back into the van and into his basket with a heavy, disapproving sigh.

I wanted to leave Bude early and get to Tintagel before the coach parties of Arthurian obsessives and pasty enthusiasts arrive. Tintagel is, of course, synonymous with King Arthur, who many historians doubt ever existed. It is here, in the castle – now owned by Prince Charles – that the King was allegedly conceived. We arrive early, but it's already moderately busy. We park in Merlin's Car Park and I pay for 3 hours, thinking we could probably spend a day here. This is the first historical (more mythological) hotspot of our trip and I'm sure Brendan will be fascinated by the place.

I walk with The Boy along the already-bustling main street with its cafes, pubs and gift shops, then suddenly we're amongst houses. That was it. That was Tintagel. Three pounds in the car park and three minutes to walk through it. That's a pound a minute! We retrace our steps, much slower, and give the place a good looking over.

Everything has an Arthurian connection: King Arthur This, Lancelot That, Guinevere The Other. There's the King Arthur's Arms Inn, the Crossbow Cafe, Arthur's Tearoom, Silver Stone crystal shop, Arthur's Codpiece. All the giftshops specialise in tat of a heraldic nature: plastic swords with ornate handles, intricately decorated plastic Celtic shields, crested helmets, Camelot related thimbles, teaspoons and tea towels and stuffed dragons. The usual pens, mugs, T-shirts, keyrings and snow globes are all on sale, but also more specialist and expensive items, such as silver goblets, statues, sculptures and a full King Arthur costume, proudly boasting UP TO ADULT SIZES! So it can be used for, let's just call it "role play".

A bewitching and mysterious lady approaches us and smiles an exotic smile. "Excuse me... You are local?" She's very softly spoken with an indeterminate accent. Presumably because she's female and diminutive, Brendan stands quietly and looks at her, possibly beguiled by her.

"I'm afraid not. I'm a visitor."

"Is there a large... *supermarket* nearby?"

"I'm sorry, I don't know the area well at all."

"A... *Lidl*?"

I do a double take. "Err... I don't think so..."

"A Tesco then?"

"I really don't know. I'm sorry. But I don't think there's any supermarket in Tintagel."

"How about down that way?" She points down a cul-de-sac of semi-detached houses.

"I really wouldn't've thought so."

She looks at me for a moment, a searching look, a suspicious look. There is disappointment in her smouldering dark eyes; she believes I'm lying.

"Right!" she says contemptuously and walks briskly away.

Brendan looks up at me with his soft brown eyes, a look that says: "You've still got it." And I realise that sarcasm works in any language and crosses the species divide.

We leave Tintagel, passing a refreshment van in a layby; it's called THE LOG BOX and boasts NICE BAPS in big, bold letters. We're back from a fictional Camelot, into the cheap innuendo of reality. I almost laugh. But don't.

We visit Padstow, which is beautiful but so busy that we don't laugh there either. We relax in a shady pub, which makes us feel a bit more like laughing, then we sign in at tonight's site, which overlooks Watergate Bay, one of the big surfing destinations in the Newquay area. It's sunny and warm and I could actually believe we're in Californ-IA. Thankfully though, we're in Cornwall.

The big tent opposite our pitch seems to be occupied by a middle-aged couple and their three grown up daughters. The poor, solitary man seems very ill at ease, outnumbered and put-upon; he regularly disappears to the toilet block or takes the dog for overly-frequent walks. It's a tiny lap dog, so he can't get any man-o-man companionship from that either. Brendan cuts it dead, because he considers it too small to be a real dog.

It's a beautiful evening. I take The Boy for a walk along the cliffs. We scramble down a rough path to the beach. It starts off looking like a navigable and well-used path, but degenerates into a sheer, crumbling and dangerous precipice challenge. By this point, it's too late and more dangerous to go back up, so we persevere gingerly. Brendan is straining frantically on his lead in his eagerness to get to the beach. He is in danger of pulling me over, so when I deem it safe, I let him off his lead so he scuttles ahead and I finish picking my way in safety. He shoots off like someone has lit his blue touch paper.

Brendan isn't supposed to be let off his lead. He's a former street dog. "Once a street dog always a street dog." they say. You're never cured. You're a "recovering" street dog, but it's always in your blood. Once they're free range they're supposed to revert back to type. I reason that this beach is a fairly safe venue, because it's currently very quiet, and it's a strip of land between the sea and some cliffs. Brendan wouldn't willingly breach either of these barriers, so I assume it will be a good place for him to let off some steam. He lets off *so much* steam it has probably contributed considerably to global warming. He races like a maniac up and down the sand in a wide circle, but so wide that I feel sure he isn't coming back. He has full-blown sand madness. I trail after him, whilst trying to appear that I'm calm, relaxed and not bothered by his display. For twenty minutes he shows no sign of slowing down.

Eventually he leaves the sand and starts threading his way through the rocks and stones higher up the beach. I'm terrified he's going to try and make his way back up the cliffs. But he finds a sandy area between the rocks, burrows in a short way then flings himself into the crater. He's made himself a sand nest. Presumably it's to expose the cooler sand below the surface. He lies there panting and isn't at all bothered as I attach his lead. It's something of a learning curve for me, because although I don't think it was ever his intention to run away – he kept a beady eye on me at all times – he wouldn't respond to me at all and seemed to completely lose himself in the moment. He's quite Buddhist in that respect.

When we set off again, he's obviously very thirsty after his long run; he samples every rock pool on the beach – and there are many – tasting them each in turn, reasoning that one of them must *surely* be fresh water and not salty. They aren't.

On the clifftops we sit and snuggle, enjoying the views out to sea of the rolling breakers, foaming and crashing. He's made me really anxious and I don't want to let go of him now. Perhaps I should be cross with him, but I'm sure he was just having a bit of fun and I'm just glad he's safe.

The breeze is warm. We sit together for a long time. I wonder what Brendan's thinking, confronted by all this sea and all this sky. Probably not much; dogs are so accepting. I wonder again if he's truly happy, if he enjoys his new life or if he misses his old life in some ways, his life of crime in Bulgaria. I don't mean raiding litter bins, chasing cats and stealing bones off other dogs; he's highly intelligent, so we're probably talking property swindles, insurance scams or even art fraud. I'll never really know what goes on in his head, but I hope he's happy with me.

The sun sinks towards the seaward horizon. By thinking too much I've made a beautiful shared moment into something poignant, introspective and potentially sad. That's so very me. Very slowly the colour drains from the landscape.

* * * * * * * * * *

Another day dawns – another fine day – and we drive into Newquay, "Cornwall's favourite resort" (Newquay's words, not mine.) The sun's shining and the surf's up. Yes, Newquay is the capital of surfin' in the UK and was voted the nation's favourite seaside town. The sand is golden, the sea is Atlantical and you might get to see dolphins here. (I won't, but you might. I *never* do; I'm like a dolphin repellent.)

After a lot of shops and concrete, we find a beach, one of many belonging to Newquay, Cornwall's favourite resort. It's a small sandy bay within a rocky cove. The sea is the most unbelievable, shimmering turquoise. There are kids zorbing along the sand: rolling along in transparent plastic spheres, which I'm very much in favour of: keep them contained. Brendan stares; he doesn't know what to make of it, so he has a sit down and thinks about it for a while.

Newquay, Cornwall's favourite resort, swirls around us in a carnival of movement and colour, waves and shops. People zip by on skateboards and run up the beach in wet suits or amble through the shopping streets eating ice cream. It's a really nice destination, but it's just not a destination for us.

We move on to Godrevy Beach, which definitely *is* a destination for us. Unfortunately it doesn't want us: the beach has a strict no dogs policy. Brendan is livid! I pacify him by taking him for a long walk along the coastal path instead, over an imposing rocky headland. Below, a sweeping bay stretches away. The first thing you notice about Godrevy is the island, situated a short way out in the bay, along with its impressive octagonal lighthouse. I'd love to be wandering barefoot along the sand, the water lapping at my feet, but you know the rules: if my dog can't come I'm not going. (By the end of the trip, the list of places I couldn't go because of Brendan will be a long one.)

Bandana Boy. Brendan at Godrevy Head.

So we walk over Godrevy Point, between heather, gorse, brambles and bracken. A middle-aged couple appear along the sandy pathway ahead and Brendan starts barking ferociously. The nice lady spots his yellow bandana and recognises it. Yes, he sometimes wears a bandana. Nicky bought it him. It's from the "Yellow Dog" campaign (www.yellowdoguk.co.uk) and is designed to alert people that the wearer needs space. Accordingly, it boasts the slogan: I NEED SPACE. And he does. And so do I. But I don't wear a bandana.

Unfortunately, for every person it alerts and deters, it attracts another two, who are curious and lean closer to try and read the message.

But this clued-up lady knows what the bandana represents just by the colour. "It's OK... It's OK," she says gently. I assume she's talking to Brendan. "I know you're frightened, but no one's going to hurt you."

This is one of the very few times anyone has responded correctly and sensibly to his various warning signs. I'm most impressed.

"He's generally OK with the ladies." I say. "But not with men."

The woman takes a step forward; the man takes a step back. A small amount of stroking is permitted and no air ambulance or emergency field surgery is required. I think the woman senses enough is enough and retreats graciously.We continue along the winding path that skirts the headland and I nearly step on a snake that's stretched out sunbathing. It is predominantly black; I think it's an adder. Brendan instinctively knows it's potentially dangerous and leaps back, using me as a human shield, watching as it lazily slithers away into the undergrowth rather than leaping towards it, which is quite unusual for him. I don't recall ever seeing a snake in the wild before.

We sit at the summit beside the Trig point, enjoying the sunshine and the sea air, sitting alone together, which is already becoming the norm. The view from here is breath-taking, over the wide, sandy bay to the lighthouse.

I love islands; I'm quite fascinated by them. I love the idea that you're somewhere segregated and private. I also love lighthouses. In another time, I would probably have become a lighthouse keeper. I would love to live on an island, especially in a lighthouse, and Godrevy is one of the lighthouses I'd most like to own. It's not too far from shore, just a short row across the bay if you have an emergency and run out of tea. The lighthouse is unusual and very attractive; the views from any of its windows must be spectacular, but I'd probably tow the island a bit further out to sea, to keep it away from the prying eyes of people like me. It would be perfect for Brendan. He could run free and bark at the waves all day, and there would be no one there to frighten him or for him to frighten. That really would be our dream. And just saying that really underlines that we are perfectly ideal for each other.

We should have stayed longer at Godrevy, basking in the sunshine, avoiding snakes, wearing yellow bandanas and dreaming about lighthouses, but we always feel compelled to move on. So we move on, heading towards the Land's End peninsula.

I drive Eagle One along narrow lanes with hawthorn hedges, out onto rough, open moorland. I see a fox cub, crawling out of his lair presumably, stretching and scampering off lethargically along the edge of the field. I assume an eagle-eyed parent is watching from the undergrowth close by.

Despite the hot day, it's cool on the moors and there's

a strong breeze. The evening is descending. There are long shadows and everything is tinged with gold. We arrive at our campsite, situated on the open moors outside Sennen Cove. There are views over the grass and heather to the sea. It's exposed and very windy. Brendan sits outside the van on his long lead and goes to sleep. The last of the day drains away into the sea and the wind-ravaged landscape is left in darkness. He's so tired, he doesn't even bark at the stars or the moon. I bring him in and he slinks into his basket and continues his sleep. He's had a very long and exhausting day. The van shakes steadily in the untamed marine wind. It's like being out at sea.

* * * * * * * * *

A new day. Another fine, sunny morning. A public footpath leads from the site across neatly farmed fields and eventually takes us to the sea above Whitesands Bay. It's scorching hot. Brendan has a sit down and barks at some seagulls for a while. I sit next to him, but don't bark. I'm caught up in the moment, enjoying the weather, the view, the clean, salty air; just enjoying being here with my dog. I don't feel the need to bark.

(It's funny how certain moments can become so significant. This is such a cherished memory, but I couldn't have said at the time how important it would be. When I think about the trip, or when I'm sitting in a park with Brendan, this moment overlooking Whitesands Bay comes into my mind. It was such a simple experience, we sat on a cliff, together, my arm around him, looking at the view, at the sea, at the sand below, at the circling seagulls; nothing happened in particular, but it seems to signify one of the most perfect moments for us.)

Rested and recharged, we follow a set of sandy steps that wind down to the beach. Once his paws hit the sand, Brendan flies towards the sea with the excitement of a young pup. It's like the biggest puddle ever! He seems to have forgotten he's met the sea before and didn't like it. He runs up to it, wetting his paws and for a moment it seems as though he's miraculously overcome his phobia, but once the waves move he backs away and remembers it's evil. I try to coax him into running through the shallow waves with me, but he isn't having any of it. I paddle and splash around enthusiastically, while he digs himself a sand nest and watches an empty piece of sky for a while.

We follow the coastal path, clambering over rocks with constant views of the sea and its unreal colour and the rushing and dragging of the waves. It's beautiful. The path opens onto a wide sandy bay packed with people sunbathing, lying or sitting on their towels, sand sticking to their salt-wet legs, staring rudely at us; it's not just the occasional person staring, but everybody. It starts to really annoy me. When we climb a slipway into the coastal village of Sennen Cove, I see all the NO DOGS signs at the entrances to the beach, not just NO DOGS, but *STRICTLY* NO DOGS and the warnings about hefty fines. But there were no signs from the side we approached, so I'm not interested. Brendan is highly delighted and walks on with a swagger.

Ironically, this dog-hostile beach is synonymous with national hero, Bilbo, Britain's first ever canine lifeguard.

He was a big brown Newfoundland with a lovely, lazy smile. He was active as a lifeguard for three years until red tape, including the NO DOGS rule, ended his career. He died in 2015 and his death was recorded in the national press. Brendan observes a respectful silence when I mention this.

We've been walking (and sitting down) for a few hours now and have covered several miles, so we feel we've earned a rest. There's a nice pub in Sennen Cove, *The Old Success*, overlooking the sea, so it seems foolish not to take advantage. We sit in the shade inside with a nice, cool breeze coming through the open window, though the heating is on full for some reason, the nearby radiator pumping out hot air like an open oven. We have a cooling beer and a few dog biscuits. The beer is very welcome, but the biscuits aren't that nice.

There's a whole array of Cornish brewery beers on offer that have old, traditional and vintage-sounding names. I have selected a pint of a dark brew called something like *Polyester Flare*, which – as it's a non-driving day – I drink as though it's going out of fashion.

When we continue along the coastal path we're both feeling happy, but very lazy. Not that Brendan's had any alcohol: the laziness is just his natural state. He's excited to be outside in the fresh air, with all the foul smells he can find. He loves being outside and sniffing, preferably in a sitting position. His tail betrays his mood: up, like a dodgem car, shows he's happy. When he's outside – but away from people, cars and most other things – this is its normal position. His upright tail makes him easy to spot in undergrowth. It's like the shark fin in *Jaws*. If it comes towards you: *run!* Tail down is fear, obviously. Tucked between his legs is *serious* fear. Straight out, like a pointer, is neutral or processing data. It's a very good indicator of how he's feeling.

Sennen Cove comes to an end and the coastal path continues along the clifftops. There is a steady throng of walkers now. We are approaching one of the most popular and iconic visitor destinations in the UK. Tourists have been drawn to Land's End for over 300 years, though people in general have been coming here for over 10,000 years... and the cliffs have been here for considerably longer. I feel quite excited. This is a symbolic landmark that means everything and nothing at the same time. Land's End is a place that's famous for being famous, more than anything. It is the most westerly point in England, the last place the sun sets on the English mainland, over 22 minutes after London.

Land's End is teeming with tourists, many of them foreign visitors; there are a whole range of wonderful languages and accents on display. I wonder if Brendan has detected his own native tongue.

It's all now quite commercial: there are fast food outlets and tacky gift shops selling Land's End pencils, Land's End snow globes, Land's End hoover bags and god knows what; all the same merchandise as everywhere else. There are several theme park type "attractions", but we avoid them like the plague. The cliffs and the timeless sea views are still here, so we sit and enjoy them, sitting apart from everyone else, at a safe distance. This is Brendan's first big British tourist attraction. I don't think he's overly impressed.

* * * * * * * * * * *

The following day is dull, grey, overcast, blowy and quite cold. It's always a shock to the system when a day like this comes after a scorcher like yesterday. We spend some time in Penzance, famous for operatic pirates. Brendan's ears are flapping in the wind; he sits on the pavement and stares at me, with a look in his beautiful brown eyes that says: "Why are we doing this?"

We continue towards the spectacular Lizard, which I love. It tries to sell itself as "the other Land's End", but it fails, and is all the better for it. It's small and essentially unspoilt. I hope it stays that way.

We follow the coast roads to the Rame Peninsular, known as the "Forgotten Corner of Cornwall" as it's an area largely bypassed by tourists, as it isn't on the way to anywhere. It's a hidden gem. The hedgerows are bursting with colour. The roads become narrower, the corners get tighter, the hedges get higher until we arrive at the end of the road: stunning Rame Head, a rocky headland crowned by a distinctive stone chapel, standing alone, high above the crashing of the waves.

I park in the car park next to a field of wild ponies and we climb the steep path up the rocky tor to the chapel, which is a well-preserved shell. There are amazing views along the coast, over the cliffs and across the sea. The wind is strong and the air is cool. It feels dramatic and open, exhilarating and life-affirming; it feels exactly how standing on the summit of a headland in a ruined chapel overlooking the sea *should* feel.

The chapel is solid and so well sited. It's commanding. It's worth coming to the "Forgotten Corner" just for this. I can't believe it isn't more famous or more photographed. It is *so* photogenic. The chapel is perfectly placed to complete this most amazing view. It looks unspoilt; it *feels* unspoilt. We sit for a long time just enjoying the breeze and the sound of the wind and the sea.

We're eventually forced to make a move because a troop of about twenty young army cadets appear, striding across the green towards us. Brendan spots them and is getting agitated; he hates soldiers. I could have guaranteed that. Like mechanics, soldiers are predominantly men, which Brendan hates; they wear uniforms, which Brendan hates; they carry things, which Brendan hates. Like guns, which Brendan hates. He does not like soldiers at all. He's also possibly a pacifist... though it seems unlikely. If they hadn't shown up, we might still be sitting there, mesmerised by the foam-crested waves and the surging of the ocean.

We hurriedly set off, trying to give the cadets a wide berth, but Brendan still barks at them incessantly, jumping up and down and straining at his lead, until we're safely back in Eagle One and he's sitting in the back with his curtains closed. He curls up in his basket, evidently pleased with his morning's work. I drive us into the middle the Rame Peninsula, to Maker Heights, a grassy upland plateau. Here there is a brilliantly positioned campsite, which offers views across a beautiful bay dotted with sailing boats, which tack in slow motion. In the distance is the imposing Plymouth breakwater. The sun is shining and everywhere looks stunning.

The campsite – probably one of my favourites so far, is a *proper* down to earth, grassy green site. No hard standings here, no delineated pitches, no electric, no neat hedges, just several open fields. The site has a strapline: "wild camping... as wild as it gets." That's not strictly true, as there *are* facilities, including showers. To me, "wild camping" is sleeping on a mountain in a survival bag and anything less is quite tame. I'm not saying I do that on a regular basis – or even occasionally – or even *ever* these days – but that's my idea of roughing it, not a pristine shower block, where even the men's has *rose scented liquid soap*!

We set off on foot from the site, along a lane which drops down towards the coast. A local lady bumps into us and begins clucking over Brendan. We go through the routine.

"What's this handsome fella called?"

"Brendan. He came with his name. Or he wouldn't be called Brendan."

"He's gorgeous. What type is he?"

"He was a rescue, so I'm not really..."

"He's definitely got some Airedale in him."

"D'you think?" I've no idea what an Airedale is. "I always think his beard has..."

"Definitely Airedale. Airedale Terrier."

"Oh…" Still no idea.

"Stands out a mile."

"Right…"

"He's lovely…"

"I think so. He…"

"I could look at him all day. I really could. Bye." And she's abruptly gone. The shoulder-high (to me) rushes at the roadside sway in her wake and then are still and we're left alone.

(I later look up Airedale Terrier. Apart from a very similar colouring – black on top, sandy underneath – Brendan bears little resemblance.)

We arrive in the village of Cawsand, a maze of crooked streets of very pretty, pastel-painted cottages. The small, sandy beach is very busy. It's getting continually warmer and the sea looks tropical. People are sun-bathing and swimming. We attempt to sit down and enjoy the sunshine and the unspoilt view, but then the air is split open by a loud, echoing crack of an explosion which reverberates underfoot. Brendan looks at me and then attempts to run for shelter. I try to comfort him and calm him down. There is a military base in the area and there is the repeated deep, hollow, thud of exploding ordnance. Poor Brendan keeps jumping and scooting off as far as his lead will allow him. I decide while the weather is so nice and Cawsand is under bombardment by heavy artillery, we should get the ferry into Plymouth.

The ferry appears in the distance, a little boat, phut-phutting into the bay. People who have been sitting on benches gazing at the sea, or lying on the sand with eyes half closed, suddenly come alive and spring into action. En masse, everyone jumps up from the sand, appears from cracks and crevices and jostles on the beach for a place on the ferry, which – as it grows closer – appears to be getting smaller and smaller. I'm concerned, because Brendan doesn't like crowds and this boat is going to be packed. There are a couple of other dogs, but they seem very well-behaved, queueing in an orderly fashion, seasoned travellers, shipmates, seadogs. I shuffle us towards them in the hope that Brendan will be reassured by their calm and learn the ropes from them, while also knowing deep down that it's never going to work.

The ferry moors on the beach and a gangplank is moved into place. The passengers alight, walking along the precariously narrow plank. It looks too complicated and frightening for my boy, but I think we have to give it a go.

We get in line behind a wise old retriever. I turn to his dad: "We're going to follow you. I want my dog to see what your dog does and learn from him."

The man shakes his head. "I wouldn't. Mine's a right wuss... He's terrified of boats... I had to carry him on yesterday."

My heart sinks. People are piling on from all directions

and I'm concerned it's going to be too tightly packed for Brendan. It comes to the retriever's turn. He tries to casually walk off in the opposite direction, pretending he's someone else, but it doesn't work. Eventually, he gives up and allows himself to be dragged up the gangplank. We follow closely. Brendan refuses to step on the narrow plank, so he's coerced and manoeuvred, coaxed and cajoled, bribed and blackmailed onto that boat in any way possible. The crew are very helpful and between us we manage to airlift him aboard – I'm still not totally sure how. We sit at the back, wedged in a tiny space on the bench seating. Brendan is suddenly fine and is wondering what all the fuss has been about; we're on the "boat" and all it involves is sitting down, one of his top hobbies.

I'm so impressed with how well he's coping with all the people at such close quarters and the bodies pressing in all around; he's amazing. But then the engine starts. The whole boat throbs and vibrates. Brendan is clinging to me for dear life. It's too late to bail. It should have been obvious, I suppose, that Brendan would hate the Plymouth Ferry. Brendan has four legs, but none of them – it seems – are sea legs.

The little boat sets off, out into the bay, rising and falling, crashing into oncoming waves, rising and falling, pitching and rolling, rising and falling, buffeted from side to side, rising and falling, going against the tide, rising and falling. Progress is painfully slow. Brendan is trembling and I feel I'm abusing him for bringing him on board in the first place. The couple next to us show a lot of interest in him and we chat about his history, the little I know of it. The man strokes him on the top of his head and survives, which shows how stressed and pre-occupied Brendan really is. Stroking a strange dog on the head is considered the height of rudeness in the dog world; you may as well flick their nose or give them the finger. They may not attack you for it, but they don't like it; only their closest family are acceptable head-patters.

It's a terrible journey and it seems to last forever. When I look up we're mooring in Plymouth at a modern landing stage. I'm giddy and overjoyed that it's nearly over. I've missed the whole voyage because I was focusing on Brendan and trying to calm him.

Plymouth describes itself as "Britain's Ocean City", so what better way to arrive than via the ocean? I don't think Brendan agrees. He isn't happy at all, but he does alight the ferry without any problems and we walk up a lightweight, vibrating metal ramp and rise into the old town. It's a maritime city; an historic city.

The harbour area is bustling; it's actually heaving. It's seething. Little cottages and shops line cobbled back streets. It's not twee, but real, solid and unpretentious. Plymouth is lived-in and it has lived. A lot. It had a famous mayor in the form of slave trader and explorer, Francis Drake, and even more famously, the Pilgrim Fathers set off from here in 1620, on board the *Mayflower*, bound for the New World.

We wander up and down the quaint streets, admiring the architecture and the feeling of the place, which is somewhat ruined by the volume of people. Brendan is coping well, but I feel very stressed on his behalf. There are too many people and there is too much traffic. I had looked forward to exploring Plymouth, but it's being ruined, so we go in search of a quaintly historic pub. Most are very attractive from the outside, but inside are just dated, lacking all character and individuality, with Juke boxes and flashing fruit machines. Eventually we find a tiny pub with whitewashed stone walls and exposed oak beams. Brendan spreads out across the cool stone and parquet floor; he's happy. I'm not. Despite the city being crammed full of tourists, we are the only customers in this particular bar. All drinks are served in plastic glasses, which I hate, and the background music is loud and intrusive. A new track starts, a soulful ballad, the chorus of which is "I swear I'll never call you bitch again". And they say music is dead. I think this proves it; it really is dead. And I don't think it died of natural causes.

I'm keeping an eye on the time, because we don't want to miss the last ferry. The little boat is much less busy. Brendan is much better, much more confident and relaxed. He learns and adapts very quickly.

As we phut-phut towards Cawsand, the Ferry driver sticks his head through the window of his cabin and shouts: "Hey, mate, what breed is he?"

I shrug. "Not sure. He's a rescue. A bit of terrier maybe."

"His beard is *cool,* man!"

"It's less cool when it's solid from his gravy binges."

"Ah, well…" He nods wisely. "He's from the north." He scratches his own gravy-heavy beard and whips his head back inside.

I smile and nod. I settle back to enjoy the rest of the ride. Then I realise, he's transposing my accent onto Brendan. Brendan *isn't* from the north. He's from Bulgaria, which isn't at all north. I consider correcting him, but he'd probably only say: "Yeah? Cool, dude." So, there isn't much point.

We pull up on the beach. Brendan negotiates the exit gangplank like a seasoned professional and we walk slowly back to the site at Maker Heights via another pub. It's a beautiful evening. As the light begins to fade across the bay, we can see yachts tacking across the hazy blue. It's idyllic. We sit outside for a long time, until the night comes down, the stars come out and the temperature drops.

* * * * * * * * * *

I wake up at 7am and get up; Brendan doesn't. I put the kettle on the gas hob for my morning tea. Nothing happens. It doesn't light. There's no smell of gas. I open the fridge, it feels warm; it works off electric when you're on hook-up, but there's no hook-up here so it's running on gas. It smells fetid. The gas has obviously run out in the night. I can't have my morning tea, which is the most important drink of the day. I'm immediately in a foul mood. Brendan is barking at birds repeatedly and I tell him to stop, so he goes into a mood as well. It isn't a good start to the day. Actually, it isn't looking like a good day at all. It's grey and breezy.

The site staff give me directions to the only place in the area that sells gas canisters. Quite unhelpfully, the shop assistant doesn't know whether she's selling me a full bottle of gas or an empty bottle awaiting refill, which is a bit worrying, but once I've installed the new canister I immediately make a brew and it seems to be working fine.

We spend the day doing a series of cliff walks. The scenery is spectacular, as is the sea, despite the day being somewhat overcast. Brendan seems to be enjoying trundling along, tail in the air, smelling everything in sight and weeing on most things.

We get as far as Cawsand, which is very quiet today, probably due to the dull weather. We call in a nice little pub with a stone flag floor. A local, perched at the bar with his own dog, comes over and gives Brendan some attention and a biscuit – which is why I think he escapes a savaging. He introduces himself as Mike. Another Mike. He looks like a surfing guru, weather beaten, suntanned, longish hair held back with a plastic Alice band. Mike seems very calm and very wise. Wise Mike. He watches Brendan struggling with the biscuit; it keeps falling out of his mouth. Mike frowns. "He's got some teeth missing... that's why he's having trouble eating... He's from Romania? Or Bulgaria, right?" I nod in amazement at his insight. "They beat them with sticks, you know... His teeth have probably snapped off." Brendan still has his canine teeth, so he can pierce your jugular and drain your blood, but his front teeth have indeed snapped off. It doesn't really show unless you're peering into his open mouth. For most people, that isn't a position they want to be in.

Mike talks for a few minutes about rescue dogs and dogs abroad. He finishes by saying: "You're doing a great thing with him." Then he returns to his stool by the bar, where his dog, Norman, is waiting patiently for his next pint. Norman is like a big fluffy, Dulux dog with big paws and a big smile. We set off on foot to find Eagle One and leave Norman and Mike with their Alice bands and Guinness.

* * * * * * * * * *

We've spent three very enjoyable nights at Maker Heights; it's been great for Brendan. We'd love to come back, preferably when it's not under heavy artillery bombardment. We reluctantly leave early the next morning under a flat, grey sky. We're leaving Cornwall, to return to Devon, the only county on a circumnavigation of Britain that you pass through twice.

We drive to Torpoint. It's something of a dusty old town, in need of a lick of paint. It seems to exist solely to channel vehicles to the ferry. The ferry is big news in Torpoint. The ferry *is* Torpoint. If there was no ferry, I'm not sure the Tor would have a point.

We're signalled onto the aforementioned ferry and park in tight lines of vehicles. With a lot of clanking the ferry sets off and we're crossing the River Tamar. Brendan is sitting upright, alert, watching and listening with trepidation. Minutes later, with a lot of grinding, the ferry docks on the other side and with an almost imperceptible rasp of tyres, we're in South Devon.

* * * * * * * * * *

Dog facts:
The most popular breed of dog in the world is the

Labrador. Famed for their gentle nature, they are the most common Guide Dogs and are often used to assist the police. Brendan also has frequently assisted the police. With their enquiries.

Brendan having a sit down near Rame Head

CHAPTER 4: DOG DAYS ON THE JURASSIC COAST

It's a Tuesday. Statistically, Tuesday is the wettest day of the week, but weirdly, also the safest day on which to drive. I *think* it's a Tuesday, but I could be wrong. It's strange how unimportant the day is when you're on the road with your dog for any amount of time. A day is a day and every day offers something new and exciting, new challenges and opportunities. The other side of the coin is that it will also bring all the usual crap that life throws at you.

We arrive at the little seaside town of Bigbury-on-Sea and Brendan scampers excitedly down to the sandy beach. The big thing about Bigbury, apart from its rather made-up-on-the-spot name, is Burgh Island, sitting just off shore, a tidal isle accessible by foot and paw at low tide and cut off at high tide. Everyone on the beach is either walking towards it or walking back from it. You don't go to the beach and ignore it – you can't ignore it. It isn't dramatic like Saint Michael's Mount; it's a gentle, low-lying green island with an art deco hotel facing the landward side, which has attracted the rich and famous... and inspired murder, most foul. (Agatha Christie was a frequent visitor and the hotel featured in several of her plots.)

Brendan glances around with interest and sniffs at the salty air. We tramp through the soft sand towards the island, just as the sea closes around it. A family get caught half way and complete the last part of the journey squealing and splashing, with their ankles wet. We've missed it. Brendan gives me a knowing look. But all is not lost, as we still have another option. We – and the two dozen other disappointed day trippers – will travel through the waves on the Sea Tractor of Terror. (Usually known simply by its commercial name, The Sea Tractor. But we know better.)

The Sea Tractor

The Sea Tractor stands incongruously on the beach. It's not like any other vehicle anywhere, ever. It looks like a section of factory shelving on big wheels. A set of steps lead up to a raised seating area largely open to the elements. It looks ludicrous and other-worldly, designed by a fool or a madman or both. We climb the steps to find the open carriage already full, but we force our way in and stand huddled together as yet more people squeeze on.

Unfortunately, it's the Plymouth ferry all over again; Brendan sits at my feet, quite relaxed, but the moment the engine starts everything shakes and rattles and vibrates. A cloud of pale diesel smoke drifts over us. Brendan starts trembling. I crouch down and wrap my arms protectively around him and tell him not to worry, but he can't hear me over the din. We're suddenly underway, trundling uncertainly towards the breakers. The journey only lasts a couple of minutes and then we're pulling up on the slipway of Burgh Island.

We climb to the top of the island; we're the first ones to reach the summit. We look back over the sea to the mainland. We're on an island! We're cut off! It's an exciting feeling. A nice couple from the sea tractor appear. Because they're carrying walking poles and probably the fact that they're people, means that Brendan barks at them incessantly, so we have to come away.

And that's it really; that's Burgh Island. Most of it is private and out of bounds, belonging to the hotel and reserved for patrons, so there isn't actually very much to see. There is a small pub, which we're told is a great place to enjoy a drink on a sunny day, but we won't get to find out, as it's closed.

We arrive back at the slipway and wait with the throng of other people for the sea tractor to return.

The tide is still stubbornly closed around the island and we are effectively stranded, so we won't be able to walk back. I needn't have worried about the traumatic return journey, because – as with the Plymouth ferry – Brendan is fine, he's relaxed, tongue lolling out, looking with interest at the landscape as we splash through the shallows.

* * * * * * * * * *

The following day is less sunny. We arrive in the yachting community of Salcombe, one of South Devon's most select locations. It clearly attracts a lot of would-be ocean-going older men, as they're out in force, wearing navy blue and white striped tops. Those that aren't trying to come across as gentrified seafaring folk are instead exhibiting a brave choice in lower garmentry. There are suddenly a lot of salmon, dusty pink, plum, burgundy, terracotta and the occasional mint slacks. None of these colours were invented to trouser a man.

Salcombe – quaint as it might be – is too busy for Brendan, so we move on, have a cliff walk, then pitch up at our campsite at Slapton. The site is nice but very busy. We set off on foot to the beach, Slapton Sands. As the sun begins to sink over the land, it suddenly goes very cold and breezy. A typical British family are sitting on the beach in deckchairs, windbreak up, wearing shorts, T-shirts and other beachwear and also wrapped in towels and blankets for warmth, but staunchly refusing to budge, because they're British and they're on holiday *in Britain* and this is what the British do when on holiday in Britain.

During the war, Slapton's beach was used for a rehearsal for the D-Day Landings, but an incident involving friendly fire resulted in the deaths of 749 American servicemen. For many years, this was covered up – quite badly – but is now acknowledged and an incongruous Sherman tank remains as a memorial. Brendan isn't used to seeing a big black tank in the corner of a car park, so he stands his ground and bravely barks at it. He can't tolerate things out of place.

We get some chips and sit on the quiet seafront. With the sound of gull calls and the rhythmic rushing of waves in the background is the best way to eat chips. I'm enjoying being with my boy, my only companion. He picks at his chips; he is such a fussy eater, which doesn't add up. He was a street dog! (Allegedly.) He had to scavenge; he had to rough it and make do! Unless, when they say "street dog", the streets they're referring to are Kensington High Street or Park Lane.

* * * * * * * * * *

The site is busy and noisy throughout the night. It's also airless and muggy, so we don't sleep very well and there is a lot of shifting and sighing from Brendan. Regardless of this, we're up early the next morning (Well, I am.), filled with excitement, (Well, I am.) and looking forward to visiting a lighthouse. (Well, I am.)

Start Point is a great lighthouse in a dramatic location. It's the only proper lighthouse in England (and Wales) that I've never visited before. It perches on jagged cliffs, bold white with unusual gothic embellishments, standing out against the sea and sky. The door is securely closed, so we sit and wait for opening time, enjoying being here, in the salty breeze with seagulls calling and circling overhead.

After a while, an elderly man comes out of the lighthouse. He introduces himself as John. He looks like a retired sailor, a captain or admiral. He comes over to stroke Brendan, but I warn him off. He continues to advance anyway, then Brendan himself warns him off, and this time John takes heed. He stands there with his hands firmly planted in the pockets of his duffle coat. He's a sailing enthusiast, he says. He's retired now, but his job had been delivering outboard motors. He has been doing the lighthouse tours for six years and he loves it.

John raises his hands as he's speaking and Brendan – assuming he's under naval attack – goes ballistic, so then we start talking about Brendan, about dogs in general and about Bulgaria. Me being allowed into the lighthouse with Brendan is down to John, so I paint a picture of this frightened dog – the same one that sits here snarling at him. John's a decent chap and the subterfuge seems to be working.

Two young women arrive on bikes. One is wearing huge, old fashioned, canvas shorts, the other is wearing dungarees. They look like they might be part of the Famous Five, or possibly women from the Land Army during the war. They come towards Brendan smiling. He isn't smiling back. I issue the usual warnings, but Dungarees says firmly: "It's OK... I know how to handle dogs. I worked in an animal shelter for five years, so I know all about... Bloody hell! He snapped at me!" She keeps a respectful distance after this.

A spritely older couple arrive.

"Are you coming on the tour?" John asks them jovially. "We're about to start now."

"I am." the woman says cheerfully. "Darling, do you want..."

The old man looks horrified. "No! Absolutely not!" He turns and walks quickly away, around the lighthouse buildings and out of sight.

The woman smiles in embarrassment. "Just me, it seems."

And those are the players: two cycling young women: Shorts and Dungarees, Older Lady, me and my boy, led by Captain John.

"Alright, all aboard!" calls John.

Brendan trails around with me and has a sit down in each of the circular rooms. There are a few occasions when John gets too animated as he's talking and moves his arms enthusiastically and Brendan delivers a salvo of barks. John apologises, pins his arms to his sides and tries to keep still as he speaks, but it's difficult because he's an expressive orator and is clearly passionate about his subject, and that's a very precious thing.

Brendan climbs the steep and narrow spiral stairs with no problems, until we come to the last proper floor, where he has to stay, as he isn't allowed to go any further. He waits patiently as the rest of us climb the ladder into the lamp room. He seems calm and very secure, as though he knows I'm coming back for him, so perhaps he's adjusting gradually.

By the end of the tour, Brendan has barked at the young women once too often. Shorts is now quite jumpy and nervous and Dungarees is quite annoyed. They leave the lighthouse, leap on their bikes and cycle off... Unfortunately, it's uphill; they get about ten yards, then have to stop, dismount and walk the rest of the way.

We say goodbye to Captain John. (Well I do; Brendan makes a series of threats.) We follow the girls up the driveway, trying to keep at a discreet distance. I'm ecstatic. I've wanted to visit this lighthouse for some time, and now I've done it and shared the experience with my boy.

In the evening we go for a walk to look around Slapton village, which is very attractive, filled with picture postcard cottages. Flowers spring from the gaps in the old stone walls, wild roses hang over the top, ivy and wisteria climb and trail.

I glance down at Brendan as he trots along the lane beside me. His handsomeness today is sailing exceedingly close to EU safety standards.

We call in the pub. Inside it's like a trip back in time. Unfortunately, it only takes us as far back as the 'Seventies. Outside however, it has a beautiful tiered, terraced, walled beer garden, surrounded by shrubs and flowering baskets. It's a mild and tranquil evening.

The sun is sinking lower over the thatched roofs and chimney pots and I'm feeling very relaxed, until Brendan has an altercation with the resident seagull, who's perched on top of a dovecote surveying his kingdom, like the dictator that he is. Each is determined to get the last word, neither prepared to back down and they refuse to shake on it. The constant barking and squawking somewhat takes the edge off the mood.

The seagull of terror

Taking Brendan for a wee just after midnight, I notice the reassuring sweep of light from Start Point lighthouse, like a searchlight moving across the sky. It's such a spectacular sight, so wondrous and so comforting. It's sad that with the advent of GPS and other technology, very soon those reassuring beams that have served mankind for centuries and saved untold millions of lives, might be no more. Our nights will be much darker, our skies much emptier and, I think, our lives a little sadder.

* * * * * * * * * *

We stroll around the port town of Dartmouth. The harbour smells of salt and seaweed. The inner harbour makes me think of Amsterdam or somewhere in Scandinavia, possibly wonderful, wonderful Copenhagen.

We follow the roads and footpaths along the riverside, heading towards the sea. A nice middle-aged couple are walking the same way, a short distance in front. They stop, waiting for a crossing light to change. Brendan rushes up and touches the woman's bare legs with his nose. She squeals and jumps, then laughs. I pull him back and apologise. She smiles and strokes him. "Oh, it's OK, I don't mind..." Her face suddenly fills with sadness. "Actually... I'm missing our dog. We're away for two weeks holiday and this is the longest we've ever left him. But he's at home, so at least I feel he's safe and in good hands. Our son's looking after him. Our grown up son. He's twenty-one."

"Oh..." I say. I'm not totally convinced a twenty-one year old left alone in his parents' home is necessarily in possession of the safest hands. "Right... OK."

"He keeps phoning to reassure us and says there are so many different people in the house giving the dog lots of attention."

So, he's having lots of people round? Those are what we call "parties". I look at the man and he returns my gaze, knowingly and nods. He'd been a twenty-one year old boy-man once and knows the score.

We say goodbye and they walk on, but Brendan pulls

frantically to catch up to them; he succeeds at every corner, every crossing and every junction, and each time he gives the woman a wet-nose sniffing. It gets excruciatingly embarrassing. It only ends when they go in a café and Brendan isn't allowed to follow.

Dartmouth is a really quaint and characterful little town, but we've been dragging along concrete all morning, so I promise Brendan we'll spend the afternoon with something soft under our weary pads. He probably excitedly pictures a mattress warehouse, but we end up at Berry Head. Think white cliffs. Think sun-bleached grass. Think sea views.

It's now blisteringly hot. We sit on the cliff edge, which plummets straight down. Brendan lies beside me, tongue lolling out, gazing lazily at the view. The shimmering sea far below goes on forever, until it merges with the perfectly clear sky. Yachts weave in slow circles. Seabirds call and wheel. This is another perfect memory, sitting here with Brendan, enjoying the moment, enjoying our trip, enjoying life. It's idyllic. But hot. But a very special, golden, soft-focus memory. But *so* hot! *Too* hot! I stroke my boy. The black part of his fur, which is the top half of him, is radiating some serious heat. He's one hot dog. We sit there as long as we can stand it, but it's unnaturally hot and there are no trees here and absolutely no shade.

I decide we should head for our pre-booked campsite and then relax for the rest of the day. This isn't a great move and just makes us hotter, because we end up snarled up in road works and then the rush hour starts. The longer I sit at temporary traffic lights on red, the hotter it gets and the more agitated I become. I have my elbows resting on the steering wheel. Red lights. Traffic. Fumes. Hot bonnets. Heat rising. Sun beating down. Sunlight glinting off glass. Hot concrete. Sticky tarmac. The world is melting. And gridlocked. The sun beats down through the windscreen. Meanwhile, in the back, Brendan is stretched out on his sofa, looking chilled and relaxed. The curtains are all closed and it's pleasantly cool for him. The driver, however, is hot, tired and stressed, whereas the passenger is relaxed and rejuvenated.

This is the first time I notice that Eagle One has started making a worrying knocking noise. I try to pretend it's nothing, but it's getting louder every minute. It's too soon for another big breakdown though, surely. When we get to our site I give the van a thorough once-over and I think I've possibly sorted the clanking noise; it looks like it was the cradle for the spare tyre underneath, working itself loose, but I won't know for sure until I drive off tomorrow.

* * * * * * * * * *

The next morning, I'm filled with trepidation as I turn the key, start the engine and drive off. The clanking noise isn't better at all, if anything it's worse; it sounds like the van is falling apart around us. Strangely, Brendan – who is frightened of men, women, walking sticks, planes, curtain fabrics, headlights, socks and origami – doesn't seem at all bothered by the constant racket. It's deafening and is getting me really agitated.

We trail around Torquay looking for shade, but the

little shade available is already full of people, so we're back on the road again, with Brendan reclining in the back and me sweating and swearing in the front. Even as we pull away I really regret not spending longer exploring the English Riviera, because we're doing a lot of travelling but I'm eager to do more living, more experiencing, more *being*. Life is for living and any moment could be your last. Serendipitously, we pass an accident on the A3022. There are police cars, a fire engine and ambulances. Someone is lying on the ground surrounded by paramedics. It's a very sobering spectacle. Like I said, any moment could be your last.

* * * * * * * * * *

I thought I was getting some funny looks today... even funnier than usual. As I'm parking Eagle One, a lady passing on the pavement stares at me and starts laughing. A smile is always nice, but laughter is a bit disconcerting. Once I've completed an excellent parallel park and pulled on the handbrake, I realise the dashboard is full of boxer shorts I'd washed last night. Ah well, if my pants can bring a smile...

We're now in Dorset. We step out of Eagle One into the charming town of Lyme Regis. It has an attractive high street leading downhill, with interesting shops and cafes housed in genuinely old buildings. Over the ornate rooftops is the horizon: deep blue sea, clear blue sky.

The beach is filled with people sunbathing. We walk along with the stones crunching beneath our six feet, Brendan is looking around for the best spot for a sit down, when a tall, broad female warden in a uniform, complete with peaked cap, comes up to us. I draw Brendan in, thinking things could go either way, but he just glances at her and then looks towards the horizon. She's very pleasant, but she tells us that the beach is closed to canine traffic and we face a heavy fine, so we must leave the pebbles.

Drenched in sunshine, Lyme Regis feels like a place to linger and enjoy. There are many characterful pubs around the harbour area, including the Pilot Boat. It is alleged that the faithful collie, Lassie, who appeared in many American films, was based on a real collie who saved the life of a shipwrecked sailor, whose ship had been torpedoed by a German submarine. Many bodies had been recovered and laid out in the cellar of the Pilot Boat, which was being used as a temporary mortuary. Lassie recognised one of the sailors was still alive and licked him and kept him warm until he came round, saving his life.

We spend an hour fossil hunting on the beach. Brendan is no help at all and just plays in the shallow rock pools, which he loves. Mainly because of his lack of commitment, we don't find any fossils, so we return to Eagle One. While Brendan has his post-fossilling nap, I slither under the chassis. This time I successfully diagnose the problem, which I've been missing because it's difficult to see in the gloom underneath. It's the rear passenger-side shock absorber. The piston has burst through its rusted casing and is bashing into the wheel arch. If left unchecked it will eventually punch a way through the metal. Brendan might hate mechanics, but I'd happily carry one as part of our safety equipment.

Instead I text our lifelong friend, Steve, asking for advice. Is he a mechanic? No, he's not, but in our teens he used to get a monthly magazine called something like *Whoops, my car!* (Part 1 comes with a free binder and miniature spanner!) So he's my best option. Within a minute he's on the phone. He asks some questions and says some technical things I don't understand, but the bottom line, which he repeats and stresses, is "Don't drive it!"

I feel crushed. It seems like something's going wrong with Eagle One every five-and-a-half minutes and I've already spent a fortune this year on repairs. There is a feeling of finality about this one which I don't want to acknowledge.

Despite Steve's warning, I hop in and start the engine. It's only a short drive to our campsite, but everyone in the county must hear us coming – the clanking of Eagle One is going from bad to worse. People are stopping on the pavements as we pass, ducking or taking shelter. I feel a weight in my chest and a growing sense of doom.

We arrive at the leafy site, which straddles the waving county boundary, so you can have a shower in Dorset and go to the toilet in Devon. If you want to.

Brendan is exhausted and flat out in his basket. I check the weather for tomorrow. We are warned that Storm Hector is coming to Britain. It seems to be the main news item and dominates all the headlines.

STORM HECTOR, BACK WITH A BANG! THREATS TO LIFE. FEAR OF POWER CUTS AND FLYING DEBRIS.

60MPH WINDS.

Reading on, the nation is seemingly nonchalant about the flying debris and the threat to life, but people are getting hysterical at the thought of a power cut and not being able to charge their iPhones. I imagine the emergency nuclear reactor has been brought online as the nation frantically uber-charges their phones. This could be the big one: a possible power cut that might last for several hours or even a full morning. The nation trembles. The electricity consumption trebles.

* * * * * * * * * *

A new day, a new start. Hopefully. The AA have been called and are due within the hour. The AA man duly arrives in his yellow van. He's called Chris and is the spitting image of one who came to my aid in Manchester. I ask if it was him. He laughs and says no. "But you're his double! *And* he was called Chris!"

He laughs. "We're all called Chris and we're made on a conveyor belt. We're all clones."

I suspect his laugh is to disarm me, because what he's telling me is clearly the truth: they really *are* all clones. Except for Mike in Portishead, who wasn't called Chris and wasn't a clone.

It takes Clone Chris a couple of hours to sort the van, including a trip out for parts. I keep Brendan away from him at all costs, though I don't think it's actually necessary. Brendan is indifferent towards him, disinterested even, as though he knows Chris is helping us... but that was how his relationship with Mike at

Portishead had begun. Chris works very fast, but then there might be more than one of him. You know what clones are like. I thank him/them, pay for the parts and off he/they go. And off *we* go, our newly fitted part absorbing shock like there's no tomorrow. It's lovely to be travelling almost silently again. As silent as a diesel engine will allow, anyway.

After a day of long, windy walks, we arrive at our next site. Their advertising states it is: "Dorset's *most* beautiful licenced camping park?" but their question mark suggests they aren't completely sure. It's certainly in a beautiful location, but it employs one of the rudest women I've ever encountered.

The lady I had spoken to on the phone earlier was friendly and really helpful. Unfortunately, she went home at five o'clock and I'm left with her colleague, a sun-wrinkled prison warder. She glances up from the counter as I walk into the lean-to that serves as reception and she actually sighs. That's before I've even spoken. I explain I've provisionally booked with her colleague.

She sighs again. "I'll check. Postcode?"

"I didn't give my postcode."

"Well, you didn't provisionally book then, did you? Or you'd have given your postcode!"

"I had a breakdown... My van, not me... I didn't know if I was going to..."

"Freeman?"

"Yes." I say, though I'm not feeling in any way free or like a man.

"She said you'd phone if you were coming."

"I actually said I'd phone if I *wasn't* coming."

Impatiently: "Well, that's not what she's put. And she's *actually written it down.*"

"Fine, whatever. I'm here, so…"

Sigh. "Right, one van, one adult, no children, no awning, grass pitch, no electric…"

"No, I wanted electric."

Sigh. I wonder if she ever gets bored of sighing. "She's written, quite clearly, *no electric!*"

"Well, she's made a mistake then. I definitely want electric."

"I'll have to move your pitch then!"

"Is that a problem?"

Sigh. She taps one button on the computer keyboard. "There! Pitch 147! Alright?"

"Thank you."

"So, one adult, no children, one dog."

"Yes."

"We don't actually allow dogs here." she says suddenly. It's an afterthought.

I look at her, because I know that's not true. I'm not going to give her the satisfaction. She stares at me. I stare back. There's a long pause. Seconds go by. More seconds pass. The pause gets longer. I've literally got all night. She gives in first and does her default sigh instead.

"Except on a lead." she says. By now those four words are too far away from their parent statement and are awkwardly alone, out of place and serve no purpose. I smile and head outside.

I climb into Eagle One. Brendan raises an eyebrow then goes back to sleep. I sit behind the wheel and look at all the literature she's given me. There's an instruction booklet of four A4 sides, containing very small print. It's a very badly laid out booklet and there's way too much to take in. There are lists of things to do, things not to do, the speed limit and regulations for everything else imaginable. There are prisons with less rigid rules. There's no music allowed – it doesn't specify no *loud* music, or no music *outside* – just *no music*. At all. Ever. No fires. Chinese lanterns are not permitted. Dogs on a lead only and at all times – which we've already covered. Do *not* park side-on. *Do* park facing outwards. Under no circumstance is anyone to have any fun or treat this like a holiday. Thanks to all these rules that isn't likely to happen.

Apart from my dad, no one would ever sit and read all

this. (He reads everything – every word. Out loud, so he can share it. "Copyright 1998. Printed by Fleetprint Limited. Telephone...") Furthermore, it's not a charity, we're actually paying quite a lot to stay here, so we should perhaps not be treated like inmates.

I pull onto my numbered pitch, which is 147. With electric. I park correctly, in accordance with the rules, whilst not listening to any music or setting off a Chinese lantern. The small, high-hedged field we're in has a capacity for twenty or more units. There are two pitches occupied. There are 366 marked pitches on this site in total and there are only three tents, two caravans and two campervans in residence, so the site is running at a fraction of its capacity, so can she really afford the bad attitude?

I had asked her if it was possible for me to stay a second night if I wanted to. She had sighed and said haughtily: "Well, it'll mean me moving you to another pitch!"

I decided at that point I didn't want to stay another night.

* * * * * * * * * *

We have a lazy and uneventful night and awake to a pleasantly sunny morning. Despite all the panic and hysteria, Storm Hector seems to have bypassed us.

The other unit in our small field belongs to a nice middle-aged couple. They seem very suburban and respectable. They seem the sort of couple who probably refer to each other as "mum" and "dad", regardless of whether they have children or not. "What's for tea, mum?" "Your favourite, dad."

As she's passing, "Mum" stops to admire Brendan, but I warn her off, because he has a look about him. She tells me she was born in Dorset but hasn't been back since. Brendan barks when she moves slightly, but she stands her ground and continues chatting, ignoring him. He doesn't know what to do, so he does nothing and stands there feeling slightly redundant, then eventually sneaks back into the van and sulks.

He's still sulking as we continue through classic patchwork fields of green and gold, fodder and cereal crops, lined with ancient hedgerows and the occasional copse. It looks like a painting. We're driving through a painting, through little villages of pale stone, past thatched cottages and sleepy little churches with lichen-covered graveyards. It's beautiful.

For a treat I take Brendan to see the famous Portland Bill lighthouse, with its distinctive red and white candy stripe livery, right at the top of the Isle of Portland. We're really ticking off the lighthouses now. I'm hoping Brendan will become as enraptured by them as I am. He's hoping I can develop a liking for sniffing gateposts. We're probably both going to be disappointed.

I drive on to Lulworth Cove, which is another of those places, like Land's End, which must be on the tourist trail for international visitors, because every other accent is foreign. We wander down to the horseshoe-shaped cove. The sun has gone and the air is damp. The tide is in and the remaining small strip of beach is full of people, who are wrapped up against the cold wind and just seem to be staring at the lapping waves. It's as though they're waiting for something to happen. Nothing does. We join them and we too stare expectant;y at the lapping waves for a while.

Brendan gets a lot of attention; if it's from other dogs he's very happy; if it's only from humans he's generally indifferent or mildly peeved. It's always quite embarrassing when someone waxes lyrical about him and he turns his back on them, or they give him a biscuit and he spits it out disdainfully. Worse still, of course, is when he lunges at them.

In the gift shop, a mother and two young girls all stop and stare at him doe-eyed: "Mum look! He's gorgeous! What type is he?"

By now my answer is automatic; I hardly know I'm saying it: "He's a rescue dog, a street dog, so he could be anything. But he's got a terrier face and beard, Alsatian colouring and possibly a bit of lurcher, because he's got a very narrow frame."

They nod vacantly, having stopped listening ages ago. Brendan sees this as a suitable distraction and uses the opportunity to try and shoplift a Lulworth Cove vanity set. Old habits die hard.

On the way to our site, we pass through Bovington Camp, a sprawling army base, specialising in armoured warfare, AKA tanks. The only fact I know about tanks is that a tank top has no sleeves and I used to have a brown one. (I was about eight.) I hope that helps.

As we're passing through the camp, I notice we keep

seeing the same cars, as though they're continually driving around the army base. Perhaps they're undercover security. The silver car behind is keeping equidistant. I slow down; it slows down. I speed up; it speeds up. There's no mistaking – they're following us. When I turn down a road leading away from the base; that car remains with the base perimeter road, but another car appears from nowhere and takes its place, following the same pattern. They stick with us for the next twenty minutes, then suddenly reduce speed, then do a U-turn and head back towards the base. We must have crossed some unseen boundary, beyond their jurisdiction.

At the campsite, we've been allocated a pitch, that seemingly no one else wants: a shady little corner that hasn't seen the sun since the oaks grew, a hundred years ago. It's secluded and looks like it will provide a perfect semi-private, gloomy garden for Brendan. It turns out not to be ideal at all. We're too close to the facilities, so people are bringing bowls of washing up or heading to the showers with a towel over their shoulders and kids are running around waiting for their parents. It's a nightmare for Brendan, who barks solidly all evening.

A little girl is running past with her friend; she comes to a sudden halt, staring at The Boy, who is sitting outside the van. "Ah... your dog is *gorgeous!*" Thankfully she doesn't attempt to stroke him, so Brendan doesn't get the chance to show how ungorgeous he can be. With her being a child, I suspect he would have been patient, forgiving and gentle, but you can't take that risk. I don't want to blink and find that only her pink flip flops and Alice band remain.

It isn't the most relaxing evening. Neither of us sleep well. I have nightmares. Brendan has nightmares. We take it in turns to have nightmares and wake each other up, because that's what pals do.

* * * * * * * * * *

It's 10.30am. Overcast, not really cold, not raining. Not really anything. We arrive at Durleston Castle, a frivolously exuberant restored Victorian folly, which now forms the hub of a country park.

We go in the café for a coffee, because that's what we do best. Brendan is very well-behaved, until a waiter starts faffing about with the empty table next to us, preparing it for lunch, setting out wine glasses, napkins and cutlery. He keeps needlessly stepping over Brendan. Brendan can't abide bad manners and is growing increasingly annoyed. He sighs and tries to get on with his napping, but the waiter – who has actually finished with the table – keeps re-arranging and titivating in an infuriatingly prissy manner, moving a fork one millimetre this way, a napkin a millimetre that way, standing back and double checking, then doing more ludicrously affected adjustments, all the time stepping over Brendan, stepping back, stepping over again. I suspect he's doing it on purpose. This isn't the Ritz and if he's got time to be so pedantic, then he's got too much time.

In the end, Brendan loses his temper; one of us was bound to, and I thought it was likely to be me. He's been very well-behaved and very patient, but suddenly he's had enough. He starts barking at the waiter, who then looks all shocked and frightened; I suspect this was his goal all along. Everyone in the café turns and stares. The waiter makes a big show about being afraid and tells us if it happens again we will have to leave. It *does* happen again, but the waiter chooses not to broach the subject.

We explore the terraced pathways around the castle, which are all so Victorian; the perfect place for gentlefolk to perambulate. The sea looks choppy and cold and it's very windy; any perambulating lady out today would surely lose her bonnet and parasol.

I begin to notice that everyone approaching us along the paths does their best to avoid us, turning off if at all possible, or pressing themselves against walls and hedges and not taking their eyes off Brendan. Their expressions are saying "Don't hurt me. Here, take my wife!" Brendan pads along beside me quite happily. Once he has passed them, they hurry away, looking skywards and mouthing: "Thank you, lord." I realise, all these people must have been present in the café. All Brendan did was bark at one waiter who was being pretentious and intrusive. I'm really annoyed; I'm much more annoyed than I should be. I need a distraction.

A short way from the castle stands a huge limestone globe, three metres in diameter and weighing 40 tonnes. I love the globe, with its slightly less than accurate carved depiction of the world as seen by the Victorians.

Brendan sits patiently on a step and watches as visitors move around it and take photographs. An older couple in gender specific waterproof coats – blue for him, pink for her – are taking photos. She has a little happy-snapper, point-and-go camera. He has a huge digital SLR with a telescopic lens. A young woman, part of a group of a dozen young people, asks the old woman if she'd mind taking a photo of them. The old man immediately slinks away and stands behind the globe for the duration, either affronted that he wasn't asked or knowing from experience that his wife is about to embarrass him. The old lady is handed the young woman's phone, given a quick instructional briefing, then the group all press in together and pose immaculately, with perfect hair and whitened teeth.

The old lady raises the phone. "Smile!" They all smile. She lowers the phone. "Oh... Am I doing it right?"

The Phone Girl smiles patiently. "Just press the red circle. OK, everyone?"

"So... like *that*. Oh... now, why's that happened?"

"It's this button here... The *red circle*... No, this one... No, you're pressing a rivet... This one. No... The red circle. The *red* circle. The red *circle*. The. Red. Circle."

"I see... Okay... sorry folks... Say cheese. There... How was that? Oh... what's that?"

"That's your finger... you've got your finger over the lens."

"Oh right, I see. Sorry. Back to your places everyone... Smile."

Good as gold. Brendan at Durleston Castle.

Brendan watches with interest as forced smiles abound for the third time.

"There. How's that?"

Evidently no better. Phone Girl has clearly given up. "Fine." she says, a little too clipped to be genuine. "Thank you."

"Did it work?"

"No, but it's fine, really. Thanks."

"D'you want me to do another?"

"No! Thank you. Really... it's fine... Thanks anyway."

"I could do another."

"It's OK really."

The young people begin to disperse and at last the older man is able to emerge from his hiding place and sheepishly rejoin his deflated wife.

As she's passing us, the Phone Girl stops to make a fuss of Brendan. I'm on pins, as usual, but he's being so lovely with her. Another girl stops and starts petting him and making cooing noises; I start to think she's swallowed a dove. Then a young man steps towards Brendan and I hear myself snapping: "*Not you!*" My heart's racing and I can't relax. I just want them to go away with their brand new designer walking clothes, their perfect hair and brilliant white teeth.

Then – without warning – everything goes into slow motion. Out in the ocean the white-crested waves surge forwards slowly and silently. Gulls freeze against the grey clouds, suspended. People walk past, limbs moving with laboured intensity. The branches of the trees swing lethargically, rhythmically, soundlessly. The young man steps backwards. Phone Girl resumes stroking Brendan's head. He raises his muzzle, gazing up at her and with his nose quivering, he starts sniffing her crotch. She's wearing skin tight black leggings. Without actually speaking, every fibre of my being yells a slowed-down, slow motion, panicked "Noooo!!!" I try to yank him away by surreptitiously pulling his lead, so as not to make it obvious, in case she hasn't noticed the shiny, wet, black nose sniffing at her with gusto.

Real time resumes. Strangely, everything happening at normal speed is *just* as excruciatingly embarrassing. I catch the young man's eye. He's biting his lower lip, which is quivering uncontrollably. He's trying his best not to laugh, but not doing a very good job. He turns away and I can see his shoulders shaking in paroxysms of laughter. I'm too mortified to laugh and it's still going on. Phone Girl starts to chuckle, so she's definitely noticed. Brendan is still sniffing away, his head raised. Then it just gets even more awkward.

"Oh!" she cries suddenly. "D'you know what he can smell?"

I don't know where to look or what to say. I just stand there with my mouth hanging open.

"Biscuits!" she exclaims jubilantly. "In my pocket. I've got biscuits in my pocket. Dog biscuits."

She produces a little bone shaped biscuit from somewhere and proffers it to Brendan. I cringe and wait for the screams, but he takes it very gently and daintily eats the body-warm treat.

Phone Girl strokes his head, says goodbye and her party set off back towards the castle. I notice the young man is still trying not to laugh as he walks away, but keeps breaking down and covering his face with his hands.

* * * * * * * * * *

It's only a short drive into Swanage, which inspired many of Enid Blyton's adventure stories for children. I used to love the *Famous Five* and *Secret Seven*. Who isn't enthralled by alliteration? I always dreamed of a time when I would be old enough to go camping with friends and sleep on the moors and have adventures. When I *was* old enough I *did* go camping with friends, though I didn't sleep on the moors on a bed of heather that Anne had gathered. But I *did* have lashings of ginger beer. And I still do. (But it now has alcohol in it and it's called Crabbies.) Somehow, real life usually falls a little short of fiction. But I'm here now with my best bud, living life to the max. And doing a lot of sitting down.

Looking over Swanage bay, everything is grey and going hazy. Flags along the esplanade are blowing, moored boats are bobbing. It looks suddenly like a winter's day and a bizarre bank of sea mist is creeping steadily towards the shore. It puts me in mind of the John Carpenter film, *The Fog*. Something sinister is surely about to occur. It's very eerie.

Colourful surf boards are stacked up on the prom, available for hire, but nobody's hiring. There are also rows of coloured, striped, old fashioned deckchairs, but not one is in use. Instead, people are sitting huddled in shelters eating chips; it's surely quite a contrast to how it would have been a few days earlier. I think that's the thing about the tourist industry in this country: it is reliant on the weather, but the weather is totally unreliable.

It's too breezy for Brendan. He flinches at every flapping

flag, every swinging sign and every billowing awning. The mist continues to roll in and Swanage disappears before our eyes.

We find our way back to Eagle One – which is almost invisible: white against white. We climb on board and drive away from the void where Swanage used to be. The tops of the surrounding hills are now missing, due to the mist and it's started raining. I park in the centre of the village of Corfe Castle, on a slope. The dramatic ruins of the eponymous castle loom over the rooftops and chimneys.

I open the sliding side door of the van for Brendan. As he's skipping down, because of the gradient, the door suddenly rolls shut and traps his tail. He squeals and his whole body reacts, but he's actually trapped – by the tail. It's awful. I open the door and free him. I examine his tail thoroughly and – unbelievably – it isn't broken or damaged in any way. Brendan has immediately forgotten the incident and is keen to carry on and do some sniffing and really earn himself a sit down, but it has ruined my day. I feel so responsible and guilty.

We have a walk round the village, Brendan has a sniff, wees on some walls, yawns and sits down at every opportunity. For me the afternoon is ruined and the village is tainted, so we move on to our nearby vast, wide-open campsite.

It's still very foggy, but despite the conditions, people are sitting outside their tents eating their tea with their hoods up, shivering. I remember similar camping experiences myself, never being able to get warm and staying awake all night because of the bone-cold chill. I don't mind enduring hardship, but I can't see Brendan readily agreeing to a night under canvas.

I take the Boy out for a walk, because I think he needs it rather than wants it. A peacock struts past us. Brendan stops and stares at it, but not in an aggressive way, just vaguely bemused, as though to say, "You! Bird! You've got something on your tail." The bird sashays past. I feel sorry for him; it's awful when you turn up somewhere way overdressed and everyone else is in jeans.

The fog is now so thick I decide it's too dangerous to walk any further in unknown territory. Besides, we're both tired and if I'm honest, I'm still traumatised about the Brendan's Tail incident. He doesn't seem remotely bothered, although he does seem really affectionate and perhaps a bit clingy. We return to the van, get the heating on and sit looking out, though there's very little to see, except the encompassing, suffocating, smothering blanket of fog. We're in bed by 8.30, warm and cosy, enjoying the atmosphere.

* * * * * * * * * *

Dog facts:
Dogs can detect an approaching storm; as a result they may act skittishly. Brendan can definitely predict a storm, but then he's constantly glued to the weather app on his phone.

CHAPTER 5: BRENDAN
THE DEVIL RIDES OUT

Milford-on-sea is a neat, prim, organised Hampshire coastal town with a natural harbour. Rows of tethered boats stretch away into the distance, towards the white tower of Hurst Point Lighthouse, which pierces the gunmetal grey sky.

We tramp along Hurst Spit, which reaches for nearly two miles out into the deep waters of the Solent, a busy strait between the south coast and the Isle of Wight. It's hard going, wading through the shingle, every step is a huge effort and doesn't seem to gain us any distance. We're also battling against a fierce wind. It's difficult for me to stand up and Brendan's eyes are screwed up against the salty blast; his ears have taken flight and are trailing behind him. It's exhausting, but exhilarating.

We reach the protective stone walls of Hurst Fort at the end of the spit. Immediately there is stillness and calm; we're sheltered from the elements by this towering edifice. I sit at a picnic table, Brendan lies on the soft grass at my feet. We're enjoying the solitude and this weird and unexpected tranquillity. It's another of those special, treasured, private moments. I'm the only person at the fort, Brendan is the only dog. In all likelihood we are the only ones on the entire spit, the only ones for several miles. In the fading light and feeling the remoteness of the location, aware of the deep, fast-flowing channel of water nearby, it all feels quite sinister. It's lonely and isolated, but utterly thrilling.

Brendan's clearly tired, but in a healthy way. He's enjoying having a sit down and he loves looking around him at what's going on. I'm sure he's happy and I'm starting to think that he's content and his feeling of security is growing, though he doesn't know he isn't going to be sent back to the sanctuary at any moment. I keep telling him he isn't, but he's not always listening. In between the occasions of severe stress he causes, there are times like this when we're calm and at peace and completely in tune with each other.

The Needles and the Needles Lighthouse.

Suddenly, the bubble of calm bursts as the fog signal on the Needles lighthouse starts sounding, a low, wailing, ominous drone, drifting across the ether. The Needles themselves and the Isle of Wight are now lost in an advancing bank of fog, which is blotting out the light. It suddenly goes very dark, very quickly, so we crunch our way back along the spit, towards the suburban neatness of Milford.

I wonder about getting a takeaway curry. Brendan reminds me he doesn't like curry. My last dog, Jake, loved his mild curry on a Thursday, but Brendan won't go near it. Again, I'm mystified as to how a former street dog gets to be such a fussy eater, but apparently it's quite common. Sometimes, when I call him for his dinner, he looks up from the newspaper with a certain expression, as though he's asking for the *a la carte* menu. I can guarantee that the food Brendan likes this week, he won't touch next week. Many of the street dogs I encounter are exactly the same. Perhaps they feel they've done their years of scavenging and eating rotting debris off the streets and now think they deserve better, which is fair enough: they do.

I stride into a near-empty Indian restaurant. There is only one table occupied. Two women are catching up on all the gossip. The smartly dressed staff easily outnumber the customers. I order poppadums, vegetable bhuna, pilau rice and a roti, to go.

"You not watching the match then?" the waiter asks.

I blink. "What match? No, I'm not... Didn't know there was one... I've been travelling... I've sort of lost touch with everything... I'm not even sure what day it is... but no."

He laughs. "That's why it's so quiet. The World Cup Qualifying..."

He carries on talking, but I tune out and start tracing patterns in the jazzy wallpaper, but I pick up that it's England playing, versus another team presumably. I think that's how it works.

So, we hurry back to the site and guess what I watch

while I eat my curry... No, *not* the football! Have you even been listening? I watch *The Famous Five* on YouTube, because its filmed at Hurst Point Lighthouse. It's lashings of fun. The baddies might as well wear tabards with the word BADDIE emblazoned across the front, because they're obvious from the first moment. And they're always frightfully working class and have regional accents.

Timmy the dog barks a lot – which Brendan can obviously relate to – and each time he does, Brendan lazily raises an eye to the screen of my laptop. Timmy is by far the most tolerable and likeable character. He is certainly Brendan's favourite of the five.

We have a cosy evening in our van, the two of us and the Famous Five, while outside the elements rage around us.

* * * * * * * * * * *

The next morning, I park up near the harbour with a view across the sheltered inlet to the lighthouse. A young couple and their dog are on the sandflats collecting seaweed. They look like alternative types; the man has a beard, the woman probably has a nose piercing. A Labrador is running energetically between them. Brendan watches them through the window for a minute, then flops down to rest.

When they return to their tatty van – parked in front of us – the woman comes over and taps on the door. Brendan starts growling furiously. I seize his collar and slide open the door. The woman is holding a dog bowl. "Have you got some spare water please? He's been drinking the sea water and he's got a right thirst." I assume she means the dog, not the man. I supply them with a bowl of water. She starts asking about Brendan. He has stopped growling and is watching her curiously, his ears raised slightly and his head tilted to one side, but the man heads towards us and Brendan immediately starts up again. I explain about his nervousness, especially towards men, men with beards, dressed predominantly in black, or without beards and dressed in white, mauve or terracotta. The woman abruptly turns round and shouts aggressively to her partner: "Go away! Go *away*! You're frightening the dog!" He smiles awkwardly and immediately veers obediently away towards their own Transit van.

The woman looks around Eagle One in awe. "What a brilliant van... This is great! You're living the dream. What a nice place to live and work..."

I feel a bond. We're van people and dog people and... predominantly *people*. But almost certainly not *people* people. We already have an understanding. She goes off to rejoin her jilted partner, but she leaves me with a bit of a glow. Eagle One *is* a brilliant van and *is* a nice place to live and work. And yes, although I don't really like the expression, I really *am* living the dream. This *really is* my dream. I'm travelling and exploring with my boy; we're enjoying life, seeing new places, having new experiences, having a sniff and a sit down... together. It's my dream and I'm pretty sure it's Brendan's dream as well. I *know* we're living the dream and have always known it, but it's really nice to hear someone else say it.

So we celebrate at a nearby little café called *Muffins Galore*. Not that you need the excuse of a celebration to eat muffins... or any cake. The café has a sign saying "DOGS AND CHILDREN ON A LEAD WELCOME", which makes me laugh. Maybe this has been taken literally or has offended parents, because there are several dogs but no children at all.

We enter the plant-strewn conservatory. A small group of older ladies are occupying a central table. I have Brendan on his short lead at my side. One of the ladies has a spaniel and when she sees Brendan, she makes a big fuss of dragging her dog into another room.

"My dog'll be fine with him." I assure her.

"No, no... it's mine. He's unpredictable and aggressive and gets out of control."

The poor spaniel doesn't look unpredictable or aggressive or remotely capable of getting out of control. What he *does* look is weary and embarrassed, because his mum goes through this attention-seeking performance every time someone appears. He looks at Brendan, his dark eyes pleading for liberation. Brendan wags his tail as a show of solidarity. Nevertheless, the woman drags the reluctant and long-suffering spaniel after her and out of the room.

I order two muffins and a coffee. (You might think that's a muffin each, but you'd be wrong. Brendan doesn't have a sweet tooth.) Once we're installed at our table, Mrs Spaniel edges her way cautiously back to her seat. As I'm eating my delicious muffins, I become aware of the conversation from the ladies' table. Mrs Spaniel is holding court, as you'd expect. "...from my thigh to my shin.... Excruciating pain... borderline hypoglycaemic... anyway, for my last tale of woe... I shan't bore you much longer..."

She's the only one who I hear speak, apart from small mewlings of sympathy from the others. "Well, it's been awful... I'm not sleeping... the extreme pain... I thought I was going to pass out... awful... terrible... dreadful..."

Another customer comes in with a dog. Mrs Spaniel immediately leaps up and drags her own little dog into the other room, as she'd done with me. She delivers the same patter: "I have to be so careful... It's him. He's unpredictable and aggressive and gets out of control." The spaniel rolls his eyes.

The new woman goes to the counter, is served, then calls over, "I'll go out of the far door, so you don't have to go through all that rigmarole again." I laugh out loud; I'm sure it's a sly comment on Mrs Spaniel's over-reacting.

Mrs Spaniel seems a bit annoyed, because she enjoys the rigmarole; she loves the rigmarole; she lives for the rigmarole. She resumes her seat again and continues with her tale: "So... they say moving is one of the most stressful activities... I'll say. In the new house the doorways are wider, they're really very, *very* wide..."

"Oh, is that for wheelchairs, seeing as it's a bungalow?"

"Possibly. But I think it's most likely for fat people. Probably fat people in wheelchairs."

I can't help spluttering into my teacup.

"It's been awful... The whole experience. Awful. Awful! *Awful.* I just wish we hadn't bothered."

I'm sure her companions are wishing the same thing.

* * * * * * * * * * *

We're in Sussex now and making a beeline for the lovely, sleepy, waterside village of Bosham. Just saying it – "Bosham" – makes me want to take a nap on a sunny, summer's day. Brendan agrees, but then taking a nap on a sunny, summer's day is one of his very top hobbies. Although most of us probably say "Bosh-ham" with the emphasis on the "shhh" – as in "Hush, I'm taking a nap on a sunny, summer's day.", it is actually pronounced "Boz-hum". Though that actually sounds even more lazily peaceful; it sounds like the drone of distant bumble bees on a sunny, summers day.

Anyway, *Boz-hum* is delightfully pretty and charmingly picturesque. It nestles peacefully, sleepily, delightfully and charmingly beside the tidal waters of Chichester harbour. It is quintessentially English, postcard pretty and chocolate box beautiful. Everywhere you turn in Bosham there is a view worthy of a photograph.

The main street ends abruptly because the tide's in; the water actually comes part way up the street at high tide. At low tide there is a small beach, where people often unwisely park, despite warning signs. Been there, seen it, done it. But that was decades ago, long before my little dog was born. I came here with Nicky and our beautiful dog, Cindy. We had parked the car on this beach, along with a dozen other hapless fools. When we returned to the car we found the tide had come in and we got wet feet. Ironically, Bosham is reputedly where King Cnut attempted to turn back the tide and he also got his feet wet, possibly because he too parked on the beach.

Now I'm here again, decades later, with Brendan. I'm finding Bosham unchanged and still as beautiful, as sleepily pretty, as peaceful and soporific... Brendan is in his element, because sleeping is one of his specialities.

A nice lady approaches us, staring at Brendan. "Oh he's gorgeous. What's his..."

"Brendan; he came with his name."

"Ah, it suits him! Is it OK to stroke him?"

"I wouldn't." I warn and she backs away rapidly and continues on her way intact.

We find the ancient church, which has the distinction of being depicted on the Bayeux Tapestry. We also find a plethora of tea shops, which most probably aren't.

Brendan recommends we have a pub lunch, so we sit in the colourfully floral beer garden of the *Anchor Bleu*. I have a hummus and salad sandwich and Brendan has a sausage roll, which he wolfs down: two bites: gone. I don't think he's actually had a pub lunch before. We sit there in the sunshine, enjoying the hum of summer and the sweet waft of blossom, with Brendan lurking under the table in the hope of snaring an unsuspecting member of the public. It's perfect.

* * * * * * * * * *

Gridlocked. Again. For ages. There are simply too many vehicles on the roads. Twice a day the country grinds to a halt because of the amount of vehicles blocking the highways. Ironically, an annual classic car extravaganza called The Festival of Speed is adding considerably to the terrible delays at the moment. It's also responsible for all the campsites in the area being full up, so we have to settle for a site in a woodland setting, far away from anywhere. Our pitch is close to a driveway and there is constant pedestrian traffic, causing Brendan to bark most of the night, so it isn't very peaceful.

The next morning, as I'm filling up the water prior to leaving, Brendan slips out of the back door of the van. I see him slink out and call him back. I offer him a treat and he comes bounding over enthusiastically, then skids to a halt a few feet away. I can see his thought process: one treat which will last a few seconds, or a good old burn off... Having made his decision, he abruptly turns and jogs off, down some steps amongst the trees.

I give chase, but casually, because I don't want it to come across as a fun chasing game. The woodland is thick with bracken which is shielding him from view. By the time I get to the steps I can't tell where he's gone. I search and call him constantly, but there's no sign of him and no sound of him crashing through the thick undergrowth. After a long and fruitless search, I go to the reception and I speak to all the staff who are going about their business and all the people on the site. No one has seen him.

I'm very good in a crisis. I keep calm, I'm organised, methodical and I do what needs to be done, but I'm growing increasingly concerned. As I walk around calling him, I'm really starting to think I won't see him again.

He is missing for 55 minutes, then he appears and runs towards me. I assume he's got frightened and is running up to me, but he runs past and disappears again. He runs past me several times, too quick for me to catch him. Eventually I hear a man calling through the trees: "We've found him! Hello? We've found him!"

I make my way through the dense undergrowth towards the sound of their voices. And there they are, a middle-aged couple, with the man holding Brendan's collar. Brendan looks very pleased with himself and is panting in a very satisfied way. The couple had seen him and called him. Brendan had bizarrely gone towards them and the man had grabbed him. Brendan had gone along with the capture willingly and offered no resistance. By this point, I think he'd had enough, was totally worn out and just wanted rescuing.

I thank them profusely. I'm overjoyed... and completely amazed. He seems very happy to get back into Eagle One. He leaps in and immediately gets into his basket and falls into an exhausted sleep. He's dog tired.

I'm really stressed and agitated and can't unwind. He deliberately and intentionally ran away. Or rather *he ran...* He went for a run. I don't think at any point he was trying to run *away*, because he ran in large circles and I'm sure he would have come back to the van in the end. He obviously wanted to stretch his legs and let off some steam, which I understand. Annoyingly, when I first got him, we hired an enclosed field at the sanctuary where Nicky volunteers, so he could have a good, safe run about. He just sat in the middle of the field looking glum and miserable, while we both threw balls and toys around him. It was a complete waste of time and money.

I'm very disappointed in him and it makes me wonder again whether he'd be better living with other dogs and whether I can provide all he needs. I live in a flat, so it's not ideal. I've brought him travelling with me; any other dog I've ever had or known would have loved this experience and would have enjoyed being with their human twenty-four hours a day. He is usually incredibly lazy, but like a whippet or greyhound he seems to need a good burn off every so often. He probably needs to be with someone with a safe and secure garden where he can be let off. Or someone who owns a soft furnishings showroom, where he can try out different beds and sofas all day long.

After this bad start to the day, I witness the Festival of Speed for myself, or rather people driving like maniacs, too fast, too close, overtaking on tight bends. It's quite terrifying. The appalling standard of driving never ceases to amaze me, and I'm sure it's borne out of the general impatience and intolerance of society. Everyone wants everything instantly or preferably sooner.

I stop at a viewpoint for a rest and a brew. Half the day has gone already and I feel stressed and exhausted, but also relieved that I've got my boy back; he dozes peacefully on his sofa, the devil.

When we continue on our way, I'm hoping Pagham will cheer me up, because I've read a lot about it and it's supposed to be beautiful, a natural harbour and nature reserve. It isn't. It never has been. Pagham *Harbour* is, but we're not there. We're at Pagham – plain and simple Pagham – a coastal village with an accompanying housing estate. I park in the central rutted cinder car park, where a car full of young men sit watching as people leave their vehicles, which is quite unsettling.

I buy some chips (again) and we walk through an estate of bungalows, towards the sound of the sea. We eventually find the grey shingle beach. We sit together and eat our chips. Brendan doesn't like vinegar, so I have to carefully select his share. We look out at the rolling grey sea beneath a hazy grey sky.

I'm quite agitated when we return to the car park, because I half expect the youths to have broken into Eagle One, but they haven't. They're still sitting there in their car watching the world go by. Perhaps this is just what they do. Brendan glances at them, but isn't remotely concerned. They watch silently as I pull out and drive away. They're still watching silently when I drive back again… and again… because leaving Pagham isn't that easy. There don't seem to be any signs at all and with my navigator napping in the back, I'm on my own. We get stuck on an eternal housing estate full of unsigned cul-de-sacs. It's a maze of dead-end streets. It's a perfectly nice, suburban estate, very well-kept and respectable, but I can visit housing estates at home. We eventually end up back at the car park again.

I spot another road we haven't tried, but this turns out to be a dead end as well, but at least it leads through Old Pagham, which is lovely and probably where we were aiming for in the first place. We park up at the end of the road, behind a tiny camper van, which has a skeleton in the passenger seat. A skeleton wearing a safety belt! (The belt is probably not necessary, but still very commendable.)

Travelling companion, Old Pagham.

The van and the skeleton suggest the owner is a black-clad goth-type, with long black hair and a pale face, but then an old man appears, not just any old man: he's bare chested and sporting a shock of white, orange and pink hair. It's things like this that put the "Great" into Great Britain. He's at least seventy, most probably a lot older, but he has the look of his choice, the vehicle of his choice and – presumably – the travelling companion of his choice. None of it seems contrived or attention-seeking; he just comes across as a man who's doing what he wants to do and getting on with being loveably eccentric in a built-up area. It makes me proud to be British.

I want to go over and engage him in conversation and ask about the skeleton and about his hair and about his life, so I leave Brendan relaxing and I walk over towards the old man, but as I draw closer, he looks so angry and unapproachable that I veer off at the last minute, when I realise he's stark raving mad and I ought to avoid him at all costs. I'm still proud to be British, but you can be proud from a distance.

* * * * * * * * * * *

We're bound for Bognor, Bognor Regis. One of us paddles in the sea, while one of us sits on the sand and licks himself. The sunlight sparkles on the water as a bikini-clad young woman emerges from the waves and shakes her long, blonde, sun-bleached hair, looking exactly like a Bond girl in any old Bond movie. Coincidentally, as a cost-cutting exercise, scenes for Daniel Craig's third Bond film, *Skyfall*, were filmed in Bognor. When word got out, the resort had a 40% increase in hotel bookings.

It's so hot. It's so bright; the light is white and dazzling. I'm concerned for Brendan's paws on the baking tarmac, so we board Eagle One and drive on. We stop in Littlehampton – which seems to be closed – so we continue to the Sussex village of Clapham, which lies along a dead-end road. I drive along that dead-end road in the early evening, with warm sunlight slanting down. Villagers are standing at their gates chatting to their neighbours. As I crawl past they stop and stare, knowing I'm not local and knowing I can't be going anywhere, because the road doesn't go anywhere. There's nowhere to park, it's teatime so everyone is home from work. Many of the houses don't have driveways, so the villagers park on the main street. There is only the one street, and it's called "The Street", which keeps things simple. Everyone can see you come and go; there are no secrets in Clapham. Apart from the black magic ones: Clapham has a reputation.

I reach the end of The Street, where Clapham village terminates at a five bar gate. I do a three point turn and drive back slowly – a little embarrassed and a little annoyed – passing again all the neighbours, who stop talking and turn their heads for the second time. They seem to stare with a steely contempt, in that way that people only do in horror movies. I wish Brendan was up at the front with me, instead of languishing in the back with his curtains drawn, because he could dish out some steely contempt of his own.

Fifty-eight seconds after leaving Clapham, we're in the depths of the South Downs, surrounded by golden wheat fields and rolling hills. It's beautiful, especially in the rich, warm evening light.

It's a lovely drive to the rural town of Steyning, to a farmhouse on the outskirts, where I've booked a pitch at their campsite. It's sheltered by a steep, tree-covered rise on one side and offers open views across the beautiful South Downs on the other.

I knock on the door of the house. I can hear a woman inside calling for her husband. It sounds like there are a hundred or more children shouting and screaming gleefully inside. The woman's tone of voice is clearly harassed. She calls her husband again, louder and with more menace.

The door opens and a smiling man stands there. "Hello." He doesn't look or sound remotely harassed.

"Sorry," I say, "Have I caught you at tea time?"

He laughs heartily. "It's *always* teatime."

I pay him and he steps outside and pulls the door closed after him. "I'll show you where everything is."

"It's OK, I'm sure I can work things out."

"No, no, no-no-no." he says, a little too eagerly. "It's no problem. I *want* to show you. I insist."

There's a wellie rack on a wall with about seven or eight pairs in various sizes, but all smaller, none of them man-sized.

"Wellies for the whole family... except you?"

"My wellies have been... if you'll pardon the pun, *booted out*. But that's fine... I've got a shed... mine are in the shed... It's *my* shed... Everything of mine is in the shed... *I'm* usually in the shed..." He gazes off into the middle distance in a momentary daze, then snaps back with a smile. "Right, I'll show you the water tap."

He leads me along the driveway, away from the clamour and chaos of the house. There are only two other people on the nice grassy site. I choose our pitch, as usual, based on proximity to others; I put us as far away as possible from the other units. Beyond us, there is a fringe of trees on the steep bank. Despite the views across the downs, it's an isolated place, a secluded place... and once the sun has set, it's a very dark and eerie place.

As the evening descends we sit in Eagle One. The curtains are still open because it has secretly gone dark and no one has told me. I have been absorbed in my work and haven't noticed, but we aren't overlooked by anyone, so it doesn't matter. I'm researching Clapham village and its mysterious and satanic associations. I've found some videos on YouTube of investigations at the woods and am utterly captivated. Suddenly, Brendan, who's sitting beside me and has been napping, tenses, sits bolt upright and starts barking ferociously, staring through the side window, out into the surrounding darkness.

It really startles me and for the first time, I look up and see the pitch black beyond the glass. Brendan continues staring and snarling viciously, teeth exposed, tail down. He's obviously been frightened by something. A chilling cold creeps over me. I turn the light off immediately and close the lid of my laptop. We are suddenly engulfed in total darkness.

As my eyes adjust, through the window I can see the tall, slim boughs of the trees in one direction and the open expanse of the Downs in the other. I can't see anyone prowling. But Brendan is adamant and remains snarling. I assure him everything is fine and we're safe, but he continues to stare and has started a low, guttural growling, which is quite unusual for him. He won't calm down – and neither can I – my heart is racing and I'm covered with sweat. I'm not easily spooked, but it has really unnerved me.

It's one of those moments when I'd really like to just pull the covers over my head and wait until the trouble has passed. But I'm not seven... and haven't been for some time, so I get Brendan on his short metal lead and slide open the side door. We step out into the darkness, to try and confront our tormentor. Brendan bounds ahead, dragging me after him. He's growling and barking; something has really disturbed him. We do a security check of our part of the site. Suddenly I regret going so far away from everyone else; there is nothing beyond Eagle One except the dark woods. If a Satan worshipper comes from the trees to collect human and canine sacrifices, we'll be the first they come to.

We return to Eagle One, shut the door, lock it and pull the curtains over the darkness. Brendan is calmer and goes back to sleep. I don't continue with the videos again.

In the night, we lie side by side in bed, listening to all the nocturnal noises, the plaintive cries, the screeches, the rustling and the stirring of branches. It's eerie and unsettling. When I eventually fall asleep, I sleep very well and when I open my eyes it's sunny, very sunny for so early, before 6am. The night has passed uneventfully; we haven't been kidnapped or sacrificed, or even just plain murdered. Everything looks cheerful and friendly again, doves are cooing, cows are mooing, lambs are bleating, and cocks are a-doodling.

Today we're investigating devilry. On this occasion I'm not referring to Brendan. With a hop and a skip, I start the engine and with a happy heart drive back to demonic Clapham.

I read a book about Clapham many years ago. Nicky read it as well. It was really chilling. It told of the mysterious woods and how four people had disappeared in the area and their bodies had reappeared several months later. It spoke of a cult of devil worshippers operating within the woods, who conducted human sacrifices.

With that in mind, I park in the middle of the village, outside the café. We go inside intending to grill the occupants, but they end up grilling us: two teacakes. I sit on the shady veranda with my dog at my feet, drinking coffee, the sun dappling the decking. A young boy brings out the teacakes and – like a shady character in a horror movie – asks if we're local.

"No," I say, a little cagily. "We're just… passing through."

Brendan shoots me a glance. This is my first mistake. I've revealed we're vulnerable and won't be missed.

After our teacakes, we set off strolling nonchalantly through the very pleasant English village, following a sign leading away from the main street, to the church. Quite unusually, the Church of Saint Mary the Virgin is set apart from the village, rather than being the hub of it. It stands alone on the edge of the woods, partially surrounded by trees. Its name also is a sinister coincidence: virgins are traditionally the sacrifice of choice amongst Satanists. Allegedly.

It's a lovely flint church, standing within its walled graveyard, surrounded by crooked, lichen-covered headstones. We sit in a shady area beneath a tree for some time, soaking up the atmosphere, but to be honest, I'm not actually feeling much atmosphere. Neither is Brendan, he's very relaxed and slightly lethargic and definitely not picking up any satanic vibrations. It's an isolated church, so it could and possibly *should* feel potentially threatening, but it doesn't. Not really. I *want* it to, but it just doesn't.

We head into the woods from the church. Brendan wafts along quite happily, showing no misgivings. We walk along a rough pathway, amongst mixed deciduous trees and shrubs, with exposed chalk underfoot. I keep Brendan on a short lead and don't take my eyes off him. Dogs have supposedly been affected within the woods and some have disappeared. I have visions of turning round and looking at his lead, only to see he's been replaced by a log or something.

Visitors have claimed to feel nauseous, light-headed, pushed by invisible hands, to feel suddenly afraid and to feel they're being watched or followed. I certainly don't feel nauseous or any other physical symptoms. I don't feel I'm being watched or followed, but I am aware that due to the thick undergrowth, I could well be.

The patches of sunlight on the ground stir as the canopy

of leaves shifts above, but all around there is darkness between the boughs of the trees. There are very few birds and no sound of movement from any animals; there are no squirrels or rabbits, which is unusual.

We've been walking for some time and we're quite a way from the village, when suddenly Brendan stops still and stares into the trees, into the darkness between the boughs. He doesn't bark or growl or jump up and down, which he would normally do if he'd spotted an animal. He just stares and seems afraid. I can't see anything, I can't hear anything, but I do suddenly feel apprehensive and I'm starting to feel that we're being watched. I pull Brendan away and we walk on, but he keeps turning to look cautiously behind him. And so do I. The fact that he hasn't barked or growled is really strange.

Brendan incarnate.

We have been in the woods over an hour and we haven't seen a soul, which is odd. It's such a hot day and the woods obviously provide some cool shade, but not one person appears to be walking their dog.

With uncanny timing, at that precise moment I hear footsteps, rapid footsteps, running. I tense. They're getting closer, swiftly closer. Brendan starts growling. (At last!) A man appears along the trackway, jogging, bare chested, just wearing shorts and trainers. I hold Brendan's lead tightly. He barks ferociously. The man nods a hello. Brendan lunges ineffectually after him, straining at his lead. The man passes us and runs on. I turn to watch him retreating. I can clearly see he has a tattoo on his lower back. It's some sort of cross, but not a regular crucifix. I only get a fleeting glimpse, but at first glance it looks like an *inverted* cross: the symbol of devil worship. It's easy to get carried away when you're filled with adrenaline and in a heightened state of anxiety. In all likelihood, the tattoo is a Celtic cross. And yet I really don't think it is.

We walk on, both of us on edge now. The trees begin to thin out and the gravel trackway broadens; the woods are coming to an end. We take an open footpath across sun-burnt grassy fields, back towards the rooftops and chimneys of the village.

I drive out of Clapham absolutely buzzing from the experience. As a teenager, my ambition was to be an investigative reporter, riding round in a van, uncovering corruption and crime. I would probably eventually have a TV series about my escapades...

Well, if that isn't what I'm doing now... But without the TV series part. Or the uncovering corruption and crime parts. But I am definitely and undeniably driving around in a van – and it really *is* my dream. I suspect it's Brendan's dream as well. I loved sharing the experience with my brave boy and I have to say, I'm very glad he was with me, because it could have been really frightening in the most remote parts of the woods.

I know I'm like a dog with a bone, but as the woman in Milford had said: I'm living the dream. It really hits home: I really *am* living the dream. Living. The. Dream. It's not everyone's dream, by any means, but it's *my* dream. ©Me.

As we leave Clapham, we get stuck behind a painfully slow-moving traction engine, chugging along at full whack of four miles an hour. The driver seems very cheerful and not at all phased by the tailback he's causing. Maybe he too is living the dream. *His* dream.

* * * * * * * * * *

Monte Carlo or Bust, Sleepless in Seattle, An American Werewolf in London, Beverley Hills Cop 2. What do all these films – and so many more – have in common? Probably every film ever made, in fact? The answer is obviously that none of them chose to use "Rottingdean" as a setting. Imagine it: *Rottingdean or Bust, Sleepless in Rottingdean, An American Werewolf in Rottingdean, Rottingdean Cop 2.* Somewhere in the quantum universe, in an alternate and probably better reality, those films exist.

Poor Rottingdean hasn't got much of a chance, has it?

Yet, the old part of the village is lovely, only its name is disappointing. Along the main road is an American-style vegan diner called *Road Shack*. It's owned and run by Anne and Julie, and it's very much a labour of love; every customer is treated like a friend. Their website claims: "Well-behaved dogs are warmly welcomed". No one ever welcomes badly behaved dogs, do they? Well, we'll give Brendan a try.

It's very strange, because from the first moment his paws touch the lino, my boy is one chilled cool cat. He seems to enjoy the calm and relaxed atmosphere. It's fairly busy and the clientele include several men , but he's being so laid back. Everyone chats together – about dogs mainly. Anne and Julie engender friendliness. My coffee cup is only ever half empty before it's refreshed and filled up. (I won't sleep for a week afterwards.)

I have a maple syrup pancake to start with, followed by a full breakfast. It's *gorgeous*. Brendan is suitably made a fuss of. Despite eating enough for eight people, I still manage to fit a cake in for pudding. It's a lovely and very memorable experience and Brendan proves just how good he can really be.

We reluctantly move on and before we know it, we arrive in Norman's Bay, where we're staying for two nights. The site is huge but surrounded by attractive flat countryside and the pebble beach is just across the road. Our pitch is way too close to the children's play area with the near-constant creaking of the swings. After sun down though, the creaking stops and the swings hang limp, unused. It's a beautiful sound. We have a relaxing evening. Brendan falls asleep half way through

The Man From UNCLE and never finds out who the undercover baddie was.

* * * * * * * * * *

We drive up the steep road to the top of Beachy Head. There is a blue sky washed with white clouds. It's beautiful. Brendan is eager to get the day started, but within five minutes of us striding along the clifftop path, he's having his first sit down.

Beachy Head is very popular, very dramatic and very English. The South Downs landscape rolls gently towards the sea, until it plummets severely to the beach with a thin line of white fringing. Beachy Head is infamous. At 531 feet, it's the highest chalk sea cliff in Britain. Because of this great height, it has become synonymous with suicide. It's one of the most notorious suicide spots *in the world.*

Understandably, there are signs for the Samaritans at various points around the area. I used to be a Samaritan, taking calls from depressed and suicidal people. It was something I was drawn to. I have a CV full of voluntary work of all kinds, but the Samaritans was the most intense. People called in who had taken overdoses; there was nothing you could do apart from talk to them and be there for them. It was very high-pressured and deeply affecting, but often very rewarding and enlightening.

Although Beachy Head is visually stunning and very dramatic, I feel it is tainted by the despair and tragedy it has witnessed.

The lighthouse at the foot of Beachy Head is one of the most iconic
and visually stunning in the UK. It has appeared in many TV programmes,
including the cult 'Sixties serial, *The Prisoner*, which we both love.
(FYI Brendan is not a number, he is a free dog!)

I cajole Brendan into continuing along the path. Considering he's frightened of virtually everything, he strangely isn't remotely afraid of heights. He canters along happily in the blinding sunlight. He suddenly throws himself down onto the grass and has a frenzied roll. The grass is parched: dry and yellow, brittle, like straw, and is already getting baked again.

We descend towards a National Trust tearoom and visitor centre. I suddenly become aware of a stench.

Sewage. Just occasionally. On the air. A foul, over-powering stink... which gets stronger every time Brendan scampers closer to me. It's Brendan! He stinks of shit! I suddenly realise... The rolling on the grass earlier... I thought it was part of his daily yoga, but it clearly wasn't. His coat is impregnated with shit. Fox shit, I'd guess. There's no way I can take him in the genteel tea cupped and doilied National Trust tearoom interior smelling like this! I'm really annoyed. Also, he needs to be clean before he sets paw in Eagle One. Them's the rules.

A solution presents itself. I spot an outside tap at the visitor centre, with a silver dog bowl underneath it. Using hand cleansing foam from the nearby toilets, I soap him all over and then rinse him off using the bowl. He stands there, soaked, his fur sticking to him, a sad, forlorn, waif-like beast, drenched and miserable. I finish and he immediately shakes himself dry, whilst steadfastly refusing to smile.

He still stinks. He *really* stinks. But I've done all I can do, so we head into the café and I do my best to avoid everyone. Thankfully that's just normal procedure anyway with Brendan. He limbos under a low table and stretches out. I have a refreshing cup of tea; he has a refreshing sleep.

We return to the cliffs and retrace our steps along the grassy pathway. There are crowds of people coming towards us from Beachy Head. They're silhouetted against the bright sky. Admittedly they do look slightly like an invading army of aliens. Brendan just keeps barking and barking at them and won't be pacified, until I discover that if I bark or growl myself, he immediately relaxes and looks away from the infringers, but he starts again the moment I stop. He just seems happy as long as one of us is barking. So we take it in turns. People must think we're barking mad.

We take a wide detour away from the cliff edge to avoid the masses along the path. Brendan finds some rare shade under a bush and we sit for an hour, watching the grasses blowing in the breeze, surrounded by things that flap or flutter, listening to the sound of bees, birds, skylarks and grasshoppers. It's quite beautiful and serene. This is how life should be lived: at a leisurely pace with time to enjoy the sights, sounds and smells around us. It's a hectic world and it isn't always possible, but when we get the chance we should embrace it. Brendan has embraced it. He embraces it a lot.

I never used to relax. I never used to stop; I was always fuelled by nervous energy. I haven't had a beach holiday since I was a child. I have always thought that sitting next to a swimming pool or lying on the sand for hours on end would be interminably boring, but I think Brendan is bringing out the relaxed Buddhist in me. Sitting surrounded by grasses, butterflies and honey bees, with Brendan's hot back against my leg, is quite blissful.

When we finally make it back to the pub where we've parked, it's obvious we need to go in. It's cool and dark inside. Very dark actually, too dark after the blinding glare outside. I have a pint and we sit and unwind further, until a coach party arrives. There is a sudden stampede for the toilets and people jostle at the bar, hurriedly buying drinks in cans. Next to us, two old ladies sit down and wait, looking at their watches continually and moaning, glancing at the bar in agitation.

Fifteen minutes go by and they suddenly stand up to leave, just as the waiter is approaching with two plates of food. It transpires they're part of the coach trip. They had been told this was a five minute toilet and drink stop... *so they had ordered a full meal each*. What were they thinking? They stop the waiter mid-flight and in the middle of the room proceed to slide the food from the plates into a series of serviettes. The waiter, in broken English, is saying. "If I am to put the plates down... please... we could... it would easier... I put the plates down... it goes on the floor! If you'll let me... It's all spilling... Please..." But they won't hear of it. A deep horn sounds from the car park; an angry and impatient coach driver. They hasten out at a speed bordering an amble, with fistfuls of grease-soaked serviettes in each hand. The waiter removes the plates and then comes back to clean up the mound of food from the floor.

Any normal dog, especially a Labrador or retriever, would strain to get to the mountain of food. Brendan just eyes it distastefully and makes a mental note about the poor housekeeping.

* * * * * * * * * *

The next morning sees us driving to do battle in Hastings. The old town at its heart is full of character. The promenade is breezy and pirate flags are a-flapping all over the place. Yesterday was the annual Pirate

Day, when everyone dresses up and goes around doing piratey things. Judging by the local crime stats, some of them take it quite seriously all year round. Once a pirate, always a pirate.

After a stroll on the pier and beach, we call into a dog-friendly eat-in chippy and have chips and peas. Brendan sits on the cool, shiny white tiles and half-heartedly nibbles the vinegar-free chips I hand him, as though he's doing me a favour.

Despite it being relatively quiet, an elderly couple come towards the table next to ours. Fortunately, Brendan doesn't react to them. Unfortunately, this means they sit down and we have to listen as the man tackles one of the staff about the OAP Meal Deal. It's very reasonably priced, but he wants to know if his wife doesn't have this and he doesn't have that and they both don't have the other, can they have a further reduction? The waiter smiles patiently and politely says that wouldn't be possible. The old man starts bartering, still trying desperately to negotiate an even better deal. It becomes quite annoying, quite quickly. They clearly aren't hard up, they're very middle class, they're just tight fisted. Try as they might – and they do try – they don't get a further reduction.

We return to Eagle One, parked on the prom. A massive camper van is now stationed in front of us; it has a collection of witty bumper stickers, including a picture of Wyle E Coyote – who really is *uncannily* like Brendan at certain times, and AN ADVENTURE BEFORE DEMENTIA. All that's missing is WE SPENT OUR KIDS' INHERITANCE ON THIS VAN, but that's so obvious it probably doesn't need stating.

* * * * * * * * *

Dog facts:
Dogs are the most popular domestic pet in the world. There's a reason for that: they have learned how to successfully manipulate us.

* * * * * * * * *

A Phone Call Away...

- In 2018, there were 6,507 suicides registered in the UK.
- Three-quarters of those deaths were men.
- Males aged 45 to 49 had the highest age-specific suicide rate.

The Samaritans are a national (UK) charity. They are available to offer support by phone 24 hours a day.

CHAPTER 6: MAD DOG AND ENGLISH MAN (GO OUT IN THE MIDDAY SUN)

We slide across the unseen border into Kent, the Garden of England. I suddenly notice the word *Invicta* creeping into business and street names. It turns out *Invicta* is the county motto; it means "undefeated". I try to think of a motto for Brendan, but give up when I realise it could only realistically include words such as "weeing", "sniffing" or "napping" and none of those are really going to make a potential enemy think twice about invading.

We're driving along a flat road between golden fields into one of the weirdest landscapes in Britain: Dungeness, a shingle headland – one of the largest expanses of shingle in Europe. It isn't an easy landscape; you either fall under its weirdly intoxicating spell and love it, or you don't – and you hate it. Personally, I love its emptiness, its flatness, its nothingness, its wide open expanses, its steady salt breeze and its slightly unsettling eeriness. I understand why people don't like it – it can seem barren, bleak and hostile, but I love it *because* it's all those things. It's harsh and unyielding. There are no trees at all (Sorry, Brendan). Instead, sea kale and odd rubbery plants sprout up occasionally between the pebbles. It's an alien landscape. This is Dungeness and it really is like nowhere else. It's like nowhere. It *is* nowhere.

Today, despite the sunshine, it's moderately windy. I imagine it's constantly windy here; a wind-ravaged terrain with grasses and plants torn by the breeze. It is predominantly a very low landscape, everything huddles close to the earth - close to the shingle - to avoid the bitter sea winds; apart from lines of telegraph poles and their swinging, clacking cables, and the other major exceptions, namely the two lighthouses and the two massive, unavoidable nuclear power stations that completely dominate the place. Rows and rows of pylons stride away into the distance over the empty landscape, taking electricity inland to the masses. I am really not a fan of nuclear power – or of any form of gambling – there is just too much that can go wrong.

You might think an inhospitable, wind-ravaged landscape wouldn't be very habitable, but there is a thriving community here. Most of the dwellings are bungalows or a variety of weird huts: shacks, sheds, cabins, chalets, lodges: wooden homes. Some look like fallout shelters, they are oddly shaped, some angular, some with smooth curved surfaces, few have any windows, some have doors with no handles. Others are shed-like, cobbled together. Several are built around old railway carriages. The buildings aren't arranged in neat rows or streets or anything so formal; they just seem to be scattered at random.

We park up and set off together over a shingle bank to the shingle beach, where a rather brown, sandy sea is churning endlessly. Brendan watches it warily. There is no one else on the beach, just the grey pebbles, the rolling tide and the buffeting of the wind. The houses facing the beach are all very ramshackle. They don't have walls or fences to delineate their land, they are all open-plan and sit there looking a little like a refugee camp in a war-torn country.

Brendan plods along beside me then plonks himself down on the shingle. The wind is making his ears flap and he's not impressed with Dungeness. We've got a warm and comfortable van and the ability to stream re-runs of *Bergerac*, so he can't understand why we're out here battling the elements.

Brendan and "Rebecca", Dungeness. (Although this looks like Brendan has been very crudely Photoshopped onto a picture of a boat, he is actually there, but it's an effect of the low, slanting golden light of sunset.)

We stroll along the roadway, passing the ominous creaking sign of the Britannia Inn, proudly and fiercely Dungeness's only pub, which looks like a building site, the whole structure seems to be wrapped in polythene sheets.

Close by is *Prospect Cottage*, which belonged to the film director, Derek Jarman, until his death in 1994. It's a typically simple building, but stands out because it's painted tar black with bright yellow window frames and sills. It's famous for its garden, created by Jarman himself, made largely of and reflecting the landscape, containing driftwood monoliths and fragments of scrap metal. It's not like a garden in the conventional sense of the word. It's barely like a garden in the unconventional sense of the word either, but it's unique and very Dungeness.

We continue along a straight, empty road that cuts along the empty landscape, to the Pilot Inn, technically at Lydd-on-Sea, which looks back across the shingle plateau. I have a gorgeous meal while Brendan has a lie down under the table. We have to sit outside because of their Draconian dog policy, but we get to look at the beautiful desolation all around us. Unfortunately, it's blowing a gale and within a minute my food is cold. It's vegan stew and dumplings, with chips. The stew is beautiful and the vegetables are perfectly cooked, it's a sheer joy to have real veg after so long of van rations. (I've eaten a lot of fruit and salad, but not proper cooked vegetables.)

Afterwards, we go for a slow, lazy evening walk. The sun is sinking towards the shingle horizon, casting long, slanting shadows and colouring everything with rich gold. It would be easy to be lonely here, especially in the fading light, but I feel far from lonely; I'm with my dog. Though he's seldom chatty, I never feel lonely when I'm with him; he exudes companionship.

Passing one of the wooden shack houses, I notice there's a handwritten sign taped to the window, reading: NEXT

DOOR STOP LOOKING INTO MY BEDROOM WINDOW! The nearest neighbour is several hundred yards away. They'd need to be using binoculars to spy on this poor unfortunate or to see the sign. Ironically, for everyone else walking close by along the road, the sign draws your attention to the window. (My suggestion for a problem of this nature, is something we have to rely on in the city; we call them "curtains". I've never bought any myself, but I believe they're quite widely available.)

We leave the roadway and go cross-country – cross-shingle – meandering. My boots crunch underfoot; Brendan's paws tread silently, making no noise at all. We come across a graveyard of boats. This is a weird and eerie spectacle, the remains of a fishing fleet, moored high up on the beach, surrounded by rusting winches, all suddenly abandoned one day and left to rot. On the outside, the wooden hulls are things of beauty, expertly crafted, paint-peeling, but still weathering gracefully.

We trudge on. I'm aware of the constant roaring from the power station. It doesn't sound too different from the constant traffic on a busy main road or a waterfall in full spate, except waterfalls don't tend to have meltdowns. I have read various leaflets and websites about the protocol in the event of a nuclear emergency. One quaintly suggests that visitors should drive away and report to the nearest hospital or police station, prior to vaporising as the reactor goes critical.

The sun is setting, the whole western skyline is a deep, fiery red, reflecting off the windows in the power station. At least, I assume it's a reflection... otherwise there's a slight meltdown in progress.

We wend our way back to Eagle One, parked in the car park of the Pilot Inn, where we will be spending the night. The pub empties, the interior lights eventually flick out and the pub stands in darkness. Only one other van remains: they too are staying the night. They're very quiet; I see them occasionally but don't hear them. Everything goes silent. The wind has dropped. The stillness is unnerving – in a surreally brilliant way.

In the small hours, I get up and go for a short walk – alone – Brendan refuses to move, as its before 10am. I step outside into a strange and alien world. It's very calm, very still and absolutely unearthly. The other van is in darkness, its curtains closed. I walk a short way across the shingle, but my footsteps are deafening. There is very little light pollution here, so I can clearly see the dusting of the Milky Way overhead and all the constellations scattered over the black dome of the heavens. And then I see a shooting star: a momentary streak of white light as a meteor burns up in the Earth's atmosphere, then it's gone. I've only seen a very few in my life, so it seems special, magical.

When I climb back into Eagle One, Brendan lazily raises his triangular little head from the bed and looks at me. His sleepy brown eyes say: "I'm glad you're back." Presumably because he likes to have his staff on hand. I get back into bed and we snuggle... We snuggle for over a minute, until he sighs heavily and inches steadily away.

* * * * * * * * * *

It's early morning, cold grey light seeps across a cold, grey landscape. It's thrilling to look out of the windscreen at the wilderness of shingle, which rises gently to create a false horizon, beyond which is the sea. It's overcast and quite cool, which suits Dungeness perfectly.

At one time I might have hated this landscape and found it bleak and depressing, but now I find it captivating; I love the almost monochrome terrain and the isolated beauty. I would live here like a shot. Me and my dog would crunch along the shingle all day long. But as the tattiest old lean-to here costs in the region of a quarter of a million, it's not likely to happen.

The coolness doesn't last long: by 9.30 it's baking again. We wander amongst the huts, taking in the sea air. A woman with a dog passes close by. She's engaged in a complete conversation with the animal. "Watch out, Brendan..." I mutter. "She's talking to her dog." Brendan just looks at me; nothing needs saying. Sometimes he's so very wise.

After lunch, I reluctantly drive away from the chilling and thrilling Dungeness, but I could have stayed much longer. I *should* have stayed much longer. The moment I leave the area I'm suddenly filled with regret and wish I was back, just wandering around with my dog, or sitting on the beach watching the sea, just soaking up the atmosphere. It really is like nowhere else on Earth. It's possibly not even on Earth. I find it captivating.

I phone ahead to check out a campsite for the night.

A man answers. Yes, he has spaces, but he's at pains to point out that although electric hook-up *is* available, it's only 6 volts, rather than 16. I've no idea what runs on what voltage, but he proceeds to recite a list of "will work" and "won't works". Kettle – yes. Microwave – no. Toaster – yes. Sunbed – no. It goes on for quite a while. He finishes his list and then I realise I haven't checked if they accept dogs. Imagine if all that detailed explanation has been for nothing…

"Sorry, I should have said at first… D'you take dogs?"

"Yes," he says cheerfully. "We take dogs."

"Oh, good… as long as I can recharge my dog on 6 volts overnight, I'll be happy."

There's a very, *very* long pause, while he may well be calculating how many volts it takes to recharge the average canine. "Yes…" he says at last, very soberly "You can recharge your dog."

Booked!

We arrive at the site in the bucolic depths of Romney Marsh. The owners, Susan and David are absolutely lovely. I'm the only person on their site, Brendan is the only dog and this proves to be very advantageous. Their field is completely sealed, almost air tight, and they say I can let Brendan off his lead. He immediately canters to the far corner of the field, where there's a strip of shade, and lies down. He doesn't move for hours. I think it does him the world of good.

We have a very nice and quiet night of peace and

freedom. Brendan really enjoys roaming around the field, sniffing at the hedges, weeing on everything and anything and having various sit downs. I keep a close eye on him at all times, because I don't trust him and I know he's wiley and devious, but he's blissfully unaware. It's lovely that he wanders back to the van when he's good and ready, gets into bed and goes into a deep sleep.

* * * * * * * * * *

Thursday morning in the sleepy little town of Hythe. I previously visited Hythe about a decade ago and stayed in a hotel on the seafront which was so badly run, so cold and so dirty it was beyond belief... though unfortunately not the worst hotel I've ever stayed in. I'm really surprised to see it's still trading.

Hythe's high street doesn't seem to have changed at all. A man with a guitar sits strumming away and singing *The Sound of Silence*. He has a good voice and sounds as though he's singing *for himself*, because he enjoys singing, which is nice. Brendan wants to sit down and listen to him, but he used the same excuse when we passed a post box earlier and I didn't fall for it then either. Basically, he just wants to sit down.

Rising behind the high street are narrow cobbled lanes leading uphill to the majestic St Leonard's Church, which peers down on the rooftops and chimneys of Hythe. We walk past the front steps of the church, where the vicar is pacing up and down with a look of consternation, speaking urgently into a mobile phone. Around the side of the church is the entrance to the crypt, which contains an ossuary – a repository for human bones – one of only two in the UK.

I ask if Brendan can come inside, but the volunteer guide, Roy, and the anxious vicar are worried that he might be like a dog with a bone. (They obviously don't know of his expensive dining preferences.) They suggest I secure him near the door, so I can see him at all times. I tell them this almost certainly won't work, but I try it anyway to prove a point. He has a neat little circular alcove all to himself and he promptly curls up and goes to sleep quite happily. This might mean he's making real progress and feels secure... or perhaps because he can see me and hear me talking, he feels safe. Or perhaps he's just exhausted and wants a nap.

The Ossuary, Hythe. No bones about it.

Roy is an engaging tour guide. He really knows his onions. And skulls. There are over 2,000 skulls neatly arranged on shelves in arches in the crypt, and stacks of 8,000 limb bones. It really does look like something from a horror film, so many hollow eye sockets, rounded pates, bared teeth, beneath a satanically vaulted ceiling. It is deeply macabre. The bones date from the medieval period and are both male and female. There have been suggestions that they were the dead from a large battle, or victims of the plague, but the most popular explanation is that they were simply dug up from the surrounding graveyard to make way for new graves, which was very common.

Bizarrely, there had been a break-in on Sunday night and twenty-one skulls had been stolen. My first thought was that they were stolen for Black Magic purposes, because what else could you want a real human skull for? Film crews had been earlier in the week and Roy had been on the local news.

It's a pleasure listening to his tales about the church and the skulls. His passion shines through and he's a really interesting chap. I stay as long as I can, but Roy wants to go home for his lunch. My boy has been as good as gold and has enjoyed his divine and holy nap. We set off along the fascinating little streets that lead back down into Hythe. Brendan tries to get into a white van we pass; he's very intelligent and has a good sense of smell, so I don't think for one moment he's mistaken it for *his* van, I think he just sees the chance of a way out, a sit down or a lift. It doesn't work.

We make it back to Eagle One and drive to nearby Brockhill Country Park. We have lunch at the popular vegetarian café there. I have shepherd's pie (No shepherds were harmed). I sit outside, surrounded by greenery. Brendan uses the opportunity to have a sit down and watch the squirrels skipping through the tall trees.

At a nearby table, an amateur counselling session seems to be underway, between two middle-aged ladies. One is clearly in need of some help and support, and the other is providing it – whether she likes it or not. The advisor has obviously been on the receiving end of some professional counselling herself and most of her advice is sound and in line with current thinking, the only let down is when she inexplicably veers into inspirational fridge magnet territory with: "You *will* smile again, I promise you." Then it gets worse with the inane: "Just think happy thoughts." But then she's back to A-Level psychology with: "Depression can't be cured… only managed." I'm waiting for the suggestion that she gets herself a dog and goes on long walks.

The healing is obviously working, because when I walk away after my food I feel very at peace. I'm not so sure about the poor "patient" though.

Brendan suggests we go for a wander around the lovely parkland and former gardens, enjoying the mottled shade. Kids are running around shrieking, armed with pump-action, pressurised, high power water Uzis; the kind of semi-lethal hardware I would have killed for as a child. Or quite possibly killed *with*. It's so hot in the direct sunlight, we have a sit down under a tree, a willow, with its long fronds hanging down around us, creating a verdant cave; I can hear the water pistol babies, but not see them through the leafy curtain. I hear the overly confident, precociously well-spoken voice of a boy of about six, saying: "What school do you go to, little boy?"

The reply comes from a much older boy. It surprises me that he would deign to reply to the upstart in the first place. "I don't need to go to school."

"Have you started your school holidays yet?"

"I told you... I don't go to school. All year is a school holiday for me."

"Oh, d'you mean you're *home ed*?"

"No..."

Then – although I can hear the hum of their voices, I can't make out their words until I hear the precocious younger boy, who probably attends a stage school, say: "Little boy..."

"What?"

"Knock knock."

"Who's there?"

I can't catch the next bit, but the punchline is "...because nobody likes you."

His parents must be very proud. This is the post-millennial generation, the so-called Generation Z. This is the future – and the future is seemingly bullying *older* children.

At the other end of the generational scale, I meet an elderly man (Baby Boom Generation, born 1940s) who is seeking shelter from the sun. He has COPD, he tells me, which means he has difficulty breathing after exertion, but especially in the heat. "We don't have seasons in this country." he wisely says, "We just have weather!"

We leave Brockhill and I drive us through the pleasant outer suburbs of Folkstone, struggling to find our next campsite. A driveway leads ever downwards through chalk scrubland with self-seeded buddleia kindly scenting the air; it's sweet and balmy, no wonder butterflies love it. I come to a fork in the road. Someone has thoughtfully put up a helpful direction sign, pointing one way for BEACH AND CAMPSITE and the other way NOWHERE. I've been nowhere and it wasn't up to much, so I steer towards the campsite.

The site is very busy and isn't really to my taste, but it's a pleasant evening and I'm with my boy. We walk to the nearby beach and sit on the sand as the sun dwindles. The beach isn't great, it's a bit scruffy, but we're together, the air is warm and it's always nice to be close to the sea. I've got my arm around Brendan; we're both quite relaxed and enjoying the moment. These times are special and I often want to preserve them by taking a photograph, but the image can never capture the whole experience, just a shadow of it.

The Dalai Lama said words to the effect that "If you're busy trying to photograph the flower, then you're not actually *seeing* the flower." That's very much Brendan's philosophy: don't try and photograph the flower... sniff it then wee on it. And be happy that you've weed on it.

I have quite a Buddhist outlook and philosophy. I try

to live in the moment; I try to appreciate all the things I have and I try to live without harming anyone or anything. I fail all the time, of course, but that's all part of the challenge.

Life's fast, so take time to stop and smell the flowers.

Brendan also is very Buddhist. He meditates for around 20 hours a day. (He often snores during it.) He has no interest in personal wealth. (He expects me to pay for everything.) He lives a communal life, in what used to be *my* flat. He owns very little. (Apart from Pink Pig, Nelliephant and OK Koala.) His is very much the spiritual path.

* * * * * * * * * *

Friday morning. It's suddenly not feeling very special. It's raining; it hasn't rained for weeks. I'm OK with that. I have long sleeves on for the first time in ages and it feels odd. I'm not sure it's just the weather; today feels very difficult. We visit a number of places, but nowhere clicks with us, nowhere feels right and we're not having much fun. We start the day off walking around The Battle of Britain Memorial in the rain, which was perhaps not a good idea. It would be a poignant place at the best of times, but in the wet greyness I start to feel really depressed. Brendan also seems sluggish and downbeat, dragging his paws.

We call at Samphire Hoe Country Park, which was created using waste from the excavations for the Channel Tunnel. It seems to be little more than an isolated car park hemmed in by high white cliffs and a huge concrete sea wall. In the still, damp air it seems rather drab and soulless: a static sort of place with no trees and no movement in the landscape. No trees, again: Brendan is *not* impressed. There's nothing here aesthetically pleasing, just an ethereal nothingness, whiteness, greyness; white chalk cliffs, grey swelling water: water vapour misting the air, nothing changing, except the cars that come, stay a very short while and then go, because there's really nothing else to do.

I should love this strange, reclaimed landscape, but it leaves me cold. The weather certainly isn't helping; the cloying damp of the air is quite oppressive and I find the location oppressive enough anyway. We have a short walk in the drizzle, though there's nowhere really to go and then we leave, long before our ticket time has expired.

Once back on the road, the SatNav starts having a meltdown: "Recalculating... Recalculating... Drive... Recalculating... Recalculating... Drive 1.2... Recalculating... Recalculating... Drive 3.5 miles. Recalculating... Recalculating... Drive... Re... Dri... Re...

Dri... Recalculating... Drive."

It goes on for several minutes and I have to give up in the end and use the map book.

In the afternoon I have an argument with an over-zealous National Trust volunteer who's trying to charge me double the going rate to park Eagle One, even though she's a small van and occupies the same space as a Fiat Panda. This exchange is conducted through the open window and Brendan is remarkably quiet throughout. We end up not parking and I drive off.

I'm fuming as we arrive in the little bay of Saint Margaret's-at-Cliffe, famous for being the closest point to France, and consequently where Channel swimmers begin their marathon 21-mile journey. We're looking forward to a walk, but no dogs are allowed on the beach.

I slam Eagle One into gear. "D'you believe this, Brendan?" Brendan remains tight-lipped. "*I don't!*" I drive off rapidly with a squeal of tyres, possibly dis-lodging half the underside of the van which is probably only held together by duct tape. "It's like the world is against us today!"

Brendan agrees. I'm furious with everything now. I'm in a rut. I feel like the day is ruined and is a stain on our perfect trip. We've overcome adversity before, but today it's not happening. It's cloudy, cold, spitting. I decide the day should be abandoned. All I want is to find a site somewhere, get the heating on, draw the curtains and curl up with my boy. But that's a problem, because I just can't find a site. I'm getting very stressed about it.

Actually I'm getting very stressed about everything.

I realise I'm no longer living the dream. As far as I can remember, this is the first time on the trip that I've been unhappy. I've been briefly stressed *a very lot*, but not unhappy. Brendan also seems lethargic and fed up. We're so in tune.

I find a large Tesco and go food shopping. When it comes to paying I see one of the till personnel, a young woman, we'll call her Mandy – partly to protect her identity and partly because that's what it says on her name badge. She seems to be hiding behind her till, with her head on the keyboard. I am automatically drawn to her. "Are you OK or are you hiding?"

She looks up wearily. "I'm actually hiding."

I admire her honesty. "So you don't need a paramedic or anything?"

"No.. no... I'm just tired." She starts bibbing my items. "This is my second job... I've been at work all day." she tells me. "I'm a primary school teacher. I work on one-to-ones with children with behavioural issues. The boy I'm working with at the moment, I said good morning to him today... he's seven and a half... and he said..." She mouths a sentence; I'm quite shocked. Not so much by the words, and not even by the fact that it was reported speech from a seven year old, I'm actually shocked because a woman on the till at Tesco has said it to me. A checkout operator has never said that to me before. Well, not to my face.

I like Mandy. I like her openness and the fact she was

attempting to remain unnoticed while sitting in full view at a till, totally covered by CCTV. She is possibly the only person I've encountered today who I didn't want to kill.

Everything is suddenly looking up, because I then get a call from a site I'd been phoning all day, but no one had been answering. They've finally returned my call and have a pitch for us.

Even when we're installed on the site, which is adequate but very expensive, I still just want to get comfortable with my dog, shut the world out and put an end to this day, because it feels sullied and can't be redeemed.

Today hasn't been a good day, but tomorrow will be another day. (Obviously). A bright new day. (Probably). And everything will be better. (Possibly.)

* * * * * * * * * *

Sandwich is a famous and historic Kentish town. It's sunny and very hot, but we find a tree-lined path alongside the old defensive town moat. Across the narrow ribbon of water, there is a cricket field with full blown match in progress. We sit down on the grassy bank beneath the shade of a horse chestnut tree – because it's what we do; my arm around Brendan, his weight against me. We watch the match in fascination. Well, I do. Brendan doesn't chase balls and he's frightened of bats, so he can't see the point of the game, which is a shame: he really ought to become an avid follower. Watching cricket is a good excuse to sit down for a very long time. He does a lazy yawn and an indignant snort, then lies down and goes to sleep.

It's thrilling to see England's game played out in a small country town: the crisp whites, the thwack of cork against willow, the smattering of polite applause. They all clap, even the opposition, after a good hit. It's so quintessentially British – and local, as cricket is believed to have been invented in Kent.

The bowler bowls, the batter bats. There's a sharp crack and the red ball sails through the hot, dry air. There's a splash as it lands in the water of the moat. Brendan raises his head and watches with interest. Bizarrely, play stops; I would have thought they'd have a bowl full of shiny red corkers, because this must surely happen all the time, but no, that was the ball, *the* ball, the one and only. The ball floats (it's mainly cork remember.) Or is it a witch? There's much consternation and talk of sending out for another ball, but two industrious blokes appear with a special ball-grabbing device: a pole and net contraption. Within seconds the ball has been scooped from the duckweed and is back in play. I'm expecting a protest from Brendan: men, dressed in a sort of uniform, carrying a long stick... But he just watches with curiosity, then flops his head down again when they walk off. Is this progress? I'd like to think so, but I suspect it's laziness.

I genuinely think The Ball In The Moat Incident is the most excitement anyone has *ever* had at a cricket match. After that, the game seems a little tame, so we move on to explore the rest of Sandwich. We turn down School Road, which not surprisingly has a school on it. I like the fact that in the olden days the streets told you where they led or what they contained, such as Vicarage Lane and Church Road. Nowadays we don't do that, which might be a blessing: Lidl Street, Aldi Avenue, Kids On Facebook Road. When the street names are not randomly generated by a council official with a lanyard and sweat-stains under his armpits, they tend to be chosen to reflect what was there before the bulldozers moved in and tore it up. Green Lane, Forest Walk, Thornhill Road. Apparently they also paved paradise and put up a parking lot.

We call into a pub to get some shade and give Brendan a break. I have a cooling red berry J2O with ice. It's so cold it hurts my teeth. We sit inside in the dark wood panelled interior with plush red curtains and furnishings. We are the only customers inside, so it's very quiet.

A scruffy work experience youth is going through a questionnaire with the polite and efficient bar man; it's obviously part of his course. The youth is reading in a slow monotone and seemingly struggling with some of the words. "Make a... *poster* for your bus... in... *business*. You may... use your computer and add... graph... I.C.S. *Graphics*. Well, that's not going to happen for a start."

"Why not?" the barman asks.

"I haven't got a computer."

A pause. "What?" A long, incredulous pause. "Seriously?"

"No."

"What… You've got *no computer?* Are you for real? How do you get by?"

He means porn.

"Why would I want one?"

"You need one for all sorts of things."

He means porn.

"Nah…"

"They're not the size of a room now, you know."

"I know. If I need something looking up I use my phone."

He means porn.

"I don't need a keyboard or printer. Everyone uses their phone. For everything."

He means porn.

The barman exhales deeply, shakes his head in a "kids today, eh?" sort of way, then moves away, dusting the bar.

Through the window there's a church on the corner, with a wedding underway.

The barman returns to the till, but he's staring out of the window. "Is that the lesbian wedding?"

I'm not sure if he still means porn, but I look up just as the two brides step from the church and are showered with confetti.

We continue through the confetti-strewn streets and complete our circuit of the town. Brendan is tired, so we return to the car park and sit in the van with all the doors and windows open, because of the heat. For tea, I'm purposefully having a sandwich in Sandwich. *Sandwiches* plural, actually. I'm having cucumber sandwiches for England, especially after the cricket match; tomato sandwiches because I like them and they were a favourite of my grandma, and peanut butter and "jelly" (it's jam) to represent our American cousins. They are all surprisingly nice. I very rarely have sandwiches, I seldom buy bread, so it's a nice change.

As all the van doors are open, Brendan is on high alert and barks at a lady walking past. I settle him down – and he is getting quite good at settling down – but she comes towards us, smiling. Brendan starts barking again, but very obediently silences himself when I ask nicely. She stands at the back door looking in. "I bet you're travelling round the country, aren't you?"

"We are."

She claps her hands triumphantly. "Thought so!"

Brendan barks at the sudden noise, but silences himself when told. I'm actually quite impressed with him.

"My husband's planning to do the same thing." She's 64, she tells me, but she looks a decade younger. She seems familiar somehow and I immediately like her. "He wants me to go with him, but I don't think I could handle it." She lowers her voice. "I like my creature comforts. I like my *things*..." She pauses, scrutinising me in a way that makes me feel both violated and treasured. "You don't need *things*, do you?"

"Only my dog." I cuddle Brendan.

She smiles. "You're not materialistic, are you?"

I shake my head. "Not at all. Neither of us are."

"No... neither's he, my husband." She sounds a bit dispirited. "He's retired. I retire next year... He wants me to go with him... I don't really want to... I'd work until I dropped dead, I would."

We talk at length about travelling, about vans, about Brendan, about her husband. She says he wants to move to Dorset.

"I love Dorset!" I say with gusto. "We've been to Dorset, haven't we, boy?" Brendan looks at me but doesn't answer. He's really not good on counties. "It's beautiful." It isn't the right thing to say.

"I know it's beautiful! It is... but he'd be out all the time and I'd be left there on my own... I get on with people... I mix easily... well, look at me now... but..." She hesitates. "I've just lost a friend of 33 years... I can make new friends, but I'll never have that again." She dabs at the corner of her eyes. "I'll never have a friendship of 33 years again. Ever."

We talk for about twenty minutes. I should really have offered her a sandwich, I suppose. Then she says: "So.... I don't want to go to Dorset and I don't want to go round the country in a camper van…" She gives a deep sigh. "I just don't know what to do."

"I think you do… You've just said."

"Yeah…" She sighs thoughtfully. "I have, haven't I…" She smiles, a brave and resolute smile. "Well, I suppose I'd better be going. Enjoy your trip, boys."

It's really odd, but I feel I've known that woman for years. When she's gone I feel quite alone. And I didn't even ask her name. I hope she makes the right decision – for her.

We leave Sandwich, feeling full of sandwiches. The Kent countryside is a patchwork of grass-green and golden wheat; it's beautiful. I drive to our next campsite, which is very busy and we're sandwiched (pun intended) between large and loud family groups.

I tether Brendan outside in the shade while I sort the van out for the evening. He's out of sight for less than a minute, but when I step outside he's gone and his lead lies there, chewed through. Behind us, beyond a large, but spartan hedge, is a road. It isn't that busy but the few cars come racing along it at a dangerous speed. I don't do panic, because it doesn't help resolve a situation, but it feels like my heart drops through my body and shatters on the ground. I look around desperately, but I needn't have worried; Brendan is standing at the rear of the van, just standing looking slightly nervous. I'm still terrified that if I go towards him he'll run through the hedge onto the road, so I approach very cautiously. He makes no attempt to move. I grab his collar, hug him and bury my face in his thick fur. He seems equally relieved and nuzzles into me. I don't know whether something spooked him, I don't know what he was thinking, what made him chew through his lead. He was taking cover, but he didn't run away. Again, that feels like it might be a breakthrough. We sit in our van, together, and I don't let go of him all evening.

* * * * * * * * * *

The next morning, we leave early in the foolish hope we'll be able to make a start on Kent's seaside hotspots before the crowds get there. Along the main roads, fruit is being sold from the boots of cars parked in laybys. "Cherries and Strawberries from the Garden of England". The "Garden of England" tag was bestowed by Henry VIII, after he finished off a dish of Kent cherries. Brendan doesn't like cherries. Or Henry VIII. But I think he's enjoying Kent.

Despite our early start and our good intentions, the crowds are already in situ by the time we arrive in Ramsgate. It's another sunny day and it's also a Sunday. We walk along the lower prom. It's very busy and very hot. Brendan's nose is quivering, his muzzle raised to the assorted seaside smells; his tail is aloft and his gait is perky. The beach is packed. People are paddling and swimming. It's like the seaside during my childhood. It makes me nostalgic. I want to do all those traditional beach activities, like get sunburnt, get stung by a jellyfish and find a cigarette end between my toes.

A colourful piece of graffito on a wall reads: I LOVE YOU TRISHA, but it's written in chalk, so it's hardly a permanent declaration. The perpetrator probably also has the word *Trisha* and a red heart emblazoned across his arm or chest – but in felt tip.

We veer into the town centre, which is disappointingly grubby. The nasty little shopping streets are dark and dingy and lined with the same tackily coloured, plastic-fronted shops as every town everywhere. It seems to lack all character and individuality. Brendan is plodding lethargically beside me. We just aren't enjoying it. We go into the generic coffee chain, Caffe Nero, because we want a rest. As we approach the door a bearded man on a bench, with eyes half-closed, calls out: "Beautiful dog, Sir." I'm waiting for some put down or punchline, but he just smiles a very genuine smile, so I smile back and give him a thumbs up.

It's apparently carnival weekend, but Brendan has already missed the dog show. A circus parade is due to begin at 4pm. I already know we'll be long gone before anyone with curly red hair, over-sized shoes and a painted smile appears on the streets.

And we are, we're in neighbouring Broadstairs, which has quite a different feel to it. Broadstairs is in full swing: in a bandstand overlooking the bay, a brass band are playing a medley of songs from the shows. I know most of them, thanks to Nicky. We sit and listen for a while. It all seems very traditional and very genteel and very fitting. I just wish Nicky was here with us – she would love it – and I know it would make Brendan's day as well.

After the band have finished blowing for all they're

worth, there's a sudden series of sharp blasts from a car horn, then a rough Cockney voice shouts: "Come round this noisy car! Come on. It's the drawing of the raffle. Come on! *Come... On!*" But he makes it sound like an order in a POW camp, a threat, and no one comes. I realise most people are southern now; we have crossed an unseen, un-named border.

I have great expectations for Broadstairs. It has a strong Dickens connection. Our mutual friend, Brendan, fits right in, because most of the time he looks like he's got mutton chops and like he's doing a Dickens. We wander along the busy, but characterful high street, with many attractive eateries and old curiosity shops. Despite these being hard times, I don't see any shuttered or boarded-up premises. On the contrary, it seems to be booming.

If Broadstairs is class, then Margate is brash. Margate is geared towards the family and beachgoers who like a pint of lager, doughnuts and candyfloss. Judging by the reddened swarms of weary people, the town has got it right. The beach is still packed, and so is the sea: the shallows are standing room only, I have never seen the sea this full before. The pavements are filled with a tide of red-fleshed, sun-exhausted people, ambling slowly with sand in their crevices, moving as one away from the beach, back to their hotels or one of the countless family fun bars.

Margate seems like a significant point in our journey, because we've turned a corner, literally and figuratively: we're no longer heading south or east, we're heading west and north, which means we're heading home – a very long way round, but still homewards.

* * * * * * * * * *

I pull up at *Highstead*, a quirky old farm house in the rural depths of the Kentish countryside. It's an eccentric place full of fascinating outbuildings, barns and sheds filled with odd antiques and sculptures, surrounded by acres of orchards and gardens. The toilet has a collection of old "saucy" seaside postcards, which are hilarious. Hilariously bad, but so traditional and an undeniable part of our seaside heritage.

A nice old chap shows me around and takes me to the camping field. He indicates precisely where I should pitch up. "We're all friends here..." he says as he saunters along. "Everyone waves and says hello." To try and prove his point, he waves at a couple who are sitting outside their caravan. Neither of them wave back. "Yes, we're all friends here..."

In the late afternoon, I'm sitting on the grass beside Eagle One with Brendan stretched out beside me. A car comes motoring through the field, a little bit too fast, turns and seems to be heading straight for us. I grab Brendan's collar and pull him aside. He's startled and starts barking. The car comes to an abrupt halt a couple of feet away from us. Surprisingly, two older women get out. I stare at them, expecting an apology or an acknowledgement of some sort, but they walk to the neighbouring tent, pointedly ignoring us. Brendan keeps on barking; he can't abide bad manners.

A few minutes later, one of the women walks past on her way to the toilet, she purposely comes far too close to us and our area. Again Brendan starts barking at her, because now he's classified her as "someone who tries to run me over". This is clearly what the woman wants: a reaction, so she can vent her spleen. She is seething. She spins round venomously. "There's the whole field to choose from, but you have to go there, right next to us. *And I don't like dogs.*"

I start to speak, but she turns and walks away. I call after her, but she doesn't stop. I wonder if I should let it go, but the answer is "No". I put Brendan in the van and stamp across to their tent. They are preparing their meal and both look up, surprised as I approach.

"Excuse me, but you don't come over, drop your poisonous little bombshell and then walk off."

"Just forget it."

"No," I say. "I won't forget it."

"I don't understand why you've parked there when there's all the field to choose from."

"I parked there because the owner told me to."

"Your dog frightened me!"

"You frightened *him*! And you frightened *me*! He's a rescue dog, he's afraid of people and you seemed to be doing your best to run him over, so now he sees you as hostile."

She flaps a hand dismissively. "Just go away."

"You started this… I'm finishing it. Keep away from my

pitch and keep away from my dog. You're both infantile, rude and pathetic." I walk off indignantly, but still furious.

Five minutes later, one of them comes sheepishly over."I'm sorry... I was in the wrong. I apologise. I'm sorry."

I graciously accept her apology, but it has soured the whole evening and the wonderfully weird site. It's sunny and there are blue skies, but it might as well be pouring down. I just want to pack up and go.

We're sitting together later on. We're trying to watch a DVD but I can't focus because I'm too angry, whereas Brendan seems calm and relaxed. Dogs are very sensible creatures; they don't dwell on things. Brendan reacts to something, fear usually, then he moves on, whereas I carry it with me and dwell on it indefinitely.

The sleep of the Just.

Brendan falls asleep and he occasionally makes comfortable little sleep noises. I am quite in awe of his species in so many ways. He doesn't care about the neighbours: they're history; he's moved on. Or so I think.

When I take him for a last wee walk before we go to bed, he immediately starts snapping and growling in the direction of the tent next door. Maybe it's childish, but it makes my day. Perhaps he *does* hold grudges after all; perhaps he's far more human than I thought.

* * * * * * * * * *

I didn't sleep well. I was awake at 4am and couldn't drift off again. I wasn't consciously mulling over the two women next door, but I know full well they were the underlying cause of my insomnia. (I told you I dwell on things.) We leave early, just happy to get away.

We stop briefly in Herne Bay, famous for Hernes. It seems like a pleasant and attractive Victorian resort, despite it being the location of the first "Brides in the Bath" murder in 1912. Close to the pier is a lifesize sculpture of the aviator Amy Johnson, who was seemingly very small and petite. She was 37 when she died in an airborne accident around Herne Bay in 1941. Brendan barks at her and keeps jumping away from her, clearly afraid. Thankfully he doesn't attempt to wee on her.

We continue to the Isle of Sheppey. The crossing ahead takes my breath away. Pairs of concrete pillars support a gracefully rising and curving carriageway. From a distance it looks amazing. I'm a bit nervous as the gradient and the height increase and there are warnings of side winds. I keep my hands gripping the wheel and eyes focused on the road immediately ahead. I don't dare glance at the view on either side, even for a second, only the camber of the road. Then we're descending and suddenly we're on dry land: the island.

We go to the middle of nowhere and then turn right, then pitch up on our site. It's quite green and smells of mown grass. On the horizon, I can see the sea. In the distance. The far distance. Just about. There's no shade on the site at all; we have all the windows open and all the curtains closed. Outside, it's like an oven. Inside, it's also like an oven, but with soft furnishings. We do nothing all afternoon, except try to keep cool. There has been an amber weather warning today, because of severe and dangerous heat. They might be referring specifically to the temperature inside Eagle One.

After the worst of the heat starts to abate, around 7.30pm, we set out to Shellness, at the tip of the island. The road becomes narrower and then degenerates into a dirt trackway. I find a parking space and we continue on foot; Brendan drags along rather wearily beside me. We walk along the top of a high, grassy, protective sea bank, which is full of wide fissures because of the heat and lack of rain. Below, the waves rush in over a sand and shingle beach with wooden groynes every few yards.

We come to an area of reeds and low shrubs. I do a double-take, as several people appear to be wandering along the sinuous sandy pathways in a state of complete nakedness. After my initial surprise – being confronted by all manner of things hanging, dangling, swinging and swaying – I'm British first and foremost, so I carry on walking as though everything is quite ordinary, purposefully *not* looking, which actually isn't a normal reaction at all. We've stumbled across a naturist beach. Brendan doesn't bat an eyelid, because he himself is a keen naturist. He hates the burden of wearing his collar, harness or the occasional neckerchief.

A few people are sunbathing. Nude. A man in shades is wandering through the marram grass. Nude. A woman stands on the beach looking out to sea, stretching her arms towards the sky. Nude. I don't ogle – I don't even film them and put it on Facebook; I leave them to their own devices. And to the devices of others probably.

We pass a naked pot-bellied old man, half-lying in the sand dunes in a catalogue or calendar pose. All I can think is: Oh my god! It's bad enough when you get sand between your toes!

The nudist beach ends; I don't see anything I'd like a closer look at. We continue along a footpath through dry grasslands, criss-crossed by dykes and sluices and drainage channels. It's a beautiful flat, golden wilderness of mosses, heath and reed beds. It's obviously normally very muddy and spongy underfoot, but the mud has dried and cracked. Brendan throws himself into a drainage ditch, which contains an inch of brackish water and a foot of foul stinking tar-like mud. He comes out looking like he's paid for an expensive spa treatment. (He stinks all night, though the following day his fur is soft and manageable and he does look years younger.)

The path takes us around the perimeter of the peninsula and we walk back along the beach as the sun is starting to set; there is a bright lilac glow over the wheat fields, illuminating a circular wind pump, which spins very slowly and lazily in the heat. We end up, completely by accident, on the nudist beach. By now, all the women have gone; it's just single men loitering about and there is an unsavoury atmosphere. I don't know where to look... just where *not* to look.

Brendan scampers along the shingle sniffing and snuffling; he's feeling quite confident, because he's naked, but I'm fully clothed and probably transgressing the rules. I'm not prudish; I'm the *opposite* of prudish, and I fully accept the concept of naturism, whilst not wanting to take part in it myself. Although I respect people who enjoy it, it doesn't escape me that the whole *concept* of nudism fails at the design stage. While part of me wants to shout: "Good for you! There's nothing more natural!" The other half wants to yell: "For god's sake! Put some bloody pants on!"

We emerge through the sand dunes, pants fully intact, back at Eagle One. We drive along the quiet lanes back to our campsite in complete, empty darkness. Brendan is already asleep and breathing steadily. I get into bed, pants still in place; even in bed I'm never completely naked.

* * * * * * * * * *

The next day we cross the frightening arched bridge back to the mainland, then across another very similar bridge over the River Medway to the Isle of Grain. There are reed beds and marshes, a flat fen-like landscape, but towering up in the background are the unmistakeable signs of industry. The road bisects a futuristic, alien city of pipes, cranes, turbines and chimneys, then continues through a housing estate. We pull up in a small, tatty car park surrounded by high hawthorn hedges, shielding it from view. There is litter everywhere; broken glass glistens in the sunlight and plastic wrappers are snagged on the thorns of the bushes. I'm really not happy about leaving Eagle One here, but I have to.

I feel like an intruder in this isolated settlement, where possibly all the houses are owned by workers at the power station and refinery. Again, I'm glad I'm with Brendan, because he legitimises my visit: I'm walking my dog. We follow a trackway that leads to the shore. The tide is in: right in and lapping at the sloping concrete sea wall. Out in the muddy brown water stands Grain Tower, a 19th-century gun tower built to repel the French, now derelict. It looks quite ghostly, stone and concrete, rising up out of the water, dark and satanic. I've come here specifically to walk out to the fort, which is possible at low tide, so I plan for us to wait.

So we wait. We wait several hours. We have a walk, we

have a nap (Brendan's favourite bit!), we have a drive around the island and then we come back. The tide is now at its furthest. The bay is just a mass of soft, muddy sand, but out in the mud is the rusting bulk of Grain Tower, with its hollow, staring windows and the threatening darkness inside.

With my trusty sidekick at my heels, I set off. There is an intermittent causeway to the fort, which is as slippery as hell. I've come clad in my flip flops, thinking it would be the best option. It really isn't. I'm slipping and sliding precariously. The causeway is covered with thick seaweed, which is so slippery, it's lethal. I try walking along the soft sand on either side, but it's quite dirty and oily and my feet sink in considerably in places. I go back to trying the causeway, barefoot now, but it's still almost impossible to stand upright. I assume I'm walking on a layer of shingle or broken shells beneath the sand layer. It really hurts, but I press on valiantly. Meanwhile, Brendan isn't having any problems. He doesn't even leave a footprint; he's so light.

We get three-quarters of the way across; it's really hard going. I have been looking down, watching where I'm putting my feet so as not to slip. I look up and see the fort looming ominously in front of us, with its gaping windows and towering rusted walls. It's really quite chilling. It looks mighty eerie. I feel a growing sense of unease. I really don't like the look of it. I don't want to go inside, even with Brendan. I find it really un-nerving.

I've already made up my mind, but as though to underline my decision, there is a deep clang from somewhere inside the bowels of the fort. Someone's in there. There's no way I'm going any nearer. The soles of my feet are really hurting and I'm concerned about the tide suddenly turning and us getting trapped inside, but the main reason is because I really don't want to get any closer. It's terrifying. We turn and head back; I feel we've been close enough to get a feeling for it, close enough to tick it off our wish list.

Going back is much easier. I seem to have found the best way to handle the stones, the weed and the mud. Once back on the sea wall, I notice there's blood on my feet. Quite a lot of blood. The soles of both feet are cut to ribbons. I don't know why it should be, but I don't think it was shingle or broken shells I was walking on; I think it was broken glass. The cuts don't seem deep enough to need stitches, but they're plentiful and painful. Brendan, thankfully, is completely unscathed.

We sit on the concrete sea wall looking over the bay. After some time, a figure emerges from the direction of the fort. I wait for ages for him, to chat about his experience inside, but he's taking so long on the slippery causeway that I give up and take my poor, sore feet back home to Eagle One.

Our campsite for the night seems to be full of regulars; many of the caravans appear to be permanently there, perhaps used by people working away from home at the island's industry. Most of them seem to know each other. There appears to be an 'Eighties disco underway and virtually everyone has gathered in a huge group in the still-warm dusky evening, all drinking and chatting and generally having a good time. The site manager, Diamond Geezer - in his army shorts and mint green vest - seems to be at the hub of it.

I'm one of the very few not taking part. Possibly the only one. Because I haven't been invited. Don't get me wrong, I'm fine with that. I'll happily be left out of a party any day of the week. It's still too hot in the van, so I sit outside in my deckchair with my exhausted dog at my feet, but I'm permanently on edge in case anyone should notice us and try and entice us over. (I needn't have worried – no one does.)

An 'Eighties compilation CD is blaring from one of the caravans via a speaker system. I know it's a CD, because it sticks repeatedly and we're treated to an unintentional dub-remix of some famous classics.

After a while I head inside to make tea, leaving Brendan trying to sleep in the sunshine. He doesn't stand a chance, because then a real life soap opera begins with the couple in the tent next door. The climax comes when the man bellows: "We're done! You hear me? We... are... done!"

Then *two* women emerge from the tent and walk off together. A few seconds later there's the cracking of a beer can. A few minutes pass, then the man – as though the beer has made him see sense – walks away carrying a large holdall. It's possibly the end of something fragile and beautiful. But more likely it's the end of something brief and sordid.

Hours pass. The sun sets. The disco stops. The shouting stops. The lights go out and we actually sleep soundly.

* * * * * * * * * *

Early morning with weather warnings. Nicky messages to say today is predicted to reach 37 degrees; one of the hottest days on record. (The hottest registered being 38.5 degrees centigrade at Faversham in Kent.)

We drive through sleepy villages and narcoleptic small towns, meandering through a flat landscape of wheat fields bordered by ancient hedgerows. The air smells sweet and balmy. We come across the Blackwater estuary, with a fjord-like coastline of islands, inlets and creeks. After many, many miles of enjoying the scenery, I have to confess to Brendan that we're lost. He doesn't care, he's none the wiser, he's fast asleep in his basket. Meanwhile I'm hot, tired and very fed up.

I'm sick to death of being so hot! I'm sick to death of letting vehicles out and the driver not thanking me. I'm sick to death of sitting upright holding this steering wheel. I'm sick to death of people not indicating. I'm sick to death of cars driving too fast on country lanes. I'm sick to death of vehicles coming round tight bends on my side of the road. I'm sick to death of roundabouts. I'm sick to death of people driving whilst on their phones. I'm sick to death of having to squint in the sunlight, even with my sunglasses on. I'm sick to death of the SatNav giving me impossible instructions: "Turn left. Turn left! Turn left *now!*" Then when I comply, she adds: "In 300 yards make a U-turn." I'm sick to death of U-turns. I'm sick to death of virtually everything.

I pull up at the side of the road and take a deep breath to try and calm down. A bird of prey soars across the washed-out blue above the road. Or it might have been a woodpigeon. Or a magpie. But it's a bird, soaring majestically, riding the thermals. Such a beautiful and natural sight should lift the heart and put all your problems into perspective. *You'd think!* It doesn't, but I'll tell you what does: the sight of my little dog sitting behind me with his big paws and his chocolate brown eyes. He should be available on the NHS.

We drive through Maldon without stopping and arrive at our campsite, surrounded by equestrian fields. Horses stand idly chewing grass and flicking their tails. Brendan barks at them incessantly, until he gets bored and goes to sleep in the shade cast by the van. We have an afternoon siesta, waiting for the worst of the heat to abate and the worst of the traffic to die down.

In the early evening, we drive to the little waterside village of Heybridge Haven at the top of the Blackwater Estuary. The tide is out and boats are sitting on the sand, stranded. There are lots of seabirds, flying in great circles, landing and strutting and calling across the mudflats.

Heybridge has some very attractive weather-boarded cottages. There isn't a great deal here, but it's a place to come and sit and take in the air, take in the view of the boats bobbing on the water – or embedded in the sand –

and enjoy the salty breeze. It's a place to relax, to let life happen and have a leisurely pint.

Never one to ignore my own very sage advice, that's exactly what we do. Heybridge Haven is blessed with two attractive pubs; we choose one based on busy-ness or lack thereof: we go in the one that seems less busy, which is the Jolly Sailor, which isn't actually all that jolly. It's very nice inside, but there's a drama going on.

6.50pm.

A very slight, camp young man at the bar makes an announcement: "We're expecting a party of sixteen at 7 o'clock, so if you want to order food you'd be advised to get the order in as soon as possible." (I very quickly get very sick of hearing this.)

6.52pm.

We sit down with a half each. (Though I have Brendan's by proxy, so it makes sense to get both drinks in a pint glass.) He slinks happily under the table to practise his limbo-ing. Behind me, at the bar, things are getting to fever pitch.

"We're expecting a party of sixteen at 7 o'clock…"

6.53pm.

"Sorry, madam, you can't sit there! We've got a party of sixteen at 7 o'clock, so those tables are reserved!"

6.55pm.

"We're expecting a party of sixteen at 7 o'clock, so you'd

be advised to order food *immediately*."

Man with sideburns: "Fish, chips and peas twice, if you please."

"That's fine, but we're out of peas."

6.58pm.

"Excuse me, those tables are reserved. We're expecting a party of sixteen at 7 o'clock. *You can't sit there!*"

7.01pm.

"Who's next? I'll just say, we're expecting a party of sixteen at 7 o'clock, so if you want to order food you'd be advised to get the order in quickly or there *will* be a delay."

7.10pm.

"We're expecting a party of sixteen at 7 o'clock, so those tables are..."

Cocky man: "Err... It's well gone seven now."

"Has it? We'll have to give them a few more minutes."

7.15pm.

"Right, we're going to phone the party of sixteen who were due at 7 o'clock."

7.20pm.

"Hello, it's the Jolly Sailor here..." (So the pub must be named after him.) "No, the pub... You've got a booking with us... Tonight... Yes, tonight... At seven o'clock... Tonight... *Tonight*... Definitely tonight... I took the booking myself... Seven o'clock tonight... What? I... Oh... But it... Oh... But I... Oh... But... Well, I... Oh... Oh... *Next* month... No... No, no that's fine... No... I'll change it... I'm... errr... I'm sorry to have disturbed your evening."

7.21pm.

"OK everyone, those tables are free now... But we still haven't got any peas."

We leave the Jolly Sailor – because we can't take the drama any more – and stroll around the village in the balmy evening, chatting with people who come up to ask about Brendan. He's so relaxed in so many ways... while being totally stressed in others. He isn't phased by the threat of the party of sixteen or by the lack of peas. He's very wise and takes everything in his double-stride. Having Brendan has made me, in turn, feel so much more relaxed with other people, with strangers. I no longer feel like a lone travelling weirdo; I feel like a travelling weirdo with a dog.

Feeling at peace with the world, we return to our equestrian site and go to sleep, surrounded by the sound of horses.

* * * * * * * * * *

At last! The weather has broken. I awake to find it's a Friday. An overcast Friday, which is very welcome. Thunder is promised for later, which is also welcome. I *love* thunder. Especially on Fridays. But Brendan doesn't.

This is our last day in Essex. Apparently, Essex has the longest coastline in the UK, with a staggering 350 milesworth! But the thing we'll remember most about Essex is the stifling heat: afternoons so hot that we just had to retreat to the site and lie down in the shade cast by the van. Brendan has loved it!

On my way back from the shower, I bump into the friendly camp site man, who asks if I've enjoyed my stay. I tell him I have. "It's a lovely site and a nice part of the world."

He suddenly becomes all serious, so much so that he feels the need to adjust his flat cap. "We get a lot of bad press, you know, with the whole stereotypical Essex person and that... but..." He smiles. "I like it round here."

We bid him goodbye and we set off; me driving, Brendan stretched out sleeping in the back. Through trial and error we've found this works best for us. We travel along A-roads in a north-easterly direction, exhaust fumes rising. By noon, the unnatural baking heat is back. The countryside seems more open now, more expansive; there are large, unhedged, unfenced wheat fields, though the wheat here is already harvested and in bales. It gives me the panicking feeling that yet another year is spinning by so quickly. We're now (slightly) nearer to *next* Christmas than *last* Christmas. We're steadily, inevitably running out of the year. But we are *rapidly* running out of Essex.

* * * * * * * * * *

Dog facts:

Dogs have much better hearing than humans; they can hear sounds four times further away than we can. So don't whisper things that you really don't want your dog to hear, especially words like "vets" or "neuter". Be warned: they can still hear you!

Brendan pretends he's in prison, whilst waiting for a manicure.

CHAPTER 7: LOW-LYING DOGGO: BRENDAN IN EAST ANGLIA

Suffolk claims (rather tenuously in my opinion) to have "More Dog Friendly Pubs Than Anywhere Else". We'll see. Anyway, that makes Brendan very pleased. He *loves* pubs. Since Day One he has always pulled to go in any pub we pass. I'm quite discerning, I like somewhere fairly quiet and with a lot of character, but he's really not bothered. I suspect the chance of a sit down is what sells the experience to him.

We arrive at our campsite in the depths of Rendelsham Forest. The site is packed to the rafters and beyond, absolutely crawling with families. Brendan does incredibly well, as hordes of noisy kids keep infringing on our pitch and coming right up to the van, but he doesn't bark or react. He isn't generally bothered by children, only adults. Obviously he has never been mistreated by a child.

After tea, I steer us down a network of narrow, winding country lanes between sandy fields. A water rig, spinning slowly, is dousing a green crop, possibly potatoes. This hot weather – that holiday makers are enjoying so much – comes at a cost; something else is knocked out of kilter. It's going to have to rain for a very long time to penetrate the top layers of soil and actually hydrate the roots properly.

We're heading off the edge of my map. I try the SatNav,

but it won't accept the postcode as a destination, which is very odd. I know roughly the right direction, so I rely on my unfailing instincts to get us there. And they *are* unfailing. On the whole.

I turn down a lane signed for HOLLESLY BAY COLONY HMP AND YOI. A minute later we're in the prison. Actually *in* the prison. Not close to it, not adjacent to it, not outside looking in through a high wire fence, but actually *in* the prison. The road goes *through* the prison! The roadway snakes between institutional-looking buildings; there are signposts for things like "kitchen", "gym", "laundry", "way out".

Inmates, men in uniform, are walking on either side of the road between the buildings. Thankfully Brendan is curled up in his basket and can't see them, or he'd have something to say; they're men *and* they're in uniform. Some of them stop and stare as I drive through. It's obviously an open prison, so these men are presumably D-Category and coming to the end of their sentences, but even so, to have a road going through the middle of it seems very odd. It could explain why the prison has been heavily criticised for the large number of escapes, which has earned Hollesley Bay the hilarious nickname of *Holiday* Bay.

Irish writer, Brendan Behan, was an inmate here, as was former Mayor of London, Jeffrey Archer. My Brendan would be able to relate to their plight, as he too – of course – was in prison in Bulgaria, in the Kill Shelter.

We pass through the prison unscathed, then set off along a winding lane between saltmarshes to our

211

destination: Shingle Street. I park up and we walk towards the solitary row of white terrace cottages which stand facing the sea. Topographically, it's very like Dungeness. It's got the same beautiful bleakness. It has a strange, unearthly, ethereal quality. I love it.

It's a very isolated spot, set apart from the rest of society, surrounded by sea and marshes, not overlooked at all. It was precisely because of this isolation that the civilian population of Shingle Street were evacuated during the war and it was taken over by the military. The pub, the Lifeboat Inn, was destroyed, blown up, not by an enemy barrage, but by the British testing a bomb.

Many strange occurrences have been reported at Shingle Street, including walls of fire across the sea, the bodies of Nazi officers littering the beach and a supposed failed German invasion. German soldiers *were* occasionally washed up on beaches around southern England, from torpedoed ships. Experiments with burning oil on the sea certainly *did* take place, but further down the coast. In all likelihood, all these disparate happenings have probably been repositioned over time to make a sensational story that's just that – a story – and nothing of any significance happened at Shingle Street, except an exercise in disinformation, misinformation and so-called "black propaganda": a fabrication designed to intimidate the enemy, boost morale and ensure the Americans got involved in the war.

We scrunch along the beach, enjoying the stillness of the evening and the cool salty breeze. The sound of church bells is drifting on the air. There is a church tower just visible over the distant treeline. It adds perfectly to the sense of mystery of the place.

The sun is dipping close to the horizon. There is a deep rumbling in the distance, which seems to split the air. It's either thunder or a nuclear attack and Brendan isn't keen on either. He digs his heels into the shingle and refuses to go on, so we head back towards Eagle One.

Brendan mingles with the shingle at Shingle Street

We high-tail it back to the site and arrive just in time. People are standing or sitting staring upwards, *oohing* and *ahhing* as forks of lightning light up the whole sky. The first heavy drops of rain are already falling, but the people stand there mesmerised. Then the heavens really open, it's like a rain white-out; everyone screams and darts for their tents and vans, as though it's unexpected.

I love watching thunder, I love rain drumming on my roof and running down my windows. But poor Brendan is terrified. He's crouching on the floor at the back of Eagle One, where he never normally goes; he's obviously assessed the van and decided this is the safest place. I coax him onto his normal seat and sit next to him. You aren't supposed to make a fuss of a frightened dog or react any differently, as that makes them believe there really *is* something to be afraid of, so I sit next to him, put my arm round him and chat to him in a calm voice, as normal. The rain is pouring in through the gaps I've left in the windows and the ceiling light, so I have to close everything. It's boiling hot. Brendan is curled up tightly – despite the heat – and trembling. I close all the curtains and put music on to try and mask the thunder. I sing to him, which is not unusual, and I completely miss the spectacular storm.

* * * * * * * * * *

It rains heavily all night, but stops mid-morning. We set off on foot into another new and rather water-logged day. According to woodland staff, it's 12 degrees colder today, which is annoying, as the forest was supposed to provide us with the luxury of some much-needed shade from the unbearable heat.

Rendelsham Forest is famous as the location of what is generally considered to be the most significant UFO sighting in the UK, when several military personnel witnessed strange crafts around the forest over a three day period in 1980. There is a leaflet-guided trail around the forest, taking in the UFO points of interest, which is fascinating and fun. At least, one of us is fascinated by it; one of us is more interested in the occasional squirrels and weeing on trees.

We walk along woodland pathways and stony forest tracks, following numbered signposts. There's no one about, no human sound, just the eerie whispering of the pine needles and the breeze, the occasional stirring of a branch and the shivering fronds of bracken and blades of grass. Twigs snap occasionally in the darkness between the slim boughs of the fir trees. Brendan is very agitated and unsettled, staring at the undergrowth and growling. It's really very unnerving. But if there *are* aliens in the trees, they don't reveal themselves to us, other than snapping twigs. At the end of the trail, the high roof of Eagle One comes into view; we have been sleeping really very close to the main encounter site.

We leave Rendelsham Forest and continue on our way, in search of other trees to wee on. En route, we suffer a fatality. The SatNav doesn't make it. She had the last of her many meltdowns and kept saying "Turn left, right. Turn left... Do a U-turn. Right... Do a U-turn... Right... Do a U-turn... Do a U-turn... " She was sending us round in circles; I kept driving round the same village and seeing the same faces sitting outside the same pub. We had become a local phenomenon. I could see the laughter in their eyes: "I tell you... just wait... he'll be back round again in a minute. See! Here he comes!" Well, no more! I put her out of her misery. It was for the best.

Nicky's dad gave us the SatNav when he upgraded and got one that actually worked. I remember him saying: "It's not great, but it's better than nothing." That's really not true. I realise now why he was so eager to part with it.

So, SatNav-free, I find my way to our next site the old fashioned way: I check the route in the road atlas and I look at the signs at each junction. Navigating by manual is a lost art form.

We arrive at the site efficiently and pitch up in a grassy field. Around the site there are several massive wind turbines, the rotors turn steadily above us, filling the air with a constant swooshing sound. Brendan sits outside on the grass and barks constantly at them. And at the people passing by. And at the people who don't pass by. And dogs, squirrels and rabbits. He barks at everyone, at everything, at no one and nothing and he won't be pacified. In the end I have to bring him in and we sit inside with the curtains and windows closed. Again.

* * * * * * * * * *

Suffolk prides itself on being one of the driest counties. But not today, oh no. It's raining cats and dogs. (No offence to either species.) It's also very windy as we arrive in Southwold. I put my jacket on for the first time in ages; it feels weird having my arms covered up.

The telegraph wires overhead are vibrating and giving out a low droning, like the sound effect from a cheap horror movie. This weather and especially the severity of it is quite startling. Twenty-four hours ago it was moderately hot. Forty-eight hours ago it was blisteringly hot. I suppose that was the summer, gone.

The pier is facing us; the hanging silver letters reading SOUTHWOLD PIER are swinging violently. Waves are crashing over the railings onto the boardwalk and the promenade. The grey sea looks furious beneath the grey sky. Waves are surging up the beach, spume is blowing in the wind. Advertising A-stands have been flung over and wheelie bins are colliding before hitting the deck. It all seems very apocalyptic.

We pass some dog water labelled BIG DOGS and LITTLE DOGS, with correspondingly-sized containers. Brendan is neither big nor little. I'd say he's medium. But also English isn't his first language, so partly to be unbiased, and partly because he doesn't like labels and categories, he drinks from both bowls.

We walk along the prom, the sea surging and thrashing. People come towards us, huddled, heads bowed. Brendan's beautiful tail is pulled to one side by the wind, so he looks like he's permanently indicating to turn right. But he doesn't turn right. That's so typically him.

The pier and sea have gone sepia now; everything looks very surreal. The sky seems discoloured with rain clouds and the air is crackling with an electric imminence. It all feels very dramatic. It's mid-afternoon, but it seems to be going dark. It's wet, it's windy, it's wild. I love it! Brendan, however, is less enamoured with it. He elects to go into the van for a sleep. I set off alone to further explore the beautiful town.

I don't last very long. I've become so used to being with The Boy, that I can barely function without him. I stay out as long as I can manage, but I just feel miserable. I go in a few pubs, but come straight out again. Although they're very quaint and full of atmosphere, I just don't feel comfortable without my dog. He's completely taken me over. This was never supposed to happen. I race back to Eagle One, we return to our site and spend all night together, while the wind and rain do their worst outside.

* * * * * * * * * *

Monday. A new day. A new week. A new county: Norfolk. We're in Great Yarmouth, just "Yarmouth" to its friends, but probably never just "Great". It has faced a lot of criticism in recent years. Our mission is to find out if it still deserves its prefix or not.

I drive down the Kings Road, which – despite its name – *isn't* a cool and happening hotbed of 'Sixties fashions, but a rather dubious, insalubrious and not very regal side street. I park outside some holiday flats, which look a bit grim. One bay-fronted hotel labels itself as a "Shabby Chic" B&B. Well, they're half right. Yarmouth has been a resort since 1760, when some of these buildings were last decorated by the look of it.

Brendan seems a bit lethargic today. I'm sure he's questioning why we need to be traipsing along another seaside promenade when we could stay in the van; *Watercolour Challenge* is bound to be on some channel somewhere. He slopes along grudgingly and refuses to smile.

It's been raining heavily in Great Yarmouth – and everywhere in Britain probably. There are black puddles by the roadside and the pavements are wet. A grey sky hangs low overhead, dark-tinged rainclouds are tethered and waiting. There is a strong and bitter wind. *This* is how I best know the British seaside.

Rides and activities along the beach and promenade are all rain-wet and unpopulated. Several bouncy castles lie deflated and waterlogged on the damp sand. The sails of a miniature windmill turn unnoticed on a crazy golf course. Brendan spots the movement and barks half-heartedly, then realises he actually can't be bothered; he stops mid-bark and sits down instead.

Yarmouth's glitteringly tacky seafront is packed full of shimmering, shining, glowing, twinkling, beeping, hooting and tooting amusements and attractions. It's got *The Golden Nugget* and *The Gold Rush; Quicksilver* and *The Silver Slipper*. It's got everything you could ever want in an amusement arcade, except perhaps amusement.

The pier has music piped along its length; *Build Me Up Buttercup* and *Morning Town Ride*: music from another era, probably a better era, but it does suggest the past, not the present and not the future. There are some head cut-outs for photos – but the faces are all empty. I suppose any kid can do the same effect on their phone now, in under five seconds, but where's the magic in that?

There is a palmistry booth... closed. There are colourful dodgems, a big slide and a ghost train. It's all beautifully traditional, but nobody is on any of them. Over the railings, on the empty beach, sad donkeys stand in the rain, looking miserable. Brendan keeps a suspicious eye on them.

We walk along in the drizzle, passing more amusement arcades flashing and whirring and doing their best to entice us over: *Atlantis, The Flamingo, The Showboat.* They're all red and pink and silver and blue: tacky and vibrant and noisy – just as they're supposed to be – but they're deserted. They're all absolutely deserted.

Bingo announcements drift across the road, monotonous and deadpan. The poor, bored bloke is probably announcing to an empty house, but going through the motions anyway. "Two little ducks..." Sigh. "Twenty two."

Things change, they call it progress, though progress is generally a retrograde step. Tourists have complained that Great Yarmouth seems to shut at 6pm, but businesses say customers don't come after 6pm, so it seems to be a vicious circle.

"Kelly's eye." Sigh. "Number one."

I love the idea of a traditional seaside resort, I love the nostalgia. But I can't see kids, who are conversant with digital technology, being entertained by a pink elephant ride or a sedate ghost train that trundles along only slightly faster than being stationary.

"Key to the door." Sigh. "Number twenty-one."

We came here as a family when I was sixteen; it was planned as our last organised holiday together as a family, so it was very memorable in that respect, but I just didn't want to be there. I'd just started work. I call it work, it was a Youth Training Scheme and I was employed at a TV and video shop for twenty-five pounds a week. I gave £12.50 to my mum for my keep and the rest was all mine. I'd asked a girl out at home and was eager to get back and continue the relationship. I didn't like Yarmouth when I was sixteen; I thought it was rough and tacky. I can't see that much has changed.

"Four-oh..." Sigh. "It's blind forty."

Brendan sniffs at a lamppost, but it can't smell very exciting, because he doesn't wee on it. The effort of raising his leg is seemingly too much.

"Clickerty click..." Sigh. "Sixty-six."

A family are approaching with a gaggle of small children. "Look out for that dog muck." the mother says. "Look out for that dog muck!" Her voice is rising in pitch and becoming more insistent. "Are you listening! *Look out for that dog muck! Look out...* Oh it's alright... that dog's eaten it." I look around. There's no other dog on the prom... and my dog is chewing.

"Seven and six." Sigh. "Was she worth it?" Supplementary sigh. "Every penny..."

We stop at a café on the prom, because I know Brendan

wants me to have a coffee and Eccles cake. The bouncy castle and bouncy slide are now fully inflated and open, but still with no customers. They just sit there and wobble amidst the hoarse rattle of a generator. Brendan sits sedately and watches the world go by. A lovely couple stop to admire him and we have a nice chat.

"He's lovely. What's he called?"

"Brendan. I didn't choose it. He came with it."

"Ah... it suits him! He's gorgeous!"

The woman strokes him and he loves it. The man, very wisely, doesn't.

We return to Eagle One and power her up for a drive around the town. Brendan is very happy to be back in his basket. We pass the funfair. A single carriage on the high monorail is going painfully slowly around the perimeter of the pleasure beach; one solitary car with one person in it. It doesn't look sad, but quite comical.

On leaving Great Yarmouth, though it's only early afternoon, it has gone dark and everyone has their headlights on and their wipers going at full speed, as there's a sudden deluge. We leave behind the bright lights, the piers and the bingo...

"Man alive..." Sigh. "It's number... oh... excuse me, I'm so tired... five."

We drive along a straight road across a very flat landscape of wheat fields and grasslands. This no longer looks or feels like Suffolk. Which it isn't. It now looks and feels like Norfolk. Which it is. There are cows grazing, horses frolicking, reed beds, marshes, rushes, dykes and ditches, peppered with windmills, both active and in ruins, used for pumping water. We drive through the rain, through the Norfolk Broads, crossing bridges over canals, past boat yards and lock gates, between wide, flat fields. It is an area criss-crossed with rivers: the Yare, the Wensum, the Waveney, the Chet, the Ant, the Thurne and the Bure – which all sound made-up to me. It's a wide open landscape and there is a whole lot of sky. It's a Constable painting; it's oil on canvas, though – especially in the rain – it ought to be a watercolour.

Brendan recharges in his basket, curled up very tightly. He starts snoring. I drive through this flat, open countryside, wipers on, headlights on, music on, singing, until we arrive in the village of Happisburgh, pronounced "Hazeborough", not "Happys-burg", which is appropriate, as it isn't all that happy, because it's basically falling into the North Sea.

We walk past a local and I say good morning. He doesn't reply "Not such a good morning when your village is being sucked into the sea!" so I assume life goes on here as normal, until the inevitable happens.

The static caravan park is in immediate danger. It is being relocated, further inland, because if it remains much longer, it will end up in the sea in a mess of pull-out divans and Porta-potties. We walk along the beach, which is essentially sandy, but already littered with rough stones and chunks of masonry: fragments and reminders of the dozens of buildings which have already come crashing down onto the shoreline. The cliff is soft and sandy and really doesn't stand a chance against the relentless action of the thrashing waves. Sea defences were built in 1959, but now need renewing and upgrading, but this is no longer funded by the government.

Happisburgh beach has an air of gloom about it, because it resembles a demolition site, so we head uphill to the village hostelry, which isn't exactly hostile, but is distinctly odd. The Hill House Inn is aptly named, but its lofty location isn't going to save it. The landlord estimates it has less than thirty years left. The pub doesn't have the charming olde worlde interior I had imagined and something strange is going on in the bar room. A middle-aged couple and the barman are playing darts and being very loud. They're acting as though they're drunk. And perhaps they are. It is a pub after all. Suddenly – and in unison – they burst into a rousing chorus of the Goons' *Ying Tong Song*, AKA *Ying Tong Yiddle I Po*. Is that even still legal? Because they're loud and annoying, Brendan insists we sit outside and I don't raise any objection.

He stretches out his front paws, sphynx-like, and watches the other people sitting around us with the avid interest of an amateur psychologist. He's so good in a pub or café; as long as people keep out of his immediate area, he's so relaxed and at ease.

When we leave, thoughts of Happisburgh stay with me. It's quite a lovely corner of the country, but it inevitably has an air of sadness about it, of imminence, of inevitability. One day in the fairly near future, it will most likely be underwater.

We return to Eagle One and trundle around the north Norfolk coast, following winding lanes between yellow fields of wheat and green fields of brassicas, through the seaside town of Cromer and on to our isolated and quite beautiful campsite in the hills.

* * * * * * * * * *

It's a wet start again as we set off ever northwards. We stop in Wells-next-the-sea and park on the outskirts. Brendan hops out and we wander along solid backstreets of colourful Georgian cottages. From around a corner, a silent and ghostly line of alpacas suddenly appear, being walked down the street on leads. They're funny animals, with Beatles moptop hairdos, flared pantaloons and a look of sneering disdain. We stand aside. Brendan – thankfully – watches them with mild amusement and doesn't bark. The strange procession passes silently by, until a woman at the back looks at us both and laughingly says: "My dog's better than yours!"

I laugh. Brendan doesn't.

We find our way into the centre of town. It's Wells' carnival week; it isn't exactly Rio, but it's lively and bustling. We go in the Raggedy Cat Café: my choice, not Brendan's. It's a tightly packed little café and Brendan lies down blocking everyone's exit. Strangely, no one attempts to leave while we're there.

Before long everyone is talking about him and asking if they can stroke him. "You *can…* but you'll only do it once." No one braves it. Brendan is very much an ambassador. He brings people together, though everyone is talking *about* him, not *with* him. He's so relaxed, as long as people understand he needs his space and it's better to admire him from a distance and not make a fuss of him.

Afterwards, we walk along the high street. The sun is shining and there's a holiday feeling in the air. People mill around chatting and laughing and being happy. We fall into step behind a young family and I catch a snippet of conversation between the father and small boy.

"Daddy, I wonder what happened to grandma and grandad."

"I don't know, Frazer."

"Maybe they got kidnapped!"

Daddy sighs wistfully. "Oh Frazer... I'm afraid we're just not that lucky."

I laugh out loud. With a glance from his wife, Daddy chuckles nervously and looks away.

The harbour is peaceful and still. I love that chinking of rigging against masts, a calming nautical pulse. We sit down overlooking the tidal channel and the salt marshes, which protect the harbour from the sea. Brendan sits, sniffing the air, his eyes lightly closed, head raised. He looks like he's posing for a catalogue shoot.

We've done Wells, so we move on along the coast. It's very hot again and it's quite a blessing when, after a day in the blistering heat, we arrive in the leafy shade of the Sandringham estate. The whole area is verdant and quite beautiful. The campsite we're staying on is on land belonging to the Queen! We're actually guests of Her Majesty!

A lovely lady shows us to our pitch. She scoots ahead on a bike and I follow her through the trees. She's so friendly, funny and personable. Our pitch isn't the greatest, because there are other people on the site, which is always a bug bear of mine. It's not really very Brendan-friendly. She comments on the Boy, saying how handsome he is, then she suddenly pauses and digs her phone out of her fleece pocket and starts flicking at the screen. "Look at this..." She holds her phone out towards me. I look and then look again, craning my neck forward to see it closer. There seems to be a photograph of Brendan on her phone. I do a double and treble take. I realise it *isn't* actually my boy, but it's a very effective clone.

It turns out the dog is her sister's cousin's or something. The similarity is astounding. I begin to worry that Brendan could be replaced by this doppelganger at any time and I'd be none the wiser, so perhaps we ought to have a secret code word, like say, "Bonio" so I'll know it's him. (Bonio is the same in English or Bulgarian.) He peers at me, with a look of love or disdain: they're very similar expressions. I suddenly feel reassured; I realise I will always know my boy because of his docile nature and soulful eyes. We have a bond and an understanding.

We sit outside the van for a while, enjoying the sunshine through the pine trees that surround the site. Two cars come trundling across the grass and take over the pitch behind us. The car doors open and close in rapid succession. It turns out to be two couples, with a noisy flock of small children. Young children.

Brendan lies on the grass and watches curiously as the two men start putting up a gigantic cityscape of a tent, hammering with mallets, inserting tent poles, and generally being men. The women unload the small and easily carriable items from the cars, like cushions, lace curtains and handkerchiefs, then they probably start preparing food and drinks, while exuding an air of calm and prettiness.

I hear a little girl of about five, suddenly announce in a precocious manner: "I'm going to watch the two annoying dads putting the tent up. Annoying Simon and Annoying Stuart."

She arrives at the Dads camp. There's a hum of general chatter and a bit more malleting, then I hear her say: "Anyway, I've got *really good* karate skills."

One of the dads laughs. "Have you? More like *Russell Harty* skills."

She tuts loudly and theatrically. *"Who?"*

"Never mind."

There's a bit more chat; the dads – Simon and Stuart – apparently both annoying – are talking to each other and trying to figure out how flap A attaches to sealant flange C, while the girl keeps making disparaging comments about how slow and stupid they both are.

The hammering of tent pegs abruptly stops and one of the dads, presumably her biological father, says in a very tight-lipped manner: *"Why don't you go and see if mummy wants any help?"*

"Nah… I'm enjoying it here."

There's a pause, then the hammering suddenly starts up again in earnest. I just know that some of those tent pegs will never be pulled free from the ground. All the time, Brendan just watches with interest, but never once raises his voice in protest. I think he's hoping this is on cable, so we can watch it at home.

The Boy, the sea, clear skies, cool air: our ideal life.

We remain sitting outside as the evening wears on and the sun heads below the surrounding treeline. The two families are installed in their tent, relaxing after tea. I can hear the clinking of wine bottles against the rims of glasses, and things seem a lot calmer. By 9.30 their tent is in darkness and silence. They are perfect nocturnal neighbours. We slink inside as it gets chilly and draw our curtains over the woodland darkness.

I'm loving staying on the Sandringham Estate, as is Brendan, though he's also finding it quite frustrating: so many trees, so little time.

We go to sleep side-by-side. I probably dream of my imminent knighthood; Brendan dreams of corgis.

* * * * * * * * * *

In King's Lynn there are a lot of sirens. *A lot* of sirens. They seem to be coming from all around. There are flashing blue lights at the end of streets and the rising pitch of accelerating engines, but I never get to see what the actual emergency is. I drive round town repeatedly, trying to park. I try a left turn and a line of cars follow me into the bus station; we drive along in convoy past all the surprised queues of people waiting at the terminals, like an automated conga, to the sound of wailing sirens. It's all quite surreal. We find a way out – following a bus – and I manage to park at a supermarket, which has a space and doesn't have a height barrier. We set off on foot. The sirens have stopped. Brendan's tail is swishing and he seems keen and perky; that's daytime napping for you.

We head into the centre of town and end up in the shopping area. Another thing we have in common: we both hate shops and shopping. We turn down a minor side street to get away from the crowds. It's a dirty back street behind the shops and seems to be filled with people, mainly men, standing in doorways staring into space, looking traumatised. Every single person on that street looks both catatonic and haunted. It's really weird, but then I remember the sirens and I wonder whether some terrible atrocity like 9/11 has happened.

We carry on regardless. One of my first thoughts about King's Lynn is, Oh God, I've had to pay for three hours in the car park! How are we going to spend three hours here? But the moment we arrive at the quayside, my opinion of King's Lynn suddenly changes. Firstly, it immediately goes eerily and unnervingly quiet. Secondly, we seem to have stepped into the heart of a beautiful historic town. The Great Ouse, which is faster flowing than its name suggests, has big muddy sandbanks at the sides, the water mid-brown, the colour of chocolate. We wander along the attractive quayside enjoying the calm and the quiet.

King's Lynn is now beautiful but deserted. Seeing as all the parking spaces are full, where the hell are all the people? Obviously in the shops. Brendan pads along happily, with no approaching people to anger or upset him. We walk over deserted cobblestones, along curved streets lined with small, rammed-in cottages and townhouses. No one passes us. No one appears to be taking in the historical splendour of the town. It's disturbingly quiet, there isn't even any sound of traffic and I'm really starting to think something very serious has happened.

We walk along the side of the Minster. I hear voices and see a couple approaching from the other end of the street. I'm quite relieved to see them. I'm about to speak to them and say how weirdly quiet it is, then I realise they're staggering along, each swinging a weighty carrier bag in one hand. The woman is singing and the man's eyes are almost completely closed. As they get nearer I can see they're both swigging from cans of alcohol and are heavily drunk. Maybe they're only drinking because of the impending disaster, whatever it is. They pass us; they don't acknowledge us at all, I'm not sure if they even see us. They totter unsteadily out of sight. Then, more worryingly still, we pass a middle-aged couple sitting on a bench. They're very respectable-looking, business people, but are also drinking cans of cider, which seems so odd and out of place.

I wonder whether the calamity is something like a release of nuclear waste and the end of the human race is in progress, hence very nice couples drinking cans of cider on benches in the mid-morning and people standing staring into space with a sense of doom. It's as though everyone else knows what's happening, the inevitable Armageddon, and I haven't been informed. I hate it when that happens. Brendan, however, is completely unconcerned.

Despite the imminent apocalypse, King's Lynn looks amazing. There are so many beautiful old buildings. We have a siesta and sit on the grass outside the Minster. It's still disturbingly quiet. I sit in the shade of a tree, looking up at the towers against the blue sky. Brendan lies beside me, completely relaxed. He's using the opportunity for a well-earned nap.

I spot a wreath of poppies on a gravestone and suddenly

wonder if today is some sort of remembrance day, possibly 9/11 itself. I don't actually know what the date is, but 9/11 is almost certainly, probably, possibly about ten or twelve weeks away. Perhaps it's some other memorial day of another tragedy and I'm the only person moving around while everyone else has stayed indoors in respectful silence.

We call into a pub opposite the Minster, it's an old building, but has a contemporary interior with sophisticated jazz playing. Only one table is occupied, but at least it isn't deserted with food on plates, still with steam rising, hurriedly abandoned. There are three young female staff standing erect behind the bar, waiting for the customers that haven't come. I order a drink and ask what's going on and why the town seems deserted. The young girl shrugs. "It's not normally like this, it must be the heat. I think everyone must have gone to the coast." But that hardly seems to explain the complete emptiness.

I sit in the window, Brendan spreads out on the cooling parquet flooring. I look out on the empty streets and the pedestrianised square in front of the minster. Suddenly, it's as though some unheard klaxon has gone off, because everything immediately, *instantly* changes. A boy on a skateboard is first, his vehicle rasping along the stone setts of the lane outside, as if that's the signal, people – as one – suddenly appear from all directions and life resumes in King's Lynn. Men, women, children. People with iPods, people walking along texting, people walking along speaking into their phones, people taking photographs. Everything is – thankfully – back to normal.

After food and drink, we have another – unintentional – tour of King's Lynn, at a much more frantic pace, as we try to locate the car park. The shopping area of the town has a very confusing layout and actually seems to be inside out. Time is seriously running out. I need local help. I approach a nice looking, prim lady with a shopping bag. Her eyes widen as I step up to her with my bad-attitude dog, as though she knows her last moment has come. I describe where I've parked and she looks around scratching her head, brow furrowed as though in pain. She eventually gives me very clear and very detailed, firm schoolteacher-like directions. I thank her and follow her advice to the letter – I wouldn't dare do anything else. We emerge at Eagle One exactly as the time expires.

We drive off promptly into the mid-afternoon heat, into the start of the rush hour: the tailbacks, the red tail lights, the rising exhaust fumes – even here – stuck in sweltering heat in a queue of traffic. We cross the Great Ouse, wide and sandy, like the Mississippi. We drive out of King's Lynn, out of Norfolk and on to pastures new, though there are actually few pastures.

Lincolnshire seems like nowhere else I've ever been. The main thing that strikes me is the flatness and the vastness of the land, which seems to be dwarfed by the bloated, oversized sky. The road cuts through farmed fields, now brassicas and potatoes, no cereals. Everything looks a bit less "pretty" though. The fields are no longer an aspect of an attractive landscape; they dominate it. There are few hedges, few trees. The word I'm skating around is *intensive;* it all feels very *intensive.*

We arrive in the agricultural countryside outside Wisbech in the late afternoon. We check in at our campsite, which is very small, surrounded by fields. We immediately go out for a walk along the lanes and trackways around the site, beneath a dull sky of uniform grey. There are views for miles across wide open fields to wind turbines in the distance. Drainage ditches run along the side of the lane, filled with papery reeds which rustle in the steady breeze. It's an eerie landscape; it feels both challenging and a little disconcerting, too open, too low down, too empty... and I love it for all those reasons. Some of the fields are newly ploughed, just rich, brown earth. A line of telegraph poles leads away into the distance like a scene from an American road movie.

When we get back to the site I try sitting out in my deckchair and Brendan lies on the grass, but it's quite chilly. Strange noises are drifting through the air: repetitive, electronic, like the cheesy jingles of a computer game. It turns out to be coming from the summerhouse office, where the site owner gives keyboard lessons on a synthesizer. He has a steady stream of customers throughout the afternoon and their electronic burblings make an appropriately alien soundtrack to this strange, man-made landscape.

Through the hedge a posse of hens are clucking and squawking and flapping continually. I find it really relaxing and Brendan strangely doesn't react to them at all. After dark, they go completely silent. Everything goes completely silent and we have a very peaceful night.

* * * * * * * * * *

I am awoken at the crack of dawn by the cock crowing through the hedge. He's in fine voice, a-doodling for all he's worth. Again, strangely Brendan doesn't react at all; he just keeps on sleeping, steeling himself for the day ahead and those strenuous parts that come between sitting down and napping.

We drive to a Tesco in Wisbech. I'm perusing the alcohol aisle when an old man sidles up to me. "Can I suggest a Bishop's Finger?" I look at him for any hint of a smile. There isn't one. "That's the one to choose if you want a nice, strong ale."

I politely refuse, because if anything I'm looking for a *weaker* drink. I end up choosing water, as I've suddenly decided I'm going to go dry for a week, partly to try and keep my weight down, but also because I'm prone to sinus attacks and alcohol can seriously exacerbate the condition. Today is a particularly bad day for my sinuses and I spend two hours parked in a layby, lying in the van in excruciating pain with a hot water bottle positioned over my face. Brendan – as ever – is glad of the down time and takes the opportunity to have a nap. To me this feels like a waste of a day, especially as I'm still in as much pain when I lift the hot water bottle from my red and swollen face and sit up. The pain seems to be worse, if anything, which doesn't seem possible.

The sunshine from the morning suddenly dissipates. The sky clouds over. We continue on our drive and arrive at a car park along a dead end lane. We go for a walk for some fresh air. This is the Wash, which

I remember from geography lessons at school, a huge area of land reclaimed from the sea. Although I can see for miles, I can see *nothing* for miles. There's nothing to see, just an empty landscape and dull, grey air, thick with water vapour. There's no colour. It's eerily atmospheric. Another line of telegraph poles disappear into the gathering mist. A sign warns about unexploded bombs. As a location it's everything I could want, but I feel terrible.

I feel too ill to continue, too ill to drive far. I feel sick from the pain. On another day I might attempt to stay overnight in this car park. That's the beauty of a van: you're always at home and always have everything you need. But right now I want a hot shower and I want electric hook up; I want warmth and comfort and a feeling of security. This area does not provide a feeling of security.

I phone a few sites in the area, find one with a space and we head there. Although it's still daylight, once in situ I close the curtains over the rain and go to bed. Brendan checks the time in disbelief, then stretches out beside me. He clearly thinks all his Christmases have come at once.

* * * * * * * * * *

I awake the next morning feeling much better. It's a sunny and fine morning, but very cold. We briefly visit Boston, statistically the UK's murder capital, but we're not blown away.

We set off in Eagle One through the farming landscape of large, flat fields bordered with drainage ditches. Hi-viz workers gather cabbages. I do like cabbage but I'm not sure I'd like to live with this smell continually. Crows circle and relocate in newly sown fields.

We visit Skegness and find it *so* bracing. Seagulls are thrown around in the air and dark clouds streak past. Skeggy offers something for everyone. Especially if you like chips and doughnuts.

We walk along the sea wall. An elderly lady with a little dog is striding briskly along the beach below, in the strictly NO DOGS area. She's local and I suspect she adamantly refuses to be told she can't walk on the beach with her dog, when she pays her taxes and has done for over fifty years. She admires Brendan and keeps saying how handsome he is. She reaches out a hand to stroke him. He is disinterested and a little bit rude, but no blood is spilled. I ask her if there's anything to do or see in Skegness other than the beach and the amusements. She thinks for a moment – a long moment – a longer moment – and then shakes her head. "No, there isn't. But he really is a most gorgeous, handsome dog."

We pull up in Mablethorpe. It's damp and grey and miserable. I'm talking about the weather, but that also describes my first impressions of Mablethorpe itself. We walk along the south shore and I apologise for bringing Brendan here. It looks very run down and a mess. A row of beach huts look derelict; they either *look* derelict, or they *are* derelict, the effect is the same. I find it quite depressing. We walk along the concrete promenade, which is dull and characterless. Brendan sniffs and wees and scratches himself, because there's not a lot else to do, but I can tell his heart's not really in it. He's just going through the motions.

There's a café, which looks like an inner-city drop-in centre. We don't drop in. No effort seems to have been made to make this into a welcoming little resort. A lady with a greyhound comes up to us and starts talking. Brendan sniffs the dog, then they studiously ignore each other in an embarrassed silence. The woman has recently moved into the area and for some reason she seems to think we've moved here the day before, I really don't know how that came about, so we have a long conversation at cross purposes. It's odd, because the first thing I asked her was: "Is this actually Mablethorpe?" I'd like to think I'd know it was if I'd just moved here. It turns out it *is* Mablethorpe, but not the right part.

"The main bit's around the corner, along the sea wall. This is South Parade."

"Oh... so the other part's North Parade, is it?"

She looks puzzled. "No... I don't think so, no."

So, that might explain why this isn't a thriving hub of resortness. But it doesn't really excuse why it's quite so horrible.

We walk along the beach towards the promised hub of Mablethorpe. We meet an old lady, who also has a beautiful sleek greyhound. She has a frolic with Brendan – the dog does, not the old lady. She's a bit boisterous for him – the dog, not the old lady – and he sits down in the sand and refuses to play. He's been trying to romance her – the dog, not the old lady (I hope), but she completely takes over proceedings and it ruins the moment for him, so he sits there stubbornly in the sand while she jumps around him – the dog, not the old lady.

The old lady recommends a café further up the prom, then we go on our way. Brendan bounds eagerly away from that emancipated bitch. The dog, not the old lady

The beach is wide open, clean and sandy. There are suddenly several cafes along the prom and herds of pensioners swarming about, preening and basking in the weak sunshine. It starts to feel a bit like a holiday resort.

We meet our third greyhound, the huge and stocky, beefy but not fat, John Boy, an ex-racing greyhound, strong but gentle, a blue-grey colour with beautiful kind eyes and a nose that's a little bit intrusive. The boys do a bit of bonding, then turn and walk in opposite directions.

We find the café recommended by the old lady. It's dog friendly and filled with friendly dogs. We choose to sit outside in the fresh air. Two women at a nearby table are discussing the prices and comparative effectiveness of kitchen roll, like people only do when they're in an advert and aren't real people. I glance around, but can't see any cameras or lights. And certainly no action. Surprisingly, they're two young women in their early twenties, which makes it quite alarming. If this really *is* the filming of an advert, I'm the one in the background staring at them incredulously as they recite their tales of absorbency versus cost.

Mablethorpe isn't too bad after all, as long as you don't go there for riveting conversation. I sip my coffee, listen to the incoming waves and we watch the world go by – mainly on mobility scooters.

Then there's sunny Cleethorpes, where we're provided with irrefutable evidence that people look like their dogs. We're walking along the promenade, with a wave of other Sunday strollers. It's like watching a dog show, there are so many four-legs. Brendan is in his element. Once he's done a micro-sniff he's not interested in them. He's like a train spotter, once he's written their number down in his little book they've lost all value to him and he cuts them dead.

We overtake a middle aged couple, each with a dog. The woman has a greyhound and she's sleek and attractive, the man has a short fat mongrel with a bad attitude. I think that proves the point.

Brendan bolts over to them, to greet their dogs, but both the people react in quite a hostile manner. The man glowers but doesn't say anything and marches off at speed. The woman explains that neither of their dogs like other dogs; though the dogs themselves aren't displaying this. They ought to let their dogs speak for themselves: bark at Brendan and he'll come away.

"Cleethorpes" is another of those resorts you hear in comedy, usually to signify somewhere naff, along with Skegness and Bognor Regis. Just saying it aloud is funny: it sounds comedic. Unfortunately, we don't laugh very much.

* * * * * * * * * *

Dog facts:
The most popular UK dog names are currently Bella, Poppy, Alfie, Lola, Max, Charlie, Luna, Bailey, Teddy and Buddy. (We know examples of all of these.) It comes as no surprise that the name "Brendan" doesn't appear on this list.

Brendan... looking a bit regal. And a bit like a rescue dog.

CHAPTER 8: DOG'S OWN COUNTRY

The drive across the Humber Bridge is a thrilling experience, but far too short. There are panoramic views in both directions over the wide Humber estuary. We're in Yorkshire, often called "God's own country" – but only by Yorkshire people. Yorkshire folk are known for their straight talking ways; they say what they like and they like what they ruddy well say.

We pass through Hull and turn down a small lane. Within minutes we seem far away from civilisation, from everywhere. A straight, single track road cuts across wide open, empty fields, fields of razored stubble. The wheat has been cut and gathered. Straw has been bailed and stands in discoloured blocks. It's a lonely, isolated sort of place. I drive for twenty minutes and nothing changes at all. There are no houses and very few trees. It's another eerie, alien wilderness.

"It's another eerie, alien wilderness, boy." I call over my shoulder.

Brendan, who's half-dozing in his basket, isn't remotely surprised. I'm not sure we agree on holiday destinations.

We carry on ahead and still nothing changes. There are very few features on the map for this area, just a lot of blank paper, but I know we're heading towards an area tantalisingly called Stone Creek. For some time I've been driving towards a house. A lone house. The house at Stone Creek; the aptly named Stone Creek House. It stands alone with a selection of ramshackle outbuildings and a fringe of trees. Balloons are flying from the hedgerows, as though there's a celebration going on. Perhaps they're expecting us. I turn into the drive and pull on the handbrake. The driveway and every spare inch of land around the house is filled with cars.

I leave Brendan to guard the van – he really doesn't find it an imposition, because he had no intention of moving – while I jog to the front door and give it a hearty knock. It's opened immediately by a small, slight, middle-aged man forcing cake nervously into his face. He has a haunted look, like someone's going to take his cake away.

I smile. "Hello. Did I speak to you on the phone?"

He shakes his head, attempting to swallow and hastily wipes his mouth. "No, no... I'm staying on the campsite... I was forced to come in and eat cake."

He doesn't actually look as though he's been coerced. He hurriedly jams more cake into his mouth, then shouts something, which I can't make out.

I realise the hallway and various rooms off it are filled with people mingling, holding glasses of wine and plates of cake. Everyone is eating cake, but not in such a frenzied manner as the chap by the door. It's some sort of party, hence the balloons and all the cars. Word passes from guest to guest and a man - probably in his fifties, with a thick head of greying hair - squeezes his way between the visitors, smiling. He's wearing a bright pink rugby shirt and he radiates good will.

"Hello, hello, welcome. I'm Simon." He grabs my hand and shakes it firmly.

"Hello," I say again. "Was it you I spoke to on the phone earlier?"

"Not me. Might have been my son. Did he sound efficient?" He smiles mischievously. "You don't have to answer that…"

"I think he did, yes."

"It was him then, my son. It wouldn't be me. Come in and have some cake."

I politely decline. "I'm blocking your driveway…"

He shrugs. "Plenty of cake." The party is evidently for his daughter. "She's *about to…*" He makes a heavily pregnant gesture with both hands. "They have a party *before* and *after* the birth now. What's that all about?"

"A way of getting more presents?" I suggest.

He nods. "Well, it's worked."

He tells me to go and help myself to any pitch. I get my wallet out.

"No, no, no… Not at all… No, no, no. Just get yourself comfortable and relaxed first. Oh, the drive's blocked… I'll get some of this lot to move their cars. Most people are going now anyway."

I sprint back to Eagle One. I reverse out onto the lane. People come flooding from the house, running to their cars, as though they've just been released. Engines spark to life, wheels spin on gravel, vehicles reverse, some do three point turns, others turn in wide arcs and exit. Within two minutes, most of the cars have gone.

I drive into an orchard, which contains the campsite. There are a few caravans, which look like they're permanent. The only other touring visitor is the Cake Eating Man, who walks past and waves, then wades through the long grass to his tiny van. It's in the middle of a field at an odd angle and looks like it's crashed there or been dropped from an aircraft.

I switch off the engine and immediately saddle up my boy to go for an exploration of this weird and wonderful place.

Stone Creek House is like nowhere else on Earth. It's like a film set of weirdness. The house stands alone on this side of the creek, a huge house, modern and not especially attractive, but full of character. And full of *characters*. Behind it is a high protective grassy bank, intended to keep the temperamental Humber at bay. There are several boats around the house, all in varying states of repair, or disrepair would be more accurate, some are way beyond repair, sinking into the earth and decaying, others could be saved but most probably won't be. I find the toilet. It's an "Eco-toilet": you flush it with a jug from a barrel of rain water.

Brendan sniffs at everything and wees on a few bushes

and trees. As we explore, he edges his way cautiously up to the doorways of the various sheds and outbuildings that huddle around the big house, peering curiously inside. Many are dusty and covered in cobwebs and no one has used them for years. It might sound like the place is a dump, but it isn't, it's exactly how it should be, largely overgrown, rambling, quirky. It's isolated: it stands completely alone. You could hate it here, but I don't. There's no village, there's no shop, there's no pub. There's no one. There's nothing.

You may have noticed, the places that really excite me aren't the pretty chocolate box villages, but the places that are somehow challenging, harsh, isolated, unusual, like Dungeness and now Stone Creek. This is one of the most exciting places I have ever been.

We trot past the front of the house. A hatchback is pulled up outside the main door, the back seats are down and it's loaded and almost completely full of gift boxes and bags; the daughter has stashed her spoils and is preparing to go home. We walk along the straight lane towards the Creek. Stone Creek is a small natural harbour, with several boats moored and bobbing on the rising Humber water. It would be easy to think the harbour and the boats have been abandoned. Stone Creek seems abandoned, forgotten and timeless.

It's windy. Something tells me it's always windy here. There is very little shelter, nothing to stop the wind coursing over the empty fields. The clouds are rolling, their undersides grey. The lighting across this bleak landscape has an eerie yellow hue. We head back to the site just as the first drops of rain begin to fall.

I knock on the door of the house, because I'm keen to pay Simon; I don't like owing money, it makes me edgy. He comes to the door, says I shouldn't have bothered and tries to force cake on me again. When I hand him the tenner, he says. "Oh, thank you for this! Thank you." as though I'm giving him a gift, rather than money I owe him.

Brendan meets a Labrador from one of the caravans and they embark on Brendan's favourite game: You wee on the tree; I wee on the tree. You wee on the hedge; I wee on the hedge. You wee on the wall; I wee on the wall. You walk off and I re-wee on the tree, the hedge and the wall, therefore I win. It's a game that he's never lost yet.

After tea, the rain stops, so we go for a walk following a footpath along the high bank which runs behind Stone Creek House. The mighty Humber flows beyond a rough grassy flood plain. Across the water is Immingham, with a skyline of cranes and gantries of the docks and the tall, slim chimneys of a chemical works. There are streaking flames, as excess gases are being burned off. The rest of the landscape around Stone Creek is dark and empty, with no warming village lights: no lights at all.

Brendan makes himself a nest under the hedge next to the van, curls up tightly and falls fast asleep. Perhaps this is a habit from his street dog days.

Very few cars pass along the solitary road just beyond the hedge. Those that do are going nowhere, because there's nowhere to go. And there are very few people living in the area. For that reason we both *love* Stone Creek. It's another of those bizarre, almost unearthly places. It's full of open space, atmosphere and not much else. Wish you were here? Probably not, but we love it.

As the darkness descends fully, I coax Brendan inside and he curls up again and goes straight back to sleep. It's windy and cold as I batten down the hatches for the night.

* * * * * * * * *

It's a bit of a grey and breezy start, but that's fine by us. Like Dungeness, Stone Creek really suits bad weather. We go for an early walk along the Humber, which doesn't go down too well with Brendan, because of his Not Before Ten rule.

We return to Eagle One and Brendan climbs into his basket, sighs heavily and tries to catch up on the missing hour of sleep, while I start the engine and drive off, along straight roads across an empty landscape. Although it's not tall, I can see the spire of the church at Sunk Island from a long way off, standing at a crossroads. This is figuratively the village centre, simply because there is nothing else. Sunk Island is a scattered community of farmsteads and isolated houses. It is reclaimed land, originally a sandbank in the river estuary. For me, it has everything, which is to say, nothing. Nothing at all.

I drive along an open road, a ditch on one side, a massive field of wheat chaff on the other. Outside it's grey and cold. Inside, I've got the heater on, I have my music, I have my dog. This is living. Again, I'm aware that I really am living the dream. Though it would certainly be some people's nightmare.

I negotiate a number of lonely lanes, knowing they're dead ends, just to see where they lead and to make the most of this otherworldly experience. It's harsh and blustery; I absolutely love it. I'm quite sorry when I eventually see a road sign at a junction, pointing to civilisation: houses, pavements, street lights, and I realise the Sunk Island continuum is coming to an end.

But even when we're back in the normal world, things are not totally normal, because we're driving on a peninsula; everything seems to be getting smaller and tighter. The sea is closing in on one side, the wide Humber estuary on the other. It feels like we're running out of land. Mainly because we are actually running out of land.

Kilnsea is a small hamlet, the last one before the narrow Spurn Head spit. Like Happisburgh and many other places along the East coast, Kilnsea is falling into the sea. The parish church was consumed by the waves a century ago and the sea has continued its work ever since. The road stops abruptly. If you look down you can see the rest of it – huge slabs of concrete – on the sandy and debris-strewn beach below.

Also like Happisburgh, a site of static caravans stands on the edge of the cliff. The nearest dull green box opens its door almost directly onto the cliff edge. A military base formerly occupied the area. Most of the buildings and gun emplacements lie on the beach, where they have fallen, and a few remain stubbornly clinging on, ready to collapse and join their fallen comrades at a moment's notice. It's a fascinating place, filled with historic remains, but tinged with sadness, because nothing *can* and nothing *will* stop this continual erosion.

Living on the edge. The cliff edge at Kilnsea.
Brendan poses in black and white – which he's not happy to do, as he feels his colours are wasted in monochrome – and he's quite right.

A short way along the beach, a man is waving frantically and comes wading urgently through the sand towards us. The wind is blowing his eyebrows upwards and he looks like a werewolf. "Where's the cliff gone?" he asks desperately.

I look to where he's indicating. At this point there is definitely no cliff, just a huge expanse of sandy soil leading from the land to the sea.

"It was right there! And it's gone!" Werewolf Ron has a static caravan on the doomed site. He tells me he comes here every fortnight. "Two weeks ago there was a cliff... an eight or ten foot cliff!"

Werewolf Ron is very animated and waves his arms liberally as he speaks. Brendan sits down and watches him with interest, but strangely doesn't react at all to Ron's aerobic workout, possibly because he recognises him as a fellow canine.

"But it's gone! The whole cliff's gone! It must have collapsed!"

There is definitely no cliff right here and weirdly, there's no sign that there has ever been one. But he's right. On my last visit there *was* a cliff. But it has evidently been washed away, leaving only a sandy plateau.

We continue along the road on foot, which is, was or should be the road to Spurn Head, a headland at the tip of a narrow spit of land that stretches for three miles or more out into the wide estuary of the Humber. But when we get to the end of the road, it's blocked off; you can no longer drive along it. A severe storm in 2017 washed away a whole section of the spit, marooning the little community of Lifeboat men and their families who lived at the Head, making it Britain's newest island.

We set off towards Spurn Head along the beach, which is littered with bricks and upturned pillboxes, sinking ever deeper into the sand. We walk almost to the new island, but Brendan is tired and really flagging. He sits down in the white sand and refuses to go any further. He reasons that we've already walked several miles and have to walk back, and he's got a point. I think this signals the end of our foray to Spurn, which is windswept, moody and unforgiving. It gets frequent bad weather and violent storms. It can be cold, wet, windy and unrelenting. Obviously, I love it.

I'm less of a fan of nearby RAF Holmpton, a military base housing a former Cold War era nuclear bunker, which is open to visitors. I had been on the tour on my last visit to the area. There were nine people in the tour party – I was there alone; the rest of the group was made up of four couples: me and four very *insular* couples, who all studiously avoided eye contact with me at all times. If Brendan had been with me, they would still have avoided eye contact, but for very different reasons.

The tour guide was a very spritely, very old fashioned retired soldier, complete with handlebar moustache and beret. The tour was quite in-depth and very depressing. It brought back a lot of bad memories. Like many generations all over the world, I grew up with the very real threat of nuclear annihilation. It was very present in our lives, but perhaps I dwelt on it a lot more than others. It was a constant threat, it seemed inevitable. It was just a waiting game.

To make matters worse, a short distance from our suburban family home, there was a bleach works on the banks of the River Mersey. Every morning they sounded a wailing klaxon to call the workers in. And every morning, *every single morning*, I lay in bed fearing it was the four minute warning. I lay there rigid and sweating and waiting for the bombs to hit. It didn't matter that it had happened yesterday and every day, because supposing today it was the real thing? It was a terrible way to start the day and it was probably the single most defining event of my life. I never expected to grow up.

So I drive past RAF Holmpton and its chain link fences, because I don't need reminders.

I pull over in a layby on the outskirts of Withernsea, so I can make a phone call, as I'm trying to book us a campsite for the night. The very bored man on the other end says: "Yes, we've got space." Then suddenly, without being prompted, he asks: "Have you got a dog?"

No one has ever asked that before. I assume it's because he's about to unleash their strict NO DOGS policy.

"Yes." I say reluctantly. "I have."

"What type?"

"He's a mongrel."

"Can you describe him?"

Of course I can describe him. I can describe him all day long... until somebody actually asks, that is, then I apparently go completely blank.

I turn and look at him, curled up on his sofa. "Well, he's... mixed race. *Breed*, I mean. Mixed *breed*. He's... medium sized, probably... But most people seem to think he's *large*, but I don't. I'd say he's at the large end of medium... or the small end of large... but I'm talking height, not build... He's very slim build... Too slim really. He's got a definite terrier face, Alsatian colouring... black and tan... Slim body...Oh I've said that...Brown eyes and... matinee idol good looks."

The man doesn't laugh, but simply says; "OK, that's fine. Call in... if you want to. Or don't... it doesn't really matter."

We continue into Withernsea, which calls itself a seaside resort, but that isn't really how I would describe it. I wouldn't call it a seaside town, I'd call it a town. It's on the coast and the beach is nice… but there seems to be very little effort to be accommodating to the visitor. Some of the shopping streets are awful, pre-fabricated concrete affairs which look like inner-city clearance zones.

Withernsea has suffered from a steady decline in visitors. If I had to use one word to describe the town, it would be *shabby*. No, *jaded*. *Shabby* and *jaded*. And *a bit tired*. Yes, if I had to choose one word, it would be those three.

Brendan is not at all impressed. We don't stop. We decide to abandon the campsite there and move on completely. We continue along winding lanes. Brendan is doing fine with travelling now. He's adjusted brilliantly and he loves being in the van. At one time these meandering roads would have had him vomiting everywhere.

We pass through some lovely pastoral Yorkshire countryside and some picturesque stone villages. A painted sign at the entrance to Aldborough, says simply JESUS IS THE ANSWER. I just don't know what the question is.

I skirt Bridlington and pitch-up at a very small site on the chalk peninsular of Flamborough Head. There is only one other pitch occupied by a caravan. When we walk past I can hear their television from inside and glimpse an older couple. From their attached awning a slim and very old grey dog moves shakily towards

Brendan, sniffing him tentatively. They stand nose to nose for several seconds. She is a beautiful, fragile dog; she's curious, but nervous and she breaks my heart. Brendan is very soft and gentle with her. He knows she's old and frail and seems to be exhibiting real compassion. Either that or he's just deftly pick-pocketed her pension book.

While I make tea, Brendan sits outside on the grass. He suddenly starts barking. He's staring through the boundary fence, across open fields. Staring back at him is what at first I take to be a huge, savage dog, but impossibly big. And deformed. It has devil horns and a long, evil pointed face. It stands stock still. It's eyes seem to be huge and fiery, and they stare like a creature possessed...

This impression probably owes something to the fact that I know we're currently within the so-called "Wolds Triangle", a location where many strange things are alleged to happen. There have been several reports of huge wild beasts, a werewolf, strange disappearances and regular UFO activity. Is it any surprise the classic horror film *An American Werewolf in London* begins in Yorkshire?

Brendan is still barking and jumping up and down, straining at his lead. I look again at the creature in the field and I realise it's not a supernatural beast, it's a deer. A wild deer. It's eyes are neither huge nor fiery and it isn't even *remotely* like a werewolf. This is how legends and rumours start. The deer lollops away and disappears through a fringe of trees. Satisfied with his conduct, Brendan chalks up another success and flops down on the grass for a rest.

* * * * * * * * * *

Flamborough Head is part of the only chalk sea cliff in the north of Britain. Brendan doesn't want to come out, because he hates chalk sea cliffs and he feels like a nap after our long morning walk. So, I set off alone into the café. At first I mistakenly think I've walked into a bordello, but it's just the exuberant trumpet flourishes of *The Legend of Xanadu* by Dave Dee, Dozy, Beaky, Mick & Tich. The café looks a bit 'Seventies, but sounds a bit 'Sixties. The next song to play is Manfred Mann's *The Mighty Quinn.*

I manage to embarrass myself, because I've run out of money and can't scrape up enough to pay for my drink and they won't take a card for the paltry sum of a cup of coffee. I stand at the till rifling through my pockets for any stray money that might have miraculously appeared, while the bored waitress yawns and sighs. All the seated customers turn and silently watch. I haven't got enough, so I have to jog back to Eagle One and raid my emergency parking fund, which is also down to the last dregs. I haven't seen a bank machine for days and I'm literally, completely and utterly out of cash. I just about manage to gather a pile of coppers and five pences to pay the bill.

I sit in the odd café, with odd people staring at me as though I'm a down and out – which technically I suppose I am, as I currently have no money. I wish I hadn't bothered. Because I don't have Brendan with me nobody at all speaks to me, which is probably a blessing, but I'm treated like a weird, dog-free pariah and I don't like it. Brendan gives me a certain credibility and a lot of confidence. And quite often a lot of stress.

I hop back on board Eagle One, awake my dog with a cuddle then drive off. I'm so excited about our next site, right on the cliffs, a short way along the coast at Bempton. It's an open, grassy site and as usual, I choose a pitch as far away from anyone else as possible. It's breezy but the sun is shining. We sit outside on the grass in this glorious scenery. We're both so relaxed and at peace... and that doesn't come very naturally to either of us.

There have been so few times on this journey when I've actually stopped and enjoyed a moment without thinking ahead, planning ahead, metaphorically looking at my watch and rushing onwards. Today, I want to sit in this field and relax with my boy and that's what we're doing.

When we're good and rested, we head along the path towards Bempton Cliffs. There's a grassy clifftop path. There's a sheer drop to the blue-grey ocean, just the wind and the rustling of the grasses. There are no buildings in sight.

For a while, we're walking towards what looks like a person, but it's stationary for far too long to be flesh and blood. As we draw closer, I can see it's a humanoid figure. Humanoid-*ish*. Then definite features begin to evolve, but they aren't very human after all, which perhaps isn't that odd, because we already know this area has an unusually high UFO tally. Its head is large, oversized, bulbous, but its face is pointed. But it turns out it isn't actually an alien. It's carved out of wood and it's a puffin: a giant puffin. A rather vexed giant puffin at that. Brendan goes up to it, he obviously recognises its vaguely human outline and is curious. He stands facing it, his ears and tail blowing in the breeze, and he appears to be having a conversation with it. When he fails to get any response from it, he turns and storms off.

Brendan chatting with the wooden puffin...
And getting bored.

We sit down beside the strange sculpture for ages, Brendan has positioned himself on my knee, and is enjoying the sights, sounds and smells of his surroundings. He's very much a watcher and a thinker. I feel totally at peace and, evidently, so does he. I regret deeply that this trip hasn't been more about enjoying the present and the experiences, living in the moment. *Being* in the moment. I've tried enjoying the experience of the now – it's the only true freedom – but it's very difficult.

I don't think I'm cut out to live in a town. I don't like it. I hate having to walk Brendan at home, or rather I hate the walks themselves; I hate trudging along suburban streets to a concrete fringed field, compared to being somewhere like this, with the openness, the views, the flora, the fauna, the fresh air and the feeling of being free. I live in a nice area, but it's not the same walking on concrete. It's not the same at all. I could live here, or I could live at Sunk Island or Dungeness; I wouldn't miss the city, I wouldn't miss shops or retail parks, I wouldn't miss the cinema or the theatre. I would only miss Nicky. She would hate living here and would miss all the things I wouldn't.

I suddenly feel annoyed with myself because I've *yet again* been tricked out of a very contented state and am now very poignant and not immersed in the here and now, but I can't shake off this rather pensive and reflective mood.

We set off again along the grassy clifftop path and I attempt to focus on the present and the beauty around me: the sea air and the calling of the sea birds and Brendan's happy tail weaving between the tall grasses.

We meet a nice couple with a beautiful Romanian dog.

Brendan introduces himself. We trade tales - while the dogs trade tails - about the trials and tribulations of rescue dogs; they discuss the uncertainty of adopting new humans. We talk and sniff for some time. I realise if I didn't have Brendan I would probably have finished the trip ages ago, because no one would have spoken to me in months.

Bempton Cliffs is a nature reserve, run by the RSPB. It is home to the only mainland breeding colony of gannets in England. Gannets have a wing span of up to two metres, making them the UKs largest sea bird. They are predominantly white, but their heads are yellow and their wing tips are dipped in chocolate. The sky is filled with them and the air is alive with their constant calling. Considering Brendan barks when a bird flies over the garden at home, he seems completely uninterested in the gannets. Possibly because he knows he's seriously outnumbered.

We head towards the RSPB centre; as it's approaching 5pm the place is in a frenzy of closing, despite it being a sunny day and the cliffs being crawling with bird spotters. It epitomises this country's "can't be bothered", half-arsed, sedentary, nine to five, "them's the rules", small town, small-minded, small change, never change, insular, indolent, intolerant attitude.

So, instead we wander back to Eagle One, we have our tea and we bed down for the night. I have cleverly picked the perfect spot for our pitch, so that I can have the curtains open and watch the lighthouse at night. Once it's dark, the beam sweeps across the landscape, it's a visual spectacle. Unfortunately, Brendan barks furiously every time the beam sails past. I manage to get him calmed down, but then on the next rotation he sets off again. In the end, I have to close the curtains on the amazing light, so my plans were in vain. I'm starting to think that apart from our affection for *Carry On* films, we don't actually have a lot in common.

* * * * * * * * * *

We're still in "God's Own Country " and heading ever northwards. Yorkshire historically had a battle with the folks across the border in Lancashire. Many would say they're still at war. There is certainly a friendly rivalry – not always that friendly. I'm actually a Lancastrian by birth. I was born in the centre of Manchester, before boundaries were rejigged for the umpteenth time and Manchester was still undeniably in the Red Rose County. Bearing in mind the War of the Roses and rivalry – friendly or otherwise – I plan to keep my secret past just that: a secret.

We drive a short way down the coast to Filey and Brendan stretches his legs in a formal little park, sniffing at the roses in the well-tended flower beds, but probably sniffing for dog wee rather than a fine floral fragrance. The park is genteel and charming. Best of all, there's an orangery tearoom.

I order from the nice lady, who might be called Janet. "In't it a lov'ly day?" she says aloud to no one in particular.

"Aye!" one of the regulars pipes up. "At least when it's like this you don't have to put your heating on!"

I suppress a smile. That isn't the *only* reason for being happy that it's a beautiful day, but it's nice that the locals are making an effort with stereotyping.

I sit outside with my boy, in the free and tax deductible sunshine. It's a sheltered spot with a view of the sea. Brendan is leaning against my legs affectionately. It's all too good, something must surely go wrong. And yes, my glass is *always* half empty, that way I'm seldom caught off guard by what life throws at me.

We meander around the park afterwards, listening to the locals:

"'Ow do?"

"Int it lovely, eh?"

"Aye, it's grand!"

A vagrant in a bobble hat, with a white whiskery beard sits dozing on a bench. There's an electronic ringing; he jerks into consciousness and answers his mobile. He isn't a vagrant at all, he's a businessman, but he certainly looks like a vagrant. But then again, so do I.

We walk to the headland, which is supposedly – according to legend – a sleeping dragon. Brendan sniffs it and concludes that it definitely isn't. We walk back via the promenade, the tide now far out. No dogs are allowed on this beach, so anyone and everyone with a dog is strolling along the prom. It's like Dog Club. (What happens in Dog Club stays in Dog Club.) There is an awful lot of sniffing going on. People are all over

Brendan, bending to stroke him. I'm really anxious, but because everyone has a dog and smells of dogs, they're generally safe.

"What's he called?"

"Brendan."

"Oh, how *lovely!*"

"*Is it?* He came with his name. I didn't choose it."

"Ah... He looks like a Brendan!"

He doesn't. He looks like a Pavlov, Dimitri or Andropov.

A strange, deep droning starts up. Everyone on the prom, in unison, looks up at the sky. And nobody moves. It's like a surreal scene from *The Prisoner* or something. There are gasps and a lot of pointing. Two planes, old prop planes, are criss-crossing the clear cornflower blue of the sky, and spiralling, as though engaged in a dog fight. It's really strange and everyone is mesmerised. I blink and they've both disappeared and the noise has cut out. Everyone stays for a few minutes scanning the skies, but the planes have definitely gone, then everyone carries on as normal and the planes are completely forgotten. My scientific mind assumes there is a rational explanation; I just don't know what it is. No one else seems remotely concerned about it, so perhaps I shouldn't be either.

Brendan sees a white van parked on the marine road and heads gleefully towards it. I point out it isn't *his* van, but he doesn't seem to think that's a problem, but

I don't let him enter the strange van, despite the side door being open.

Once back in the correct van, he has a nice sleep while I drive along the coast to our site just outside Scarborough, Britain's first seaside resort. We walk back into Scarborough via clifftop paths, over a headland and down steps to the end of the prom. There is a nice sandy beach, full of people engaged in traditional family seaside activities, paddling, building sand castles, burying their dads, sunbathing, checking Facebook, smoking and arguing.

A grandad holding the hand of a young child is coming towards us. "Elliot," Grandad says, "There's a pub over there. Are you going to have a pint of beer or a glass of wine?"

The little boy sighs wearily. "Neither, Grandad... I'm going to have *water*, because I'm *six!*" It's delivered with such disdain, a cynicism way beyond his six years. That child will surely go a long way.

We find our way into Peasholm Park, where the boating lake water is famously dyed green, which has caused some controversy over the years. Brendan trots alongside me, a little wearily, but perfectly at peace with the approaching people. He's being remarkably relaxed in fact. Brendan doesn't bark at the green water, nor at the ducks, nor at the dragon-shaped boats or the cascading waterfall. I really hope this isn't the calm before the storm.

There's a nicely placed café overlooking the lake with a

lovely terrace. It's only 3.30 but the café is closing. Staff are waddling about and every time someone stands up, the chair is whipped from beneath them. On a sunny day in summer this is too early to be wrapping up business; the park is crowded and people are being turned away.

We find a way back to the sea. Poor Brendan is getting tired. He again tries to gain illegal access to a white removal van, but is cast out. I think he's had enough now, so we walk very slowly back to the site.

Once in Eagle One, Brendan installs himself in his usual place on the settee, taking up 87% of the available space. He prepares himself for a long and welcome evening of napping.

* * * * * * * * * *

It's a Friday. Again. Probably. The weeks are spiralling by so fast. I'm sure time should be going slower for me, because I'm doing new things, seeing new places; I'm getting a lot of new sensory input, which is what scientists believe determines how fast time appears to pass for us. For children it's slower, because everything is new to them, so there is a lot of data to process, but as we get older we do less and less that's new and different. It really is healthy to do something new every day, or at least once in a while.

I'm seeing places I've never seen before, so why is time going so fast? I love travelling and I love exploring and I love spending all day with Brendan, but every morning – especially when I'm having a wash, I think "What, a new day, already?" And the same at night, when I'm brushing my teeth – "Another day's gone, already?" I'm pretty sure Brendan feels the same. His brown eyes have such a depth, he's clearly either contemplating existentialism or planning a heist.

It's still grey and cold as we step down onto the rain-wet pavement in Ravenscar, a remote coastal village that was planned as a holiday resort to rival Scarborough and Whitby. Roads were laid out, sewers were dug, but no one was interested. Ravenscar remains the town that never was.

We set off for a walk in the light drizzle. The first building we pass is the foreboding Raven Hall, a solid and rather sinister-looking house on the cliff edge. It's every inch the sort of brooding, isolated house where you might host a dinner party, late one thundery night and murder each of your guests. We're already planning our guestlist.

A footpath joins the cliff edge and there are good views along the coast. We walk for quite a way to a 1940s Radar station, made up of a crumbling Nissen hut and other low brick buildings. This base was replaced by the famous trio of "golf balls" at Fylingdales, out on the North York Moors, which I love. Loved. Still love; they may be gone but they were so iconic; they are part of our history and heritage.

Back on the cliff path, a couple and their miserable looking greyhound come towards us. They both have their hoods up. Brendan makes a beeline for the dog, who doesn't have his hood up. I say: "Is he OK to say hello?"

The woman points to her ears and says overly loudly: *"I've got music on! I can't hear you!"*

I hesitate, thinking she means "One second, I'll turn my music off." She doesn't; she doesn't turn her music off or remove her earphones. They both walk past me.

I stare after them. "How bloody rude!" I say to Brendan, but he ignores me and walks off.

I hurry after him. The rain is getting steadily heavier; Brendan is on a mission to get back to the van. He doesn't stop and sniff again, he doesn't wee on any trees or gateposts; he presses on, pulling slightly with a dogged determination. He hates rain.

Back in Eagle One, I slide the door shut over the bouncing raindrops and we towel ourselves down. We leave Ravenscar, skirting the North York Moors: rolling, open moorland, yellowed grass, bleak and naked; it's dramatic and beautiful. I spot the aforementioned RAF Fylingdales in the distance on the top of a hill. The station was built in 1962. Its main function was to detect incoming missile attacks: the dreaded "four minute warning" which haunted my childhood. It also spies on spy satellites; it's the spy's spy. The motto of RAF Fylingdales is the Latin *"Vigilamus"*, which – although it might sound like a cream for an intimate complaint – actually means "We're watching". And I don't doubt that.

The three original 'golf balls' or "radomes", were replaced in the 'Eighties by the stark, white, oddly angled and incongruous structure visible today. It's known as "the Pyramid", though technically it's a truncated tetrahedron. It's full title is the Solid State Phased Array Radar – or the SSPAR. So if someone says "I'm just nipping down the SSPAR" – they may be gone a while.

The windscreen wipers scrape rain from the window. Outside the air is heavy and grey. Perhaps it's me, but nothing is delivering today.

We drop down into Robin Hood's Bay, which is attractive enough, but is essentially a "tourist village" full of cafes and gift shops. It now seems to be filled with "locals" who aren't remotely local, who have their second homes here and complain all the time about holiday-makers.

The main street heads steeply downhill, right onto the beach. The last building on the left is the aptly named Bay View Hotel. The seats outside seem to be the province of dogs and men, but not a single woman. I don't know if it's a fluke or a Yorkshire thing, but it seems odd. Brendan pulls to go over; I'm not sure whether it's to see the dogs or have a pint, but I resist.

Today I feel like we're tourists. Tourists with a capital "T". We're tourists in a tourist village, wandering about with the other tourists who are wandering about, actively looking for something to do to occupy ourselves. Brendan trails along with me, but it isn't his sort of place either.

We decide to move on along the coast to Whitby, where

I part-own a car park. At least that's what I gather, judging by how much I pay to park. I assume I'm buying a share in the business.

Whitby is the most gothic place in Yorkshire and probably the most gothic place in Britain, thanks to its dalliance with Dracula. In his classic novel, Bram Stoker tells how the Count arrives via a ship, *The Demeter*, which is washed ashore here. The dominating and inescapable ruins of the abbey on the East Cliff really help the gothic image. It looms menacingly over the town; it is Whitby's oldest and most prominent landmark.

The abbey, Whitby.

Now, I do like Whitby. I came a few years ago, but Brendan has never been... unless he was washed ashore here when he came over from Bulgaria... which wouldn't surprise me. The problem is, everyone else likes Whitby as well and its tight little streets are packed with holiday-makers. It's far too busy and Brendan is jittery and nervous, so we abort almost immediately.

We end up with the next best thing: a perfect little campsite with views over the abbey and the sea. This is more like it. Brendan thoroughly approves and has a sit down on the grass to celebrate, but not for long. The only other campers are a middle-aged couple with their fluffy little dog called Bobby. Bobby and Brendan have an instant rapport and roll about on the grass together.

The couple are very friendly and ask about our plans for tomorrow.

"We're moving on." I tell them. "This is just a stop-over for us."

"You going round the coast?"

"Yes."

The wife nods knowingly. "Thought so. That's *his* thing." She nods towards her husband. "He wants to do that. He was thinking of getting a camper van and doing it."

She seems less keen. That seems to be the way; the men are keen, the women are very resistant.

The boys play for a while until Bobby has to go in: "Bobby, come on. You can play out later, but your cup of tea is getting cold." And off he scampers.

I tried Brendan with tea when he first moved in. He hated it. He is such a fussy eater. I can only assume that when he was homeless in Bulgaria he checked the Michelin star rating of a restaurant before he went through their bins.

We haven't had a great day, but at least we've been together. We watch the light fade over the satanic ruins of the abbey, until it's lost from sight. It's cold and windy outside, but it's warm and cosy inside.

* * * * * * * * * *

Dog facts:
Dogs find it much easier to see a moving person or object than a stationary one. With that in mind, next time I need to run away from a dog, I'm going to stand still and pretend to be a tree... surely the worst that can happen is I get wet feet.

CHAPTER 9: RUNNING OUT OF ENGLAND.

The weather is dull and overcast as I drive through dull and overcast residential areas towards the coast of County Durham. We arrive at what was once known as *the Poisoned Shore*, because large quantities of colliery waste were dumped here. We have a short walk along one stretch, which looks like it's made out of clinker. Brendan tiptoes along, but doesn't stop and sniff anything, which is very unusual. It's barren, it's desolate; the ground looks dead and nothing grows. I don't like it, so I pack the boy back in the van and we move a short way along the coast, where there is a marked contrast. There is a sandy beach, though the sand is unusually dark, and above it is a grassy wildflower meadow. This is where Michael Caine gets got in *Get Carter*, not that it bears any resemblance.

Brendan skitters about in the long grass, barking at butterflies. Out in the turbulent sea, half a dozen big ships and tankers are moored towards the dark horizon. When he notices, he starts barking at them as well.

The campsite I've booked is part of a farm. It's basic, but has a sea view. The mutton-chopped farmer comes and taps on the rear door of Eagle One. Brendan goes frenzied; he hates people tapping on the door of his van. I hold his collar and open the door. Without speaking, the farmer looks around the van.

"You haven't got a toilet, have you?" I'm not too sure if he's just checking or actually wants to use it.

"No."

"I always say "own san essential"."

"I booked online. In the search it came up as "pet friendly" and "has a toilet"."

"I can't be responsible for that. I say "own san essential"."

"Right. But it didn't say that."

"There *is* a toilet."

"OK. So..."

"But it's for backpackers."

"Right..."

"They come here, the backpackers... They get off the train and they walk here... They can't carry a toilet with them."

Brendan is still snarling.

"No... they can't."

"Not when they're on foot, walking, they can't."

"No..."

"So it's for them, the toilet."

"Right."

"But there aren't any."

"There aren't?"

"Backpackers... No. Not at the moment. There's only you. And you're only here for one night."

"Yes..." I say thankfully. "I really am. Just one night."

"So you can use the toilet."

"Right... Thanks."

"So it's not going to cause me a big issue."

I was under the impression it already had done. "Right. OK. Good."

And off he goes, muttering to himself.

As it happens, I don't go anywhere even *remotely* near his toilet, because it's in the farmyard, outside the farmhouse – in the vicinity of the farmer – and I'm worried that he'll see me from the window and come out and subject me to another pointless and bizarre conversation like the one I just endured. One was enough.

On the site there's a large rally underway. They are all members of a caravan rallying club. There are around a hundred people in that one group and just me and my dog in the other. As usual, we're the odd couple on the outside looking in. I wouldn't have it any other way.

They have a big top and there's entertainment on. I keep hearing the compere through his PA system. They seem to be auctioning cabbages to raise funds for the club. The current lot has got up to an exciting 30 pence as we set off to the beach.

The rollers are rolling, the breakers are breaking; the tide is coming and a flock of little terns are nesting in the sandhills. Brendan suddenly starts barking. It could be a little tern, or a wave, or some sand, or a shell, or some air. He's looking out to sea. He's again spotted the line of moored ships and for some reason perceives them as a threat. I have to drag him away.

Back on the site, the inevitable evening of Karaoke has started. An older woman sings Abba's *Does Your mother Know*, which makes the whole concept *even more* disturbing than when Bjorn sings it. Through the windscreen the ocean is blending into the sky. The lights are coming on in those isolated, lonely vessels. And here am I, in my isolated, lonely vessel. Brendan is asleep, sleeping off his tea, or his walk, or something, he generally doesn't need an excuse. He wakes up suddenly and starts barking at the twinkling lights on the ships – he's really got it in for those ships – so I have to close the curtains.

The karaoke finishes, which you'd think I'd be grateful for, but during the entertainment, all the ralliers were contained in the marquee, now it's over they're free range. They're everywhere, laughing and shouting. I resign myself to a night of non-stop barking.

* * * * * * * * * *

Sunday morning. Windy, grey. It's an exposed spot. The front curtains are open, giving me a view out of the windscreen to the distant ships. As if he hadn't got enough mileage from them yesterday, Brendan barks at all the ships again, then gets resettled and has a quick nap after the exertion.

A group of little terns fly across the sky, white, slim, stream-lined. There are about fifty of them – and one solitary, ungainly, dirty pigeon. How does that happen? Did he get caught up in the big white confusion? Or was he seeing them off his land? Or was he being kidnapped? And if so, ought I to call for help? Or perhaps he was actually part of the posse, part of the family: a brother from another egg. Whatever the case, there is surely a metaphor or a nursery rhyme in there somewhere.

We're going to leave old Durham town, almost as soon as we've arrived. We hit the road and cut through Tyne and Wear. I love the northeast accent, with its odd stresses, its singsong quality, its expressiveness and the range and effort they put in. It's an accent to be proud of. By comparison, my local accent – Mancunian – is lazy and flat, smoking a spliff and wearing a shell suit.

We arrive early at our campsite in South Shields. I've been to this site once before, many years ago and it was a very odd experience. Instead of having a defined pitch, I was told to wedge my van on a patch of grass next to the wreck of a caravan that had collapsed in on itself.

This time, the collapsed caravan has gone. Instead, I'm told to pull up on a rough area of gravel at an odd angle, sandwiched between a wooden bin enclosure and the main driveway, overlooked by the neighbouring housing estate. The majority of the site is tightly packed static caravans, with just a small, scruffy, haphazard area for a few touring vans. For the extortionate price they're charging, I really expect a lot better, but it's the perfect location for visiting Souter Lighthouse. Over the roofs of the static caravans I can see the sea, which looks very dark and brooding.

Souter Lighthouse dominates this stretch of coastline. It's red and white, and one of the few lighthouses owned by the National Trust, so you can have the full sanitised experience and also buy some jam. I don't do either, thanks to Brendan. But we do sit as far away from the crowds and look at the lighthouse for a while.

We then wander in the direction of the beach, but pass a makeshift shrine at the top of the cliff, with photographs and flowers, to a young man who committed suicide by driving his car off the cliff at this point. As with Beachy Head, there is a sign for the Samaritans. TALK TO US. I had never really associated this place with suicide, but it turns out to be a suicide blackspot. Some places are obvious, like Beachy Head and the Humber Bridge, but here? But then again, this is a densely populated conurbation, and these cliffs provide an opportunity, so of course they've been utilised.

We're in a very sombre mood as we descend the narrow steps to the beach. I sit on a boulder, Brendan lies in a rockpool. Nestling at the foot of the cliffs, is Marsden Grotto, a pub built against the rockface, but extending back into it. We sit outside on the veranda. I have a pint of lager; I'm hereby breaking my alcohol fast on purpose after seven days, because I feel it's appropriate. There are dogs everywhere, but none of them get as much admiration from passing drinkers as Brendan.

We return to Eagle One and close the curtains over the driveway, the bin closet and the housing estate. If it wasn't for Brendan I would be quite depressed now. We get comfy in bed. Well, Brendan does. He has most of the bed, while I lie as compactly and as still as I can, so as not to disturb him.

* * * * * * * * * *

Brendan has a dream in the early hours of the morning. He's twitching and yelping, as he sometimes does. It obviously isn't a happy dream. It makes me really sad to think of all the terrible things he's experienced, all the cruelty and violence that's been thrown at him, and how he's probably scarred for life.

I also have a bad night. I don't sleep much; it's a very negative night. Being parked virtually on the main drive, every car or person coming or going disturbs us. But apart from the constant cars and Brendan's nightmares, the whole suicide thing has got to me. I keep thinking of all the people I've known who have died. Through work and volunteering I have encountered several suicides, including drug overdoses, hanging and a woman who jumped into the murky waters of the Manchester Ship Canal and drowned herself.

I think I first started thinking about death when I was very young. Too young. We had a family cat; he was a tabby called Tinker. He'd been brought to us as a kitten, as a stray. We'd had him for many years and he was very friendly and loving. He was hit by a car on our quiet suburban street. He survived, but he had to have his tail removed and he had internal complications and was never the same again. I remember holding him one day and realising that Tinker, who I loved, was going to die, mum and dad were going to die and everyone was going to die and we were all just treading water and awaiting the inevitable. It was a harsh realisation and I think it scarred me.

When I wake up the next morning from my fitful sleep, I'm in a very black mood. The sun comes up, the seagulls start calling. We go for a walk. I watch Brendan scamper ahead, tail high, sniffing, surveying the scenery. Every so often he will turn and look up at me, sometimes raising his head towards my hand, or turning and rubbing his body against my legs. It's impossible to stay in a black mood when he does this.

We sit on a bench at the top of the cliffs looking out to sea. Brendan is totally captivated by the view. At 8.45, two policemen appear, walking along doing a clifftop check. They're on suicide patrol; they probably do this route every morning, looking for bodies. Brendan barks aggressively at them both, of course. They laugh and smile politely, whilst giving us a wide berth.

Although Brendan has cheered me up, the weather is doing its best to send me down again. We drive towards Whitley Bay, under low, oppressive clouds, which are smothering the landscape. We pass a Fisherman's mission, where JESUS SAVES. (There's nothing wrong with being thrifty.)

I park at the St Mary's Island car park, just north of Whitley Bay. The parking machine isn't working, which is causing consternation amongst the other parkers.

"The machine's not working."

"Oh no, what are we supposed to do? The machine's not working."

"Isn't it? Oh, that's a problem. Apparently, the machine's not working."

"Are you sure? *They've* got a ticket."

"It's from last Thursday."

"Excuse me, the machine's not working."

"I'll just try it."

"Fine. I just did. But it's not working."

"No… it's not working."

"I told you. Excuse me, the machine's not working."

And so it goes on. A frenzied Mexican wave of parking panic. Not without reason; if the machine isn't working you can't get a ticket, but it doesn't mean you won't get a fine. Some people are literally standing in the car park with their jaws hanging open in confusion, as though re-enacting the Eddie Munch painting, "The Scream".

I leave a note in the windscreen and walk towards the beach, so now they stand open-mouthed at my audacity.

The tide is out and the causeway to the island is fully exposed, so it's safe to cross. The lighthouse stands out starkly in the rocky bay, a plain white tapering tower. We spend an hour walking round the lighthouse, sitting down looking at the lighthouse and standing up looking at the lighthouse. (The middle activity proves to be Brendan's favourite.) Then we cross back over the causeway, board Eagle One and we're off.

And that's it for Tyne-and-Wear: it came and it went. Auf wiedersehen, pet. We're entering Northumberland, which makes me feel uneasy. I'm very aware that this is the last coastal county of my trip, so it feels like things are drawing to an end. I had hoped this journey might enlighten me, might provide some answers, but

I don't feel I'm any closer to knowing what I want from life, what I want to do, apart from *this*: travel around, explore, see things, experience things and then write about them. All with my dog. That's all I've ever really wanted.

Newbiggin-by-the-Sea doesn't help my uneasiness. Newbiggin is nearer the sea than it really wants to be. It's had major problems with erosion in the past – and probably will again in the future. Brendan doesn't seem at all interested in Newbiggin. And he absolutely couldn't care less whether it's By-the-Sea or not. He refuses to get out of Eagle One, so I leave him napping while I walk to the beach.

Out in the middle of the horseshoe bay is a brass statue of a couple – a man and a woman – called, imaginatively, *Couple.* I find it something of an eyesore; it looks incongruous and tacky. I just don't get it. But all art is subjective and that's just my opinion.

I walk around the Maritime Centre with its big windows. Inside, there's some sort of staff training or team building exercise going on. The team players in question are sitting in a semi-circle, wearing name badges and looking towards a wipe clean whiteboard. It brings back memories of mandatory training at work. *Bad* memories. Nobody amidst the group looks like they're enjoying it or learning anything. They look uncomfortable and fidget restlessly.

I round the grassy headland to a nice church with a tower built of rough stones. Until recently, the graveyard was jutting over the cliffs; bones and body parts kept getting washed up on the beach in a macabre horror movie scenario. Walking round the little church, it all seems well and good now, with a new, sturdy all-encompassing boundary wall. I want to look inside the church, but it's locked.

When I get into Eagle One, Brendan raises an eyebrow, but not his head. He gives me that lazily annoying "told you so" look and promptly goes back to sleep. He's so wise.

I turn the key and start the engine. I notice an old couple in the car adjacent. They aren't talking; they're just staring straight ahead. Not at the sea, not at the beach, not at the statue, just at the car park, at the parked cars, at the tarmac. I can't decide whether it's silent despair or quiet peace they exude. I release the handbrake and pull away.

The town is solid, but unmemorable. It's got that hard, northern, built-to-withstand-the-weather sort of feeling. Two minutes later, we're back in the car park again with the old couple; they turn their heads very slowly in unison to look at me, then very slowly turn their heads away again and continue their silent vigil. Perhaps, in their youth, they too had tried to leave Newbiggin and had eventually just given up and are waiting helplessly, hopelessly, wordlessly for the end.

"I think we're trapped here forever, boy." I tell Brendan.

He looks at me, then looks away. I know full well that he's thinking "It wouldn't be a problem if you hadn't broken the SatNav." But he's being very diplomatic.

"Let's try again, boy."

On my third circuit of the town – quite by chance – I make it out. As the buildings end, the landscape suddenly seems *bigger*; there are farmed fields, some ploughed, some pasture, there are trees, but there is also a backdrop of outlying hills, *big* hills, distant but unmistakeably powerful and immovable. They give the landscape some scale and some dynamism, because it's so long since I've seen hills of any significance. They look and feel majestic, dark and slightly purpled, snagging the low clouds and brooding silently.

We drive back towards the coast and pitch up on a big, but very nice site. We have a meal. We have a walk. We return to Eagle One, the sun goes down and it gets dark. Very dark. Much darker than it ought to be, because it isn't late. The site has very little lighting. Brendan decides he'll stay stretched out on the settee, so I walk to the shower and utility block. I'm trying to find the showers. I walk round the building three times. It's *so* dark. I can't find any signs for what's what and what's where.

I start tentatively pushing doors open. I find the dish wash. I find the laundry. I find the chemical toilet disposal. There seems to be only one door I haven't tried, so I cautiously enter. It's painted a very pale pastel green; they don't always have "his" and "hers" colour co-ordinated pink and blue facilities, but you wouldn't ever find men's toilets painted pink. Green can be a somewhat gender-neutral colour, but this hue seems very pale and quite feminine. Also the whole place seems too clean and neat and pristine. It looks like a new building, only completed last weekend, as though it hasn't been open long enough for hordes of men to ruin it. The giveaway that you're in the men's is always the urinals, but I can't see any.

The place is like a maze. Thankfully a very quiet maze. I creep apprehensively around a corner and bump into someone combing their moustache. I'm pretty sure it's a man. We both jump. "Sorry..." I say, "I was a bit wary because I thought this might be the women's."

He laughs. "I've been coming in all week and I'm pretty sure it's the men's."

I get in the shower and as far as I know, no women come in. I have my shower, turn off the water and then stand there, dripping and freezing. It's then that I realise I've forgotten my towel. I stand shivering for a while, then shake my limbs and drip dry, not too successfully.

On trying to leave the block, I find the urinals – so I really *am* in the men's, but this time the exit door eludes me.

* * * * * * * * * *

We wake up and it's another day. A grey day. A *Tues*day.

My phone rings, which startles me, because everyone I know knows I'm away. Not that anyone calls me anyway. Ever. I don't like the phone and if I can avoid a phone conversation, I will do. I only get two types of call these days. The first is a business cold call: would I like double-glazing or to change energy supplier? The second type of call is along the lines of: "Hello, I'm your dad's carer. I've called round and he's disappeared again."

This turns out to be the second type. My dad has carers calling in three times a day to make sure he has something to eat and takes his medication. When he fell last year he was in a terrible state and seemingly wouldn't get better, but he's bounced back and defied medical science. He's got a lot wrong with him, but he goes on. Thirty-something years ago he had a triple heart bypass, which he was told would last him for up to ten years. Everyone else on his ward has since died, but dad soldiers on. His mobility isn't great, but he can still elude his captors (carers) and make it to freedom (the pub). He's got so well, he currently doesn't really need the carers, but he does enjoy being waited on hand and foot. So, he's missing. Again. Except he isn't missing, because it's a Tuesday. On Tuesday he goes to snooker. He's forgotten to remind the carers, but that's where he'll be. (And that's where he was.)

We set off for a walk. A strip of woodland runs along the edge of the site. We follow the footpath through it as the trees rattle overhead. We come to a junction of paths and have a difference of opinion. I want to go right, because it's the correct way, whereas Brendan wants to go left, because that's the way we went last night and he doesn't see why we should change things and make life so complicated. He stands his ground, digging his paws in the dirt and eyeballing me adamantly. I'm so impressed he knows which way we went yesterday. I don't care what the other dogs say, he's a genius.

We stand there in a deadlock as the woodland moves and shifts and sways around us. The wind is getting steadily stronger, tearing at the trees and sending down a blizzard of leaves. A typhoon is promised for later today, lasting into tomorrow. In the end I win; we go my way. We come out of the woods and cross open fields, through stunning pastoral countryside. It's so windy I keep thinking my dog is going to take to the air, but he seems unphased.

We arrive at the sea and sit watching the waves roll steadily in, enjoying the sound of the ocean. There are some lovely dog people on the beach. One little dog is wearing a life jacket. She bounds into the oncoming waves after her fluorescent toy. The lifejacket has a handle, so in an emergency her dad can pick her up and walk along with her like hand luggage. He demonstrates this for us; the little dog doesn't react at all. She sits there quite happily, suspended in mid-air, surveying the beach from her new elevated position.

A nice couple stop to admire Brendan.

"He's lovely. What's his name?"

"Brendan; he came with his name." I don't even know I'm saying it anymore.

"He's gorgeous. He's so chilled, isn't he?"

"Well…"

"But then he probably picks it up from you, doesn't he? Because you're very laid back, aren't you?"

"Oh…"

I said they were nice; I didn't say they were rational.

Brendan has a run about, a sit down, a sniff, a snuffle and a shuffle, then we stagger back to the site, battling against the wind. There have been weather warnings and this time I really believe them, because I can see and feel the evidence. Many of the older people on the site are sitting outside their caravans on deckchairs, watching other people's tents and awnings being torn apart. They've lived through the blitz, so a mere life-threatening storm isn't going to deter them. A round sewage cartridge goes rolling along the driveway with a woman running after it, shrieking for it to stop, but it isn't listening.

Brendan flinches at each bang and clatter as people's possessions are thrown about. We make haste to Eagle One and close ourselves inside.

We huddle together in the van in the evening. It's cold, it's windy and it's dark. We get into bed and argue over whose turn it is to sleep on which side. We sort it out and go to sleep, while Eagle One rocks and rattles around us.

* * * * * * * * * *

Wednesday. Again. But this Wednesday is different, because weather warnings have been issued for today: severe gale force winds.

I go to the site office to book a further night, because

there are warnings not to travel when the approaching and much-anticipated typhoon is at its worst later on and my next port of call would be very exposed, with winds coming straight off the sea. Many people have already fled the site, cutting their holidays short, leaving at first light in order to get safely home before the worst of the storm hits. No one wants to be in a high-sided vehicle or towing a caravan on the motorway in the grip of the typhoon.

Last night had been bad enough. Many tents and awnings had suffered and been torn apart and scattered across the site. Two women are already being served when I enter the reception office. They're asking advice about local hotels, because their tent has been destroyed in the night. Others, like me, have opted to stay put to avoid driving in the oncoming storm. It's going to be quite an experience being thrown around in a van, but – as they say – what doesn't make you stronger kills you. Or words to that effect.

It's so windy already, it's difficult to stand. Brendan isn't happy and wants to return to the van. I'm genuinely concerned that he might be blown away or a tree might come down on us, so it seems safer to stay in the van during the storm. This might be a mistake, but it's borne out of logic.

It's strangely disorientating in Eagle One during the afternoon, like being airborne and riding turbulence. The whole van is rising up then falling down, while being buffeted from side to side. I'm convinced we're going to be blown over.

Most people have taken their awnings down in preparation for the storm. Some, of course, haven't and have gone out for the day as normal. When they come back in the evening, most will find their awnings in shreds, or gone completely and all their possessions scattered across the site. These people really annoy me. The awnings don't just collapse, they explode, sending tent poles, tent pegs, guy ropes and whatever raining out like bullets. Someone could be hurt or even killed. It's very irresponsible to have left them up. There are weather warnings and everyone is talking about it, so the severe weather is *not* a surprise. There is potential for a serious incident.

It's so windy it's disturbing Brendan's nap. He sits next to me, shaking. I chat to him in a slow, soothing voice, speaking clearly, so he can understand. His soulful brown eyes look at me as though to say he trusts me and knows I will protect him. I sing to him for a while, which seems to calm him a bit. We sit huddled together as the van rises and falls. It's quite unnerving. I don't think I've ever experienced such violent weather. There are several sudden squalls when the van lurches and it seems we're going to go over, then Eagle One rights herself and bounces on her suspension. I think we're both starting to feel seasick.

The wind forces its way through the various air vents and through the thin gaps in the doors and windows. It sounds like screaming; the screaming of souls in torment: cliches are borne from reality.

I cling onto Brendan. He's stopped shaking now, but

is very wary and on edge, but he's doing surprisingly well. We're thrown backwards and forwards. The floor beneath us rises and falls, rocks and reels. You'd pay good money for this at a funfare... but it isn't fun. And it's not fair. It goes on for hours and we're helpless. All we can do is sit there and let the storm rage around us. And it rages. And rages. And then – eventually – it very gradually begins to abate. The buffeting gets less severe, the sound begins to die down.

We're both feeling quite ill. I decide some fresh air is what we need, so we go for a walk. Brendan is very pleased to be out in the open and scampers ahead to the full extent of his flexi-lead. It's still very windy; it's difficult to stand. In the fringe of woodland the path is littered with leaves, twigs and branches, but also several full trees have come down. The grass in the fields is combed flat against the earth. The clouds are streaming.

Brendan's ears are pulled back. He's putting on a brave face, but I know he doesn't like it, so we return to the van for the night.

* * * * * * * * *

Friday – the current in a line of rapid-fire Fridays. Brendan slept well and seems to have completely forgotten about the storm. He awakes grudgingly, yawns, grumbles and goes back to sleep, so all is normal.

It's a cold and grey day. Everywhere is wet after a night of heavy rain. It's breezy, but it's a normal breeze, no longer hazardous to human and canine health.

Winding lanes take us through a relatively flat farmed

landscape: ploughed fields, dark brown furrows of earth, wet with rain. Those background hills to the northwest are getting continually less background.

We drive through Seahouses, which is classed as a large village, but looks like a small town. The centre is very modern and quite characterless. I don't have good memories of Seahouses. We came here, unexpectedly, on a family holiday when I was possibly ten or eleven. In those days you generally had one week's holiday a year, when you'd probably go to a seaside location and stay in a caravan or a B&B. But the new thing was "weekend breaks", which we now all take for granted.

I remember playing out in the street the day before and telling my friends I was going on holiday tomorrow. They couldn't understand, and neither could I for that matter. We'd already had our summer holiday that year, it was autumn now and the weather was very bad, plus – and this was the really surreal part – mum and dad hadn't decided where we were going yet. They hadn't booked anywhere! We were just going to set off after work and school, and drive randomly until we ended up somewhere. It seemed like madness! I assumed there would be men in white coats waiting to seize them if they tried to go through with this insanity, but those men never came.

We set off and drove through the rush hour at dusk. The rush hour ended and we kept on driving. It went fully dark. We kept on driving. It got well past teatime. We kept on driving. I felt like I was being kidnapped. We kept on driving. I wondered if I was experiencing Stockholm Syndrome, then I wondered what it was, because the term wasn't in everyday usage yet. We kept on driving. Then they stopped driving and we were on a grey council estate. It was called Seahouses. Then they started driving again, driving up and down cul-de-sacs and backstreets, stopping at every B&B sign, knocking on doors, getting refused, with either: "We're full up." or "What, at this time of night?" or "We're closed until spring." or "Well, have you booked?" So it *was* madness, after all!

We ended up in a modern, grey, semi-detached house with a family that included several very young children. We had breakfast with them in the morning, at their table, in their kitchen, while the mother was getting the kids ready for school. It was excruciating.

As we'd arrived in the dark we hadn't really had a good look at Seahouses, but I remember it being very grey: grey houses, grey shops, grey streets. I hated it. Driving through now, it really doesn't look that bad. It's modern, but it looks bright and clean.

We drive on to a wide, sandy beach. It's blustery but the sun is shining intermittently. The moment Brendan's four paws touch the sand, he gets sand madness and is racing around and pulling at his lead. I want to let him off so he can enjoy this vast open space, but he can't be trusted and the road beyond the sandhills is too busy to risk it. I keep forgetting that technically he isn't my dog, I'm just fostering him, a long term foster, but nevertheless, I am bound by the rules of his sanctuary. But I could never part with him now. To do so would be abusive. To both of us.

Back in Eagle One, after an on-lead walk and run, Brendan gets comfortable, takes up all the sofa and goes immediately to sleep. There have been times on this trip when I've really enjoyed his company, when we've had a play and a snuggle, but there have also been times when I've thought he's been less of a companion than a box of dried lentils would be. You don't have to clean up after a box of dried lentils; you can let a box of dried lentils off their lead and trust it not to tear up your home while you're out. Also, Brendan has stopped me going in a number of places and has completely ruined many experiences by getting me stressed. You can go anywhere with a box of dried lentils; people do look at you strangely, but you can still go in. The Spinnaker Tower in Portsmouth springs to mind. But we've reached the point now where we've completely bonded, we've adapted and grown together and there's no going back. I absolutely love him in a way that I could never love a box of dried lentils.

I sit in Eagle One with a brew, looking out at the sand dunes and the sky above, feeling pensive, unable to escape the inevitable fact that the trip is coming to an end and a very large part of me is sorry that it is, because real life is currently suspended and when I get back I need to get back to reality – and reality isn't always great.

I'm getting myself quite depressed and not reaching any conclusions. I decide I need to move on and have a change of scenery, get out of this rut of thinking. I rouse my dog and we walk back into Seahouses along the beach and cliff top path.

The tide is quite far in now, so everyone is condensed on the remaining slim crescent of sand. Most people are in couples, many of them holding hands. It makes me feel very alone, then right on cue, my boy looks up at me, bounds over and nuzzles me and it makes me really happy. We continue with a spring in our step, but this has dissipated by the time we've reached Seahouses.

I have always thought this is a very attractive piece of coastline, but someone had put Seahouses in the middle of it and spoilt it. The harbour isn't pretty or quaint, it's practical. It's concrete and stone with some water around it. The Bamburgh Castle Inn overlooks the harbour and the sea. I decide we need a pub experience to cheer us up, Brendan never disagrees about going in a pub, so in we go.

It's nice inside with good views over the sea, though we have a corner table, a semi-booth, with no window, no light, no view; it's a bit like being imprisoned in a very small cellar, hoping that someone will pay the ransom and they'll actually release you alive. Despite this, we have a nice pub experience and it manages to break our mood, so we're feeling much happier as we walk back along the cliff path.

There are surreal views over the sea, across the bay to the dark and sinister silhouette of Bamburgh Castle. The lighting is very strange. It's obviously going to pour down imminently. And then it does. A sudden and absolute downpour. It's torrential and really rather wet. Brendan isn't happy: he hates rain. We get soaked, as do all the other people we pass along the cliff path, hoods up, grimacing, eyes screwed up, some screaming. A brave few battle with umbrellas, which probably doesn't end well. No waterproof would be water proof in this deluge.

We make it to Eagle One. We each have a towelling down and a change of clothes/collar and sit and watch the rain for an hour, until the dark clouds clear and the sun comes out again. Car bonnets steam and streams of water trickle down grids as the landscape drains.

Storm brewing, Seahouses.

We drive on to our site for the next few days, just outside Seahouses, across the road from the beach. A nice chap shows me to our pitch; I'm behind the wheel and he gives me the lowdown through the open window.

"The men's facilities are just there... Are you alone?"

"Just me and my dog."

"What type of dog?" he asks with enthusiasm.

He leans back to look into the rear of the van, but Brendan always closes the curtains on the side where he sits, to keep the sun out. Not that it's always sunny, but I think it's become a habit for him.

The bloke calls to Brendan, hoping he'll appear in the cockpit. I know that won't get Brendan to move. I go through the motions of calling Brendan myself, but he doesn't appear. It's like Mrs Bates in the big house behind the Bates Motel in *Psycho*. I'm sure he doesn't believe I actually have a dog. He seems disappointed in me and excuses himself, leaving me with my make-believe dog.

It's a beautiful evening, so we go for a walk along the beach. Waves are rolling in quite violently, but the sound is muted. The beach is eerily still. There are a few lone dog walkers. The sun is setting, breaking open on the landward horizon and the sky is lilac and warm gold. Brendan poses for photographs. In them he looks a little poignant, a little sad, but I don't believe he's ever been happier.

* * * * * * * * * *

The next morning, I park outside Bamburgh and we walk along the wide and sandy beach towards the village and castle. It's a grey day, windy and bitterly cold. The light is stark and white. Waves crash in. I have my hoodie hood up and big waterproof on. Brendan's ears have taken off like kites.

The Castle dominates the beach; it dominates everything, high on its rocky crag: it's commanding, stunningly impressive, impenetrable, impregnable, visible for miles. There are tenuous connections with the Arthurian legend, as the castle is often cited as Sir Lancelot's house.

I remember this beach from the childhood holiday. It was a really cold, blustery grey day. Northumberland seemed a bit bleak at that time, in the autumn. The beach was empty and windswept. We walked a short way, then my dad spotted a sign that warned of unexploded bombs and the danger of mines being washed up, so we hurriedly left the beach. There are no signs now, so presumably there is a fairly low likelihood of exploding.

A large group of people approach along the beach, wearing purple hats, with dogs wearing purple coats. Brendan is fascinated by them and stares rudely. A lady right at the back of the 30-strong group breaks formation and comes towards us. She explains they're walking to raise awareness for safeguarding in the North. She's lovely and very informative; she gives me a pen and won't accept a donation. She's a brilliant ambassador. However, her twenty-nine companions, who just walk past chatting and ignoring the general public, raise no awareness whatsoever.

Brendan meets a lot of lovely dogs on the beach, but his favourites are a pair of brothers, twins, little white Scotties, whom he calls "the ingredients". The couple with them are friendly and chatty. Brendan sniffs the woman's legs, after which one of the Scotties wees on her to re-scent her. She stands open-mouthed in disbelief and says very little after that.

The sun keeps coming out in fits and starts between the clouds. I walk with my boy, around the castle and down into the pleasant stone estate village of Bamburgh. In the centre of the village there is a café called *The Copper Kettle*, which I remember *exceptionally* well from the family trip, despite it being over thirty years ago.

We sat inside at a table at the back. Me and mum had prawn cocktail. The prawns tasted very odd, sour and sort of acidic. I didn't like them and only ate half of mine. Mum never liked waste, so she ate all hers. I moaned to my dad. He tasted the prawns and agreed they were off. He complained to the staff and the woman was quite rude, saying nobody else had complained. I don't recall whether he got money off, but it would be unlike my dad to pay for something inedible: always firm but fair. Later that day, mum took ill and started being violently sick. We had rooms at a different B&B than the previous night, an older house run by an old lady. I had to share a double bed with my brother. To get to the bathroom we had to go along a corridor, then cut through mum and dad's room; it was quite an odd set up.

In the night I started feeling sick – very sick. I put up with it for a while, then I realised it was coming, I was actually going to vomit. I hurried along the corridor, into mum and dad's room. It was dark and I lost my bearings, then my footing. I fell headlong into the darkness, spun round on the carpet and on my hands and knees I projectile vomited all over their room. I was sick repeatedly, violently and rather colourfully.

For some reason we had to go home the next day, rather than staying until we felt well enough to travel. Perhaps dad had work commitments, I can't remember. We set off and had to keep stopping at the roadside so I could throw up. It took us hours and hours and was a nightmare. It wasn't a great holiday for a number of reasons, but it has always stuck in my mind. I didn't revisit the county until recent years, when I came camping with friends.

The Copper Kettle is still open, but seems very different inside. I sit in the garden with Brendan. There are seven dogs in total and – remarkably – Brendan is the best behaved; he's calm and placid and keeps himself to himself. Most of the other dogs are little yappers with constant, high-pitched, whining barks. The majority of them look like the decorative pompoms from someone's poncho, whereas Brendan is a fine figure of a dog. I'm really proud of him.

* * * * * * * * * *

It's Sunday. I'm sure it's less than a week since the last Sunday. Anyway, we're driving along the coast, ever northwards. It's a beautiful sunny day again, but cold. I've had a nose bleed and have sinus pain in my head and face, so things are less than great. Brendan is in a slight mood, because we've set off before 10am again and – he keeps reminding me – this is supposed to be a holiday. (It's *not* a holiday… it's a *trip*.)

"I'm looking forward to today's location, boy." I tell him. He probably pictures miles of shingle, a grey, empty wilderness with no trees and no anything, because he's learnt my landscape preferences the hard way. In fact, the opposite is true, because we're actually heading for Lindisfarne, also known as Holy Island, a tidal island off the Northumberland coast which is holy. Apparently.

Reaching the causeway, the island stretches out ahead of us. I love crossing to an island; it's so exciting. To the right, the sea is silver from the sun and shimmers. To the left, brilliant green sand dunes shiver. The island is a mile from the mainland and is completely cut off for several hours at high tide every day. I know Brendan will love it.

I pull into the car park on the outskirts of the village. I don't think Brendan's going to like it, after all. There are already 120 cars here at 10.30am. (And yes, I counted them.) It's going to be busy. We walk into the island's solitary village, which is pleasant, largely stone-built, red roofed. It feels quiet and tranquil, despite the number of people wandering about. There are several cafés, but they are nearly all closed, possibly because it's a Sunday and this is, after all, a holy island, if not *the* Holy Island.

Pilgrims Coffee House is open, so we call in. It's unpretentious, rustic in a modern way. I join the already sizeable queue at the counter. The service is so slow and the server is so laid back; he's possibly hung over. He has enough hair for two or more people and is probably called Bobdylan (one word). He's chatting to the man in front of me, who is local. If I hadn't waited so long already, I'd walk out. Bobdylan comes across as a stoner; he moves and speaks in slow motion. A queue is mounting behind me and people are shifting impatiently; several at the back walk out mumbling, but Brendan stands beside me, patiently, observing the proceedings, but very calm and relaxed.

I'm eventually served. I have a cake ("our own take on a flapjack"). It's gorgeous. And nothing like a flapjack, which is always a bonus.

Back out in the village, people are ambling and dawdling everywhere. It's way too busy for me and I'm on pins with Brendan, because people are drifting into his bite zone, but he's actually fine. As it's a Sunday, I pray to anyone's god who'll listen, for it to be considerably less busy after one o'clock when the causeway has flooded and the island thankfully reverts to being an island. (With me not having a subscription to any of them, it doesn't work.)

We sit by the harbour in the cool sunshine, watching the boats bobbing. Across the small bay, the dramatic castle on its steep crag looks somewhat Transylvanian. We wander to the eastern shore of the island, which feels isolated and remote. We sit on the grassy ridge above the beach. We do seem to do a lot of sitting down. The wind is strong and cold, the sea is vast and empty. There is no sight of the mainland, just the North Sea rushing in, powerful and violent. We watch the breakers. It's beautiful and I feel quite contented sitting here with my dog. This is what travelling is all about. This is what life is all about.

I make the mistake of asking myself what I want out of life. I already know the answer: this. I want to live

near the sea. I want to sit near the sea with my dog. I
don't mind routine if it isn't a routine that I despise. I
hate taking Brendan to the local field or round the block.
I hate the bickering neighbours. We can't always have
what we want in life and if we get one thing it's often
at the expense of something else. I don't want to live
in a town in a landlocked county. I feel trapped. I could
move here and get a little job. Maybe a job I could take
my dog to. Or he could get his own job, perhaps a life
model, because he enjoys sitting, he enjoys being naked
and he's got the looks. But it's all irrelevant really. We hit
the same stumbling block: I live where I live because of
Nicky and she would never move.

Everything is suddenly different. I feel dejected and
hopeless. We set off walking again between green
fields, cutting across the middle of the island. That
introspection has ruined my afternoon. For the past
half hour I've been ranting on about everything and not
getting to any conclusions... because there aren't any.
It's ruined a magical moment and I feel very sombre.

I go back to the Pilgrim Café for a reviving caffeine fix.
It's gone 2 o'clock, long after the causeway has closed, so
I expect it to be quieter, but the queue is out of the door.
I wait for a few minutes, but the staff are serving so
slowly, it's like a joke. A slow joke. A.v.e.r.y.s.l.o.w.j.o.k.e.
The queue isn't moving at all and they don't deserve the
custom, so I walk out. At normal speed.

I go in one of the island's two pubs instead, the
Crown and Anchor, which is bright and friendly and
the staff move at a suitable speed. I have a pint and a
chip butty. It's lovely. A little girl comes up and starts

poking Brendan, in his face, while her mother stands there and watches, smiling. I tell the little girl to stop. Her mother gives no reaction at all. I start to think she's had a stroke. The fatal type, not the petting type. Not that petting Brendan can't be fatal. I needn't have worried, because Brendan is very patient and shows no signs of aggression, though it would have been quite understandable if he'd bitten her.

There are many locals in the pub; the bar staff seem to know most of the customers. Of course, it's a Sunday. It isn't standoffish or hostile or cliquish. There is a lovely, friendly atmosphere. A sign says "lots of people come to Lindisfarne for lots of different reasons. And the island is a better place for that". I really like that sentiment. The island relies on visitors and tourists and the locals seem to acknowledge that and have the right attitude. Considering the island gets thousands of visitors in a week, it isn't tacky and it doesn't feel like a show village; it feels natural and unspoilt. Lindisfarne seems to manage itself exceptionally well as a real place, a real community and a tourist hotspot.

After lunch, it's a lovely afternoon. Now the causeway is fully submerged, it's suddenly like a ghost town. There are still eighty cars in the car park. (Yes, I counted them. *Again.*) There are many camper vans, with the curtains closed but the doors open, probably with the owners inside having a lazy nap, while their dogs sunbathe outside. And that's what *we* do for a while, then we decide to walk around the island. It's beautiful as we pick our way along the deserted shore. The lighting is warm and golden.

Out across the bay, I can see cars glinting in the sunlight. There is already a queue of traffic on the mainland waiting to get on to the island, perhaps locals coming home. Bizarrely, there is also a queue of traffic waiting to get *off* the island. Even though there is nearly two hours until the causeway is passable again. I'm not sure what the hurry to get away is. Or why you'd rather spend time sitting in your car on a road than being on the island in the open air with a view.

At 5.30, nearly a full hour before the causeway is officially safe and passable, there is a slow but steady, sneaking exodus. Quite a few cars crawl out of the car park. A few wet cars have made it across and drive along the road into the village.

At 6.15, the sunlight suddenly stops; it has gone below the horizon and it goes freakishly, instantly very cold. We're going to cross the causeway, reluctantly leaving this little island paradise, (as they have a strict no camper van policy). Tonight's site is only a mile away on the mainland and offers unparalleled views of the bay, the island and out to sea. There are thirty vehicles left in the car park as I sadly drive away. I would have loved to stay on the island overnight.

The road is wet and glistening and everything seems like a film; a film fading from colour to monochrome as the light dwindles.

The campsite doesn't disappoint. At least the views don't. As darkness falls, isolated lights come on out at sea. There are also views inland, over a pastoral plain.

A train snakes through the darkening countryside, all lit up inside and looking like a scene from a Film Noir. It's so filmic that Brendan starts barking at it. The little yapper next door starts as well, in competition, but it's no competition. A while later Brendan spots the haunting white globe of the moon and starts barking again, setting the other dog off. And so it goes on, all night.

* * * * * * * * * * *

Berwick-upon-Tweed is a town in Northumberland, but it's been all over the place. It's flitted between England and Scotland repeatedly, but it's currently the northernmost town in England; the last town. Or the first town, if you're going the other way.

It's a very grand, handsome, solidly built stone town. We stroll along the medieval walls; I stop to read an information board and Brendan uses the opportunity to have a sit down.

"Your dog is waiting very patiently."

I look up. A nice couple from Buckinghamshire have materialised out of nowhere. The man approaches, offering the back of his hand for Brendan to smell. I tense and issue the regulation warning. The man persists and Brendan graciously allows him to stroke him for a minute, then suddenly turns and starts growling. The woman has a go, but gets the same treatment. They're very good about it.

Trying to change the subject, I say: "Berwick seems very nice."

"Yes," the man agrees, "Except it's shut. Everything's shut. We've come specifically for the museums and galleries. All shut. All of them. Everything. Shut."

I smile apologetically, then hurriedly lead Brendan away before I need to apologise again, because he seems to be getting a bit restless.

We look at the various majestic bridges that span the shimmering Tweed, then call into a lovely, quirky café down a back street. It's a relaxed place with bookshelves lining the walls and odd tables and chairs. Brendan gratefully dives under the table and stretches out. As I'm sitting enjoying my second piece of sponge, I become aware of a middle-aged woman talking to the staff at the counter. She's the type of woman who speaks quite loudly and isn't in any way self-conscious.

"I just want a friend essentially... That's the main thing. I'm happy being single, but I'd like a friend to share things with... A "friend with benefits", if possible."

I send vanilla sponge spraying across the table. This is not tearoom-approved conversation. I'm quite shocked that she's so open and so loud. But I'm even more shocked that she assumes all these wide-eyed cake bingers around her want to know. Nobody says anything, but everyone concentrates a little bit more studiously on their Battenbergs from this point on.

I like Berwick a lot. I think it's safe to say we both do. It's a handsome town and we're sorry to leave. I drive over the bridge, high above the Tweed and away towards the Scottish border, though we won't be crossing it.

This feels like an ending of sorts, because we're now very sadly leaving the sea and the coast behind. We're heading home cross country, the long way round.

* * * * * * * * * *

Dog facts:
Beagles and Border Collies are supposedly the breeds of dog that bark the most. Brendan is not convinced and would like to challenge any of these varieties to a bark-off.

Brendan in Beadnell Bay

CHAPTER 10: CROSS COUNTRY: THE LONG WAY ROUND.

It's weird not being near the sea. Of course, I haven't always been able to *see* the sea, by any means, but I've always known it was there, never too far away. Now we won't see it again on this trip – and that's sad.

"That's the last of the sea, boy." I tell Brendan. He raises his eyes slightly, then sighs. He's as gutted as I am. I really love the sea. There's something so reassuring about its rhythms and repetitions. Without the sea, the beach would basically be a quarry.

We drive on through beautiful scenery and the sun is shining. The mountains we're heading towards are no longer low-lying hills, they rise up majestically, they're treeless, dark and brooding. It all feels very Scottish now, because the mountains are high, the forests are dark and there's a certain vast, open grandeur to the landscape, but it's still England, still Northumberland; there are several yellow and red Northumberland flags flying, presumably hung by people proudly declaring their allegiance. I have never seen so many flags.

We cross a vast area of bleak moorland, with just this tarmac strip bisecting the empty landscape.

I have no maps for this area, which instantly wrong-foots me. I like to know where I am, what's around the corner and what's over the horizon. I decide to treat it as a surprise, but that doesn't work. I always find surprises work best when you've planned them carefully in advance.

Brendan, inside looking out. (Just how he likes it.)

We reach a plateau – I don't know where it is because there's no sign, just a viewpoint: there are views in all directions of open countryside, open, barren countryside as far as the eye can see, mile after mile, just moorland and the occasional conifer forest, no human intrusion. It's reassuring that this type of landscape still exists in England – this vastness.

Ahead, the hills are shrouded in cloud, which is probably rain. The air is going a sickly yellow and the grey sky seems to be getting lower. Everything looks surreal, tinted and slightly false.

We arrive in the village of Bellingham, which is comparatively a thriving metropolis, as it has four pubs and several shops. It provides the amenities and accommodation for people visiting the nearby Kielder

Forest. Our campsite is just outside the village. It's a nice green site and the staff are very friendly.

"Where are you from?"

"Stockport. It's just south of Manch..."

"*Thought so!* Our daughter lives in Stockport!"

My accent – which I don't think I have – has given me away. They aren't local, but they've accumulated a vast Northumberland knowledge; there isn't anything about the area they don't know and they love it here.

In the evening, I walk into the village with my boy. Bellingham isn't such a metropolis after all, as all the cafes are shut at this time of the evening, but so are half the pubs. The thriving hub of the village seems to be the beckoning bright, white lights of the Co-op, slap bang in the middle. Tourists and locals alike are pulling up outside, running in for last minute ingredients or alcohol and then running out and driving off into the night. By contrast, close by is the subdued lighting of the Chinese takeaway, which seems much less frenetic, much calmer, with a relaxed lounge feel, filled with people leaning back in comfortable chairs, flicking idly through newspapers: these are the opposite of the hurried people in the Co-op, these are the people too idle to cook, enjoying a few moments of sizzling calm while their food is wok-ed in the background.

Bellingham is a nice village, surrounded by the largest working forest in England. It has something of a "final staging post" feel to it, because most of the roads from here lead nowhere – except to trees. An almost full moon hangs over the rooftops and chimneys. There seems to have been a full moon for days. It must surely be on the wane by now. It's a *huge* moon. Thankfully, Brendan is busy sniffing the hedges and gateposts and doesn't notice it.

Apart from the over-sized moon, the Kielder area is renowned for having the darkest skies in England and is allegedly the largest "dark sky preserve" in the whole of Europe.

Back at the site, I realise a large amount of the lighting is red, presumably to keep light emissions to a minimum. I want to make use of these famed dark skies and do some sky watching. But I also really want to follow Brendan, who has sloped off to bed. After a few minutes of looking up at nothing, bed wins. I go into the van and join my slumbering companion.

Goodnight.

* * * * * * * * * * * *

It was very cold in the small hours. Brendan got me up at 3pm, asking to go out. There were clear skies, no clouds and an array of blinking stars cast over the heavens.

The day slowly develops into a chilly, overcast Tuesday. Brendan has a rough 'n' tumble playtime with a boisterous puppy from next door. Young Harry is a collie cross. Always better to meet than a cross collie. They do some canine wrestling; Brendan wins.

We're spending the day in the Kielder Forest and around

Kielder Water, deep, grey and choppy. We walk along winding pathways between the trees. A couple riding bikes overtakes us. The man has a little dog, a Jack Russell, in a rucksack. She's quite happily sitting on her dad's back looking at the world passing her by. The woman stops to chat. The dog is thirteen, so not able to do the walks and rides with them anymore, so this way she can still come out, which is clearly what she wants. She'd rather be with them than left in alone. Brendan watches them quizzically. He's probably wondering why we don't have a similar arrangement.We carry on. I stop for a moment to take a photograph of the reservoir. When I walk off again, less than a minute later, I realise there's no resistance on Brendan's flexi-lead. I look down. He's trotting ahead quite happily, tail in the air, sniffing and weeing and going about his business as usual, but he isn't attached to his lead; only a frayed fragment remains, trailing from his collar. He's chewed through it. He's not allowed off his lead (technically I'm only fostering him), but he's already off and he clearly isn't going to come to me willingly to be restrained.

He doesn't run away, but he also doesn't respond remotely when I call him. So, I walk along trying to exude calm. He scampers close by, but is very purposefully keeping an eye on me and making sure I don't come into grab-range. He's very calculating. If I lunge at him and miss, this will immediately be a power game.

I reason that the only way for me to maintain control is to act like this is part of the plan and I'm not bothered. This seems to be working well. He's not running wild, he's keeping equidistant to me. He definitely doesn't want to lose me, but he is completely ignoring my calls and my commands and if I approach him, he bolts away amongst the trees to a safe distance.

I'm getting anxious, because we're drawing nearer to the car park, so there is the danger posed by moving vehicles. But more immediately, we're not alone in the forest, there are other people. A jogger and then a cyclist suddenly appear. Both times Brendan makes a lunge for them, barking savagely, because they come too close and he's warning them off. It's time to initiate the emergency protocol. For some dogs it might be an edible treat, for others it might be a ball or special toy, but for Brendan...

"Right, Brendan... I'm going to have a nice sit down now. Just here, I think."

I perch on a grassy bank beneath a tree. Brendan stands, head cocked slightly. He's calculating the variables, but it's too much for him to resist. He bounds over and sits beside me. I slide my arm slowly, casually around him, so we're sitting as we would normally sit, with his weight against me.

This is very revealing. Firstly, he could have sat down anywhere in the forest, but he clearly wanted to sit next to me. I feel quite touched. Secondly, I think it proves that while he does want to have a run about and he's naturally mischievous, he absolutely doesn't want to run away and he doesn't want to get lost.

After a prolonged sit down, I slip his metal emergency lead on and we continue back to the car park. Once in Eagle One, Brendan goes into a deep sleep after the exertion of being rebellious.

* * * * * * * * * * * *

Wednesday. Very windy and very wet. It's suddenly our last full day. I'm filled with mixed feelings, glad to be seeing Nicky, but everything else is a negative. I love travelling. I love being away from home and seeing new things. I don't think I'm made to be stuck in one place.

We visit Hexham, apparently England's favourite market town. Brendan asks to stay in the van, so I set off on foot, alone, which I'm not happy about; as it's the last day I feel we ought to be spending it together. On the rare occasions he's not with me it feels very weird.

Overlooking the market place, is the splendour of Hexham Abbey. Inside there is calm and quiet. Stone floors worn smooth by centuries of sandaled feet. The smell of dust, stone and candle wax. Subdued lighting and colourful stained glass. Echoes and muted conversation.

The Abbey has a wealth of sculptures, carvings, gargoyles, effigies and statues, which have been incorporated into the fabric of the building; they stare down at you from the walls and corners, many of them look quite demonic. There is a three-headed man and many very weird and sinister animal carvings; it all feels a little bit *Wicker Man*.

Also there is a rood screen, intricately carved and featuring medieval painted panels, including four "Dance of Death" scenes, which depict Death as a skeletal Grim Reaper type, wielding his sickle and seemingly having a dance-off with a cardinal, a king, an emperor and a pope. The moral of the grisly story is: it doesn't matter what your rank, Death will still get you – and presumably dance at you – whether you like it or not.

As usual, I don't last very long without Brendan. When I get back to Eagle One, he wearily raises his head. He has slept so soundly he needs a nap to recover, which he duly has, as I drive ever westwards.

It's still windy and there's rain in the air, but we go for a walk along Hadrian's Wall, the largest Roman artefact *in the world*. It runs across the neck of the country, from east to west, for 73 miles, but we're only going to do about one seventy-third of it. Brendan scoots along, sniffing the Wall repeatedly, and out of respect – presumably – he doesn't even attempt to wee on it.

This trip – or the original trip rather, before I had Brendan – featured Hadrian's Wall on the first day, where it begins on the shores of the Solway Firth. Here we are again, on the last full day, alongside the wall. It wasn't intentional and I've only just realised, but it seems suitably serendipitous. I'd like to walk further and even Brendan looks like he could ramble up and down the undulations for a while longer, but our extortionate car parking is due to expire, so we head back. We just make it to Eagle One as the heavens open, and it's northern rain: it means business.

We continue to Haltwhistle, a grey stone town beneath the stone grey rainclouds. It cheekily claims to be the centre of Britain, which is a statement somewhat impossible to quantify. Driving through it in the heavy rain, it doesn't seem like the centre of anywhere; it seems to be half day closing, because everywhere seems to be half-shut.

Our final site is just outside Haltwhistle, on the banks of the South Tyne. Our final site, our final night. We could have driven home from here in a couple of hours (2 hours 13 minutes to be exact, according to Google), but we're staying to prolong our experience.

Brendan is having a nap. I have a can of Guinness and look out at the now-heavy rain. Our last evening turns into our last night. We spend it as we have spent all our previous nights: quietly together. There are no bells and whistles and certainly no fireworks. We're warm, we're comfortable, we're relaxed; frenzied barking is kept to a minimum.

This time feels like a bonus; we've only stayed overnight in Haltwhistle to delay our inevitable return to the real world. The real world isn't all it's cracked up to be. We've had a fantastic and memorable trip. I think we've bonded, I think we've grown even closer and I don't want it to end.

Our evening and our last day fades out into darkness.

* * * * * * * * * * * *

It's the last day. It's damp but not raining. We leave Haltwhistle. We're on the way home. The countryside is undulating, unmistakably northern, north-western. Brendan is curled up in his basket. His curtains are drawn and he's sleeping soundly. I wonder if he knows we're going home. I have told him, but he doesn't always listen. But animals can sense things. I wonder if he can even remember home, or perhaps he thinks this travelling metal box *is* his permanent residence now.

We pass a WELCOME TO CUMBRIA sign. I know Cumbria well, so it gives the illusion that we're almost home.

Nicky texts: "Don't forget you've got the hosp this aft." I *had* forgotten. Completely. The reason we're coming back today is because of this appointment, or I'd probably find some excuse to extend our trip further. I'd forgotten the appointment, but I also wasn't aware of the day or date anyway. This adds quite a lot of stress to the journey. I've been driving along slowly, enjoying the scenery, but I put my foot down and focus on getting home: if the traffic is bad on the motorway there's every chance I'll be late.

We join the ubiquitous M6. There is an almost clear blue sky, with a single vapour trail billowing across it; it looks like a tear in a blank canvas. It's too hot through the glass. We pass over the unyielding, craggy moorlands of Shap, desolate and remote – apart from the six lanes of tarmac slicing through them and the never-ending stream of heavy traffic.

We pass a sign, a graffito, sprayed on an overhead bridge: DEMOCRACY IS FRACKED. I'll vote for that.

Typically, there is little traffic until we reach the outskirts of Manchester. Joining the M61 we're trapped in a queue of crawling vehicles, wedged behind a caravan for ages. A sticker on the back features two palm trees forming the shape of a heart with the words ALAN and LINDA beneath it. Another sticker says ON AN ADVENTURE BEFORE DEMENTIA. I think I've seen that one before, but I can't remember.

The traffic comes to a complete standstill. There has been an incident at Junction 13. Unlucky. Brendan looks up briefly, questioning why we've stopped. His head flops down again. I drum my fingers on the steering wheel and check the time, which is rapidly running out.

The traffic starts to move again and we're off. There's no sign of any incident. We join the M60; the junction numbers are counting down. As we're approaching Junction 1, Brendan can sense we're nearing the end of our journey; he doesn't stand up, he doesn't sit up, but he lies down a little more alertly. This is it: the end of our voyage of (self) discovery.

* * * * * * * * * * * *

Dog facts:
If you have mental health issues a dog companion can really help you. If you *don't*, a dog can help you get mental health issues.

CHAPTER 11: BRENDANS ARE FOREVER

After much stress rushing back from our trip, I dropped Brendan off with Nicky and continued up to the hospital to have a cyst removed – from my head. It was quite a bizarre experience. When I arrived, the waiting room was packed with grim-faced people. Several hours passed and the numbers went down until I was left completely alone. I was the last one. The staff were no longer walking past and the continual background hum of the hospital had stopped. I was starting to think I'd been forgotten. Through the window, it was getting dark over the hospital rooftops. There was no longer anyone at the reception desk, no one to ask. It was like a scene from a sci-fi film. (*The Day of the Triffids* or *28 Days Later* spring to mind.)

I sat there, abandoned, thinking how surreal this all seemed, but weirdest of all was not having Brendan by my side. Nicky sent me a photo of him stretched out on her sofa, looking miserable. She said he was missing me. It's more likely that he was annoyed because she wouldn't let him be in charge of the remote control. But whatever the case, *I* was missing *him.* This wasn't the best end to our trip.

Eventually a nurse walked past; she jumped when she saw me. "Oh!" She laughed nervously and then collected herself. "I bet you thought you'd been forgotten!" she said cheerfully.

"Yes." I said, because they had forgotten me.

"No...no." she said. But they *had* forgotten me. She laughed again. "You're next."

Obviously. There was no one else.

I was dressed in a gown and then wheeled through the now-deserted hospital corridors to the operating theatre. The staff were all really nice, but they yawned an awful lot and were obviously waiting to go home. I had my local anaesthetic: several injections directly into my head, but I was still aware of the cutting and manhandling. It wasn't an experience I'd like to repeat.

Later that night, feeling a little bit sore and with a bandage on my head, I was released into the cool darkness. I don't remember getting back to Nicky's, but I did. Brendan was pleased to see me and was a bit clingy. I made a fuss of him and he made a fuss of me.

Although the procedure had forced the end of the trip – all along it had been the only date I had to stick to – it was quite useful in a way. I was in considerable pain and had to take it easy. I was on extra-strong pain killers, though they didn't actually help very much. I had to stay indoors for several days, apart from taking Brendan for short walks (and sit downs) to his beloved field. Being unwell, in pain and on medication kept me occupied or I think I would have found being back at home unbearable and would have been very depressed about our travelling being over.

* * * * * * * * * *

I had wondered whether Brendan would remember his home, our flat. Of course he did; he's a genius. He pulled me up the stairs and waited impatiently at the correct door, wagging his tail, peering round at me repeatedly in anticipation. When I let him in, he ran into the room and did a high-jump onto the bed, like he always did. He celebrated being home by having a nice nap. I can't actually remember what I did, but I assume I would have celebrated being home by having a cup of tea. We're both creatures of habit.

Brendan reunited with the bed.

Brendan loved his reunion with the field the next morning. He instinctively remembered the way and pulled to get there. He had a sniff and a few wees, then went and sat down on the low hill in his usual place and surveyed his kingdom proudly. I could almost hear his thoughts: with this on our doorstep, why did we ever need to go away?

* * * * * * * * * *

Days passed. With my bandage off, the stitches removed and an end to the mind-altering medication, life started to feel a bit more normal again. By "normal" I mean, exactly the same as before we went away. We visited my dad almost every day. Dad's health had suddenly started to deteriorate; in particular his Alzheimer's was getting much worse, very quickly. My aim was to keep him independent and in his own home as long as possible, as he had requested.

Being back home was disconcerting, because – apart from all the happy memories I had stored away of our travels – nothing at all had changed. In many ways it was like our trip had never happened. I had envisaged that after this journey, this experience, we would come back changed – bonded, but worldly-wise, relaxed, perhaps surfers, philosophers, artists even. Something. *Any*thing. We had definitely bonded, but when we actually resumed our normal lives, it quickly became evident that Brendan still had quite a long list of things he didn't like. Numbers one and two on this list were (still) men and women. Put these two together and what have you got? Well, babies actually, if you're not careful. But the answer I'm looking for is *people*. Brendan still didn't generally like most *people*. He might have been travelling and come back home, but people were still people – and he still wasn't a fan.

In particular, Brendan had a special hatred for anyone with a walking stick. He was always quick to warn others that you should avoid these people at all costs, as they were basically carrying weaponry and were not to be trusted. He was also still very vocal towards anyone wearing a uniform, hi-viz gear or loud knitwear.

He had also retained his dislike for methods of

transport, namely planes, trains and automobiles. He didn't actually mind trains so much, because they had the decency to keep themselves to themselves, but he didn't like the noise they made, which sometimes sounded like thunder. He still didn't like planes or cars at all, so he barked at them. All the time.

Brendan was the same. And so was I. I didn't feel worldly or wise, or well-travelled or more confident. We were both still the same. Distinctly odd.

* * * * * * * * * *

I was quite shocked when the call from the sanctuary came; it was so unexpected. By this point, Brendan had been with me for nearly a year, yet they called out of the blue suddenly demanding money for him. I was technically fostering him, but we had arranged that it would be a permanent foster and he would never be rehomed elsewhere because of his behavioural issues, so effectively we would be together forever. When I queried this, they immediately became all aggressive and insisted I returned him to them. I refused. I said we had bonded and Brendan had adapted to his new life. Yes, he still barked at everything, but I could tell he was a happier dog now, probably happier than he had ever been in his life. This was his home, we were a unit and to change that now would be abusive.

The sanctuary were very unreasonable and inflexible. What appalled me the most was that it seemed they were thinking purely in monetary terms, when they should have been thinking of what was best for the dog. They wanted someone to *buy* Brendan: they wanted the cash. We had a heated discussion, at the end of which I agreed to pay them the money, but at this point they withdrew the offer and demanded I returned him immediately. The discussion got even less cordial. I promised them Brendan would be staying with me and they would not be getting him back under any circumstances.

I hung up and looked at him. He was sitting on the settee, looking back at me with his soft brown eyes. To take him back now would surely be very damaging for him. I sat next to him and clung onto him. He gazed at me, knowing something was wrong, but not sure what it was. I felt devastated.

I texted Nicky and asked her to call in on her way home from work, because there was a problem. She didn't question me, she just agreed.

I spent the afternoon going over and over the exchange with the sanctuary. I was disgusted with their mercenary attitude. I started to think about Brendan and what would genuinely be best for him, but I kept coming up with contradictory answers. Surely, to take him back would severely undermine his confidence, possibly irreparably. How could he ever relax in future and think he had found a home? Surely he would be better here with me. James, the dog psychologist, certainly believed he would be better here. But I started to question – again – whether this was the right set up for him, whether he needed to be with other dogs, whether he might be better off if he was rehomed with someone who owned a house and had a nice garden. If it would be better for Brendan, then that was how it had to be.

We went to the field for a very sad and serious walk, then we went and sat in the van to wait for Nicky. She arrived on her bike and climbed inside. We all sat in the back. I was quite nervous as I explained what had happened. Brendan and Nicky hadn't really bonded at this point. We'd been travelling for months, so she hadn't seen that much of him. There were times when she said she felt nervous of him, because she thought he might go for her. I never believed he would – and he never did. Brendan had severely restricted our social lives, so he had hardly endeared himself to her. She was annoyed with the way I had handled the sanctuary, because I had lost my temper. I expected her to say technically he's still their dog, so you have to take him back. But she didn't. Her reaction surprised me. She burst into tears and said "But he'll *die* without you!"

I value her opinion immensely and that was all I needed to hear: taking him back was definitely not an option. Whatever happened, Brendan was staying with me. If that meant us going on the run and living in the van or in a tent in a forest, to avoid detection by the sanctuary militia, then that's how it would be. I was prepared to give up my flat and everything to ensure his safety. Strangely, I suddenly wasn't at all stressed, because I knew this was the right thing to do and there were no other options. In a way it almost felt like perhaps this was our calling, that we were destined to live our lives on the run; maybe this was the opportunity I'd been waiting for. I'd travelled round Britain looking for meaning to my life and had come home and found it.

Nicky said she would continue to negotiate with the sanctuary via diplomatic channels; it was better if *she* attempted to resume talks, because they had clearly closed the door on me and there was no chance of any further dialogue. On the one hand, I didn't expect them to back down, because they were unreasonable and neurotic, but on the other hand, I had every faith that Nicky would succeed. She had said she'd deal with it, so I knew she would sort it out. The fact that she had cried and often displays her emotions doesn't in any way mean she's weak. If she's fighting for somebody else she is unstoppable. She didn't approach the sanctuary aggressively, she was very calm and reasonable, but totally unrelenting.

All night they rebutted her and said they wanted Brendan back. She offered – on my behalf – the adoption fee for Brendan, plus a generous donation to continue their work, but they stubbornly refused.

She had a terrible evening, receiving one communication after another from them, some hysterical, some plain nasty, all unreasonable. Each time she countered their hysteria with calm logic, but it was very difficult for her and very upsetting. Meanwhile, I was with The Boy in our flat, sitting on the settee, feeling eerily calm. I had every faith Nicky would be successful and even if she wasn't, there was no way my boy was going back, so it was all in the hands of fate. We belonged together and we were staying together, no matter what.

The next morning, the sanctuary women wearily gave

in to Nicky. Perhaps because of the offer of money, possibly because they knew they were never going to get Brendan back and most probably because Nicky had ground them down and they knew she was never going to stop. I transferred them the money, which effectively made Brendan – my scruffy, maladjusted street dog from Bulgaria – more expensive than a top of the range pedigree.

The sanctuary sent his passport and certificates. Yes, he had a passport and I didn't. He could go travelling abroad and I couldn't.

So, in reality, what I gained from our trip was Brendan; I got Brendan legally, which makes the trip was a huge success after all. We're inseparable pals. We bonded whilst travelling and then I paid a fortune for him. He is the most expensive dog I know… which could explain his very exclusive tastes. Apart from my van, he is the most expensive purchase I have ever made. By a long way. But there is no price on his value; he's priceless.

* * * * * * * * * *

Once I'd officially adopted him, the strangest thing happened; Brendan changed overnight. He changed completely and utterly. We had been together for exactly a year, so that might have had something to do with it. From the beginning, countless people with rescue dogs had told me it takes twelve months or more for them to bond with you. Or perhaps it was because he was a year older. He was six now, he was no longer a wilful and belligerent five year old. Perhaps for dogs, turning six is like a coming of age – though technically, he'd be 42, so that seems unlikely. Perhaps he's a late developer.

I feel though that it had a lot to do with him being adopted. I think he sensed something was different and he knew this was going to remain his permanent home and he didn't need to worry about getting carted back to the sanctuary. Dogs can pick up many human emotions and perhaps he could sense that our relationship was now different. He suddenly seemed more confident, more relaxed, more secure. I could now let him off his lead and he would stay close by and not head for the hills.

Brendan the franchise.
He's quite the businessdog! He's *everywhere!*

He's not a model citizen, of course, but he's so much more laid back than he used to be. And when people at the park now say: "Oh, he's so chilled, your dog!" I agree that about 62% of the time, he actually is.As I've said, I came back from the trip exactly the same person, but once Brendan was adopted he changed and I also changed. In so many ways.

Firstly, Brendan imposes a routine on me. On the one

hand routines might seem boring and predictable, but they also provide structure and security. I have to get up in the morning whether I want to or not, because I have to take Brendan to the field. Come rain or shine, no matter how I'm feeling or what's going on, we have to go out. Brendan's walks provide the frame around which the rest of our day hangs. Dogs thrive on routine: Brendan *loves* routine. Sitting down and napping are big parts of his daily agenda. He's forever telling me that a good routine can't be a bad thing.

Before I had Brendan, I would often go for a walk to get some fresh air. I would have my earphones in, partly because I enjoy listening to music (and singing) whilst walking, but also to create an audio/aural barrier between myself and other people, so most often my walks were decidedly isolated activities; I wouldn't speak to anyone. But now, going out with Brendan, walks have become very social affairs. I can't go out without meeting fellow dog walkers or even strangers who stop to admire Brendan and ask what type of dog he is. Before breakfast I've usually interacted with at least half a dozen people, which is more than I used to speak to in the average week. We stand at the field and chat. We talk about our dogs first and foremost, then we talk about the weather and sometimes we exchange a few words about current affairs. (At the moment, the impending Coronavirus and the Trump administration are the most frequent topics.)

I used to be a very shy and insular person. Now I can't be. I have to speak to people. Often it's to apologise for my dog. All these encounters have helped to make me more socialised and increase my confidence. This is solely down to Brendan. He is my life coach.

Apart from the social aspect of walking, it is – of course – good, regular exercise: a cardio-vascular activity, so it's good for the heart, the lungs and the waistline. I walk for at least a couple of hours a day; Brendan usually walks for considerably less. Our trips to the field often result in me walking around the perimeter on my own, while he sits in the middle and watches in a bemused manner.

After the trip: Brendan attempts to bring the beach into the home.

Walking is also very beneficial for your *mental* health. Exercising releases endorphins into the bloodstream which promote a feeling of well-being and can even reduce the perception of pain. I always feel good after a walk. Even if it's cold or raining, it's lovely to get back home, get warm and get the kettle on. Brendan gets the same rush of endorphins by sitting down at the field and watching me exercise.

Being close to Brendan, touching him or even just looking at him lifts my spirits and changes my mood. He is completely addictive. It's a fact that having an animal is good for your mental health and reduces stress, anxiety and has a calming effect, whilst also boosting self-esteem. Brendan is a mood altering drug and I think I could market him as an anti-depressant.

I spend an inordinate amount of time just staring at him and telling him how handsome he is. He spends an inordinate amount of time agreeing with me.

Brendan is such a huge part of my life. He's usually the first thing I see in the morning and the last thing I see at night, lying next to me on the bed, taking up most of the space and sighing moodily. He's my boy.

* * * * * * * * * *

Dog facts:
Humans and dogs have been living together for at least 16,000 years – possibly double that. Either way, that's a hell of a lot of sniffing, weeing, walking and snuggling. It clearly shows that something about this special human-canine relationship works.

POSTSCRIPT: BRENDAN
LOOKING BACK

Yesterday, I bumped into a former colleague. She asked what I'd been doing since we last met and I told her about travelling. This chance meeting underlined to me the fact that the trip with Brendan in Eagle One had been the highlight of my life in recent years. It was an ambition fulfilled; it was such an amazing experience and to have shared it with my boy was the very best part. I loved travelling around with Brendan. He's been my constant companion and he's never once complained. Hardly ever. Not verbally anyway.

I think about our trip a lot. The most special memories are the moments that didn't actually mean that much at the time, but now have a golden, magical quality to them: they have come to encapsulate our journey. Sitting together at Godrevy Head, sitting together overlooking Whitesands Bay, sitting together at Land's End, sitting together on Bempton Cliffs... and so many other occasions. These events have one thing in common; it's the *sitting together* that made it special, rather than the view or the location. When I sit with Brendan now at our local field, I have flashbacks of those beautiful places and the perfect memories, but I appreciate where we are now and the warmth and companionship that we share.

I have a few regrets about our adventure. I'm sorry we didn't take it slower and really savour it. Brendan is totally with me on that. We very often did have a relaxed pace, but there were several times I felt a compulsion to move on and get the trip completed. However, Brendan didn't feel this compulsion at all, ever, and if he was leading the expedition we'd still probably be in Portishead. Sitting down. Or most likely he'd be stretched out on that Persian rug in the waterside cafe, snoring peacefully.

A lady stopped us on the field the other day. She was gazing at Brendan in awe. "What a lovely looking boy! He is a boy, isn't he?"

"Yes, he's a boy." (He's actually *The* Boy: the definite article.)

"What's he called?"

"Brendan. He came with his... Oh, never mind..." I heard myself say. "He's called Brendan."

"Oh, how lovely. And original. I think it suits him."

I smiled. "Yes... so do I. I didn't used to... but I think he's grown into it."

Brendan: he came with his name and he stayed with his name. I'm now glad I didn't change it. It's part of who he is. It occurred to me that I have started to love my dog's name.

On his next birthday, Brendan will be older than me. Technically he'll be in charge. I envisage a lot more napping on the agenda and a mandatory increase in weeing – though that comes naturally with age in humans anyway.

ıe once-matted, narrow-framed, exhausted boy who ∧ad climbed wearily up onto my lap and went to sleep, chose me and I feel blessed that he did. I'm not saying a dog will solve *all* your problems... it won't, in fact it will bring along with it a host of other problems, different problems, problems you didn't have before, but probably less serious and less dark problems. A dog will almost certainly help with improving your mental health.

Our trip around "pre-Corona" England now seems a lifetime ago. At the time of writing the coronavirus is approaching our shores and the future is suddenly looking very uncertain. There won't be any travelling for a while, but I know that at some point in the future I'll be back in my van with my dog – because there's a whole lot of world out there for us to explore together.

This has been the story of Brendan – he came with his name – a former street dog who crept into my life when I needed him, changed it around to suit himself and then had a nap.

<u>The End</u>

What's new about Social Distancing? Brendan's been doing it for years.
(Brendan – alone and aloof – at the field)

AFTERWORD

This book has been a joy to write, as much joy as it was to live through. If you have enjoyed reading it, please consider putting a review on Amazon. Thank you.

You may like to join our mailing list for exclusive content: the2underdogs@outlook.com

Dog facts:
There are approximately 600 million dogs in the world, 400 million of which are estimated to be strays. You could help reduce that number.

ALSO BY GRAY FREEMAN

DOG DAYS:
underdogs II

Finding they were unable to return to a life on the road as the coronavirus cast its black shadow over the world, Gray and Brendan decided to use the time to try and improve themselves, and – most importantly – to try and find positivity in every day. This began well, but it wasn't long before their world started to fall apart.

Dog Days is a diary of that unprecedented period in history. It is in turns touching, funny, optimistic, poignant, tragic and very human. Despite everything going wrong in the world, *Dog Days* is about the joy of spending every second of every day with your best friend.

The Long Goodbye
& Other Plays

NOTHING IS AS IT SEEMS.

The Long Goodbye was a play. It was staged twice in Manchester. People laughed, people cried, people said how much they could relate to it. You will also be able to relate to it. It is funny, tragic and touching; it leaves a lasting impression.

WAKE UP AND A WHOLE NEW LIFE HAS BEEN WRITTEN FOR YOU – A LIFE WHICH YOU KNOW MUST BE A LIE.

The Long Goodbye made a humorous, moving and memorable piece of theatre, and here it is presented as a "reading script" – between a script and a novel. It is accessible, at times laugh-out-loud funny and also deeply poignant. On the page it doesn't lose any of its humour or haunting impact.

EVERYTHING IS BIZARRE AND SURREAL, LIKE A 'SIXTIES TV SHOW. YOUR LIFE IS A PRISON; YOU ARE THE PRISONER.

the underdog

TRAVELS BEFORE BRENDAN

The Prequel to underdogs

THE RIVITINGLY EXCITING PREQUEL TO underdogs

Gray Freeman sets off in a van on a voyage of self-discovery - to fulfil a dream and travel around the coast of Britain. Without a dog! What was he thinking?

The plan was to see hidden corners of Britain and to explore remote coastlines, clifftops and forgotten byways, backwaters and other places that haven't yet been used to build shopping malls.

This was to be a life-changing experience, but not everything went according to plan.

The underdog is travel writing, but it is humorous and accessible, light-hearted and quirky. It is a celebration of travel, a love letter to the British coast.

This was to be the journey of a lifetime – and this is where it all began.